More Praise for *The Guns of John Moses Browning*

"Nathan Gorenstein goes beyond the bounds of a typical biography. He masterfully weaves the story of John Moses Browning's life with the social, cultural, and political impact of his inventions. Peer inside the mind of a genius whose work, like that of fellow titans Henry Ford and Steve Jobs, transcended an industry and revolutionized the world. The scale is epic, but the book's best moments are the most relatable. A simple, unassuming man was driven not by fame or fortune but, rather, an innate desire to overcome obstacles that perplexed himself and his peers. The story and its ramifications are truly remarkable."
—**Jeffrey Richardson, author of *Colt: The Revolver of the American West***

"If you already know the difference between a 'locked' breech and 'blowback' pistol, here's a chance to understand the life of history's premier gun designer. If you haven't encountered those phrases before, here's a chance to see how a guy growing up poor in a remote Western village became one of the greatest mechanical engineers of his time, transforming the world. This very engaging biography of one of America's most creative minds is set in an era just remote enough to startle modern readers."
—**Clayton E. Cramer, author of *Lock, Stock, and Barrel: The Origins of American Gun Culture***

"The perfect combination of technological and social history—a feat rarely attempted and even more rarely achieved with such thorough attention to detail."
—**Ashley Hlebinsky, former cohost of Discovery Channel's *Master of Arms* and founding president, Association of Firearms History and Museums**

"Nathan Gorenstein's *The Guns of John Moses Browning* tells the surprising story of a genius inventor who changed the course of American history. It will captivate readers interested in firearms and the process of innovation. I highly recommend it."

—**Paul M. Barrett, author of** *GLOCK: The Rise of America's Gun*

THE GUNS OF
JOHN MOSES BROWNING

THE REMARKABLE STORY
OF THE INVENTOR WHOSE FIREARMS
CHANGED THE WORLD

———————•———————

NATHAN GORENSTEIN

SCRIBNER

New York   London   Toronto   Sydney   New Delhi

Scribner

An Imprint of Simon & Schuster, Inc.

1230 Avenue of the Americas

New York, NY 10020

First Scribner hardcover edition May 2021

SCRIBNER and design are registered trademarks of The Gale Group, Inc.,
used under license by Simon & Schuster, Inc., the publisher of this work.

For information about special discounts for bulk purchases,
please contact Simon & Schuster Special Sales at 1-866-506-1949
or business@simonandschuster.com.

The Simon & Schuster Speakers Bureau can bring authors to your live event.
For more information or to book an event, contact the Simon & Schuster Speakers
Bureau at 1-866-248-3049 or visit our website at www.simonspeakers.com.

Manufactured in the United States of America

1   3   5   7   9   10   8   6   4   2

Library of Congress Cataloging-in-Publication Data

Names: Gorenstein, Nathan, author.
Title: The guns of John Moses Browning : the remarkable story of the
inventor whose firearms changed the world / Nathan Gorenstein.
Description: First Scribner hardcover edition. | New York : Scribner, 2021.
| Includes bibliographical references and index.
Identifiers: LCCN 2021005893 (print) | LCCN 2021005894 (ebook) | ISBN
9781982129217 (hardcover) | ISBN 9781982129231 (ebook)
Subjects: LCSH: Browning, John M. (John Moses), 1855–1926. | Firearms
designers—United States—Biography.
Classification: LCC TS533.62 .B76 2021 (print) | LCC TS533.62 (ebook) |
DDC 683.40092 [B]—dc23
LC record available at https://lccn.loc.gov/2021005893
LC ebook record available at https://lccn.loc.gov/2021005894

ISBN 978-1-9821-2921-7
ISBN 978-1-9821-2923-1 (ebook)

CONTENTS

ILLUSTRATIONS

AUTHOR'S NOTE

Of all the mechanical devices invented since the Industrial Revolution, only firearms indisputably occupy both ends of a moral spectrum starting at good and ending at evil. A gun can save a life, or take a life, and can do either, or both, with a single shot in a single instant. Whether that outcome is laudable or deplorable depends on who asks and answers the question and whether you're in front of the muzzle or have your finger on the trigger. Pistols, rifles, and machine guns can defend a nation and liberate a people, or conquer a land and slaughter its inhabitants. A shotgun or the "obsolete" lever-action rifle can put food on the table, or wipe out a species. One is hard-pressed to cite a major historic event since the mid-nineteenth century that was not started, finished, or changed by a gun.

A case can be made that the influence of mechanized firearms on human events is exceeded only by that of the automobile, the airplane, and the practical application of electricity. Henry Ford, Wilbur and Orville Wright, and Thomas Alva Edison imagined and then created, or at least perfected, devices that define the modern world.

During those same decades dozens of firearms inventors throughout Europe and the United States attempted to apply the era's chemical, mechanical, and manufacturing discoveries—which gave birth to the Wright Flyer's lightweight combustion engine, for example—to the creation of new guns that fired lead projectiles faster, farther, and more accurately. Most of those engineers and mechanics failed. A few succeeded, none more remarkably than self-taught John Moses Browning, the man whom contemporaries called the Edison of guns.

AUTHOR'S NOTE

Just as Edison invented, with much help, an array of modern devices including the lightbulb, phonograph, movie camera, and storage battery, Browning created firearms that ranged widely—from tiny pocket pistols to five-foot-long aerial machine guns. His mechanisms were so ubiquitous that, as decades elapsed, fewer and fewer realized that a single mind had created them.

What follows is the story of one of the world's least-known, and yet most influential, American inventors.

TO THE READER:

Please note that a glossary of key terms can be found at the back of the book.

PROLOGUE

Nineteen-year-old Gavrilo Princip, a self-styled patriot but a terrorist to the Austro-Hungarian monarchy, was a slight, dark-haired youth with a thin mustache atop his upper lip. On the morning of June 28, 1914, he slipped a small pistol into his jacket pocket. It weighed barely more than a pound, so no saggy bulge could betray him to the Sarajevo police. The machine—and by any standard it was a finely made machine—was an expensive bit of modernity, but then Princip and his handlers were serious men. To kill the future king they'd chosen the very best tool.

There were six assassins. Two carried grenades and four were armed with handguns newly manufactured in Belgium, designed by an American and selected by a Serbian colonel in the "Black Hand" terrorist underground. Like so many other revolutionaries of the left and right, the Balkan nationalists hoped to cut their way through history with a murder.

The first attacker threw a grenade. He missed his target, the Archduke Franz Ferdinand, who sat in the back seat of a slow-moving touring car with his wife, Sophie, the Duchess of Hohenberg. The grenade bounced onto the ground and detonated beneath a trailing automobile. Arriving at city hall, the unharmed archduke scolded the Sarajevo mayor, "I come here on a visit and I am greeted with bombs. It is outrageous!" and then drove off to comfort the now-hospitalized wounded. En route the archduke's driver took a wrong turn, the car slowed to a stop, and there on the sidewalk was Princip.[1]

The gun that appeared in his hand represented the pinnacle of small arms manufacture. In design and function it demonstrated an unrivaled combination of mechanical invention and aesthetics. The curved and contoured steel, combined with the ornate initials "FN" on the grips, gave it visual cues that echoed the elegance of Europe's "Belle Epoque," the era Princip would soon end. In the hand—and the gun was meant to be fired with a single hand—the weapon balanced well, was easily gripped, and pointed naturally at a target.

A short movement of the index finger fired a round. The exploding propellant shot the bullet down the barrel. The effect was to make the gun jump in Princip's hand as the recoil energy operated the semiautomatic firearm. The slide, a steel cover surrounding the barrel, flew backward, ejected the spent cartridge, cocked the mechanism, and loaded a fresh cartridge. Faster than could be seen, almost faster than could be conceived, the gun was ready to fire again. It was like a small combustion engine, only held in your hand.

The gun was no sharpshooter's weapon. Made by Fabrique Nationale d'Armes de Guerre and named the FN 1910, it was meant for self-defense or close-in police work. It slipped smoothly from a pocket and was very accurate over a short distance. And as Princip proved when he fired two bullets, one striking the archduke's neck, the other Sophie's stomach, it could also be used to start a world war.[2]

Its creator was the American John Moses Browning. Thanks to the scope, variety, and particularly the mechanical ingenuity of his inventions, there were 1.25 million Browning pistols circulating in Europe by 1914.[3] His name was synonymous with pistols of all types. (The French referred to any pistol as "le browning.") Across the Atlantic, however, Browning remained unknown to the general public, even though millions of Americans owned or used a firearm he'd invented and then sold or licensed to famous firms, including Winchester, Colt, Remington, and Savage. They were rifles, shotguns and pistols, and soon machine guns. As Henry Ford was to automobiles, and Thomas Edison was to electricity, Browning was to firearms, and his inventions had similar world-changing influence. Unlike those contemporaries, Browning sought no publicity. His relative obscurity lasted until

1917, late in his life, when the United States entered World War I and Browning found himself suddenly elevated to the status of a national icon.[4]

He was a straight-backed man, over six feet tall, whose most visible luxury was the elegant brick and stone home with splendid oak woodwork he shared with his wife, Rachel, and their eight children. That Browning would live a life that curved history was inconceivable when he was born, before the Civil War, in the isolated frontier settlement of Ogden, Utah, where in 1865, at age ten, he began a career in guns.

CHAPTER ONE

FRONTIER LESSONS

John Browning's first firearm was a crude shotgun, fashioned from a discarded musket barrel as long as he was tall. He built it in his father's workshop in less than a day and afterward went hunting in the grass of the high plains with Matt, his five-year-old brother and future business partner.[1]

The 1865 Browning home in Ogden, Utah, was adobe brick, situated a few steps away from untrammeled land filled with grouse, a small wildfowl that made tolerable eating once it was plucked, butchered, and cooked, preferably with bacon fat to moisten the dry flesh. Utah's five varieties of grouse could fly, but mostly the birds shuffled about on the earth. The male "greater" grouse reached seven pounds, making a decent meal and an easy target, as yellow feathers surrounded each eye and a burst of white marked the breast. A skilled hunter could sneak up on a covey picking at leaves and grasses and with one blast of birdshot get two or three for the frying pan.

Such frugality was necessary. The closest railroad stop was nearly one thousand miles east, and the largest nearby town was Salt Lake City, thirty-five miles to the south and home to only ten thousand people. Ogden's settlers ate what they grew, raised, or hunted. Water for drinking and crops depended on the streams and rivers that flowed west out of the mountains into the Great Salt Lake, and irrigated wheat, corn, turnips, cabbage, and potatoes. Each settler was obliged to contribute labor or money to construct the hand-dug ditches and canals. They made their own bricks, cured hides for leather, and made molasses out of a thin, yellowish juice squeezed from sugar beets with heavy iron rollers and then boiled down to a thick, dark bittersweet liquid.

The rollers were made by John's father, Jonathan, himself a talented gunsmith who also doubled as a blacksmith while pursuing a variety of entrepreneurial adventures that never yielded more than mixed success. Jonathan's shop was his son's playground, and John's toys were broken gun parts thrown into the corner. At age six, John was taught by his "pappy" to pick out metal bits for forging and hammering into new gun parts. Soon the boy was wielding tools under his father's direction.

To build that first crude gun John chose a day when his father was away on an errand. From the pile of discards John retrieved the old musket barrel and dug out a few feet of wire and a length of scrap wood. He clamped the barrel into a vice and with a fine-toothed saw cut off the damaged muzzle. He set Matt to work with a file and orders to scrape a strip along the barrel's top down to clean metal. With a hatchet John hacked out a crude stock. The boys worked intently. On the frontier a task didn't have to be polished, but it had to be right. Basic materials were in short supply, and to make his gun parts and agricultural tools Pappy Browning scavenged iron and steel abandoned by exhausted and overloaded immigrants passing through on their way west. Once, he purchased a load of metal fittings collected from the burned-out remains of an army wagon train, and as payment he signed over a parcel of land that, years later, became the site of Ogden's first hotel.

John used a length of wire to fasten the gun barrel to the stock, then bonded them with drops of molten solder. There was no trigger. Near the barrel's flash hole John screwed on a tin cone. When it came time to fire, gunpowder and lead birdshot would be loaded down the muzzle and finely ground primer powder would be sprinkled into the cone. The brothers would work together as a team: John would aim, Matt would lean in and ignite the primer with the tip of a smoldering stick, and the cobbled-together shotgun would, presumably, fire.

This wasn't without risk. There was no telling if the soldered wire was strong enough to contain the recoil, or if the barrel itself would burst. Then there was the matter of ammunition. Gunpowder and shot were expensive imports delivered by ox-drawn wagon train, and early settlers, surrounded by game, suffered pangs of hunger when foodstuffs were eaten up, powder was exhausted, and their firearms hung useless on the wall. Even as a shotgun—which fires lead pellets—the Browning brothers' makeshift weapon might prove ineffective. John could miss, and anger their father by using up valuable gunpowder with no result. Despite the risks, John pilfered enough powder and lead shot (from Jonathan's poorly hidden supply) for one shot.

In ten minutes the brothers were in open country. Ogden's eastern side nestled against the sheer ramparts of the Wasatch Mountains, and to the west lay the waters of the Great Salt Lake. To the north the Bear and Weber rivers flowed out of the Wasatch to sustain the largest waterfowl breeding ground west of the Mississippi River. Early white explorers were staggered by seemingly endless flocks of geese and ducks. In the 1840s pioneers described the "astonishing spectacle of waterfowl multitudes" taking to the air with a sound like "distant thunder." Mountains rose up in all four directions, with one range or another flashing reflected sunlight. It was a striking geographic combination, magnified by the bright, clear sunlight of Ogden's near-mile-high elevation. A settler's life was lived on a stage of uncommon spectacle.[2]

John carried the shotgun while Matt toted a stick and a small metal can holding a few clumps of glowing coal. The idea was to take two or three birds with a single shot, thereby allaying parental anger with a show of skilled marksmanship. Barefoot, the brothers crept from place to place until they spotted a cluster of birds pecking at the ground. Two were almost touching wings and a third was inches away. John knelt and aimed. Matt pulled the glowing stick out of the embers, almost jabbed John in the ear, and then touched the stick to the tin cone to fire the shot. The recoil knocked John backward—but in front of him lay a dead bird. Two other wounded fowl flapped nearby. Matt scampered ahead and "stood, a bird in each hand, whooping and trying to wring both necks at once."

The next morning, as Jonathan breakfasted on grouse breast and biscuits, John listened to sympathetic advice from his mother and chose that moment to tell Pappy the story of his gun, his hunt—and the pilfered powder. Jonathan sat quietly and when John was finished made no mention of the theft. He did ask to see the weapon and was unimpressed. "John Moses, you're going on eleven; can't you make a better gun than that?"

Matt snickered. John choked down his remaining breakfast. "Pappy has drawn first blood, no doubt about that. He hadn't scolded about the powder and shot, and the sin of stealing. But he'd hit my pride right on the funny bone," John told his family decades later. A moment later he followed his father into the shop. He unrolled the wire from the barrel, "whistling soft and low to show how unconcerned I was," and then stamped on the stock, snapped it in two, and tossed the pieces into a pile of kindling. "I remember thinking, rebelliously, that for all Pappy might say, the gun had gotten three fine birds for breakfast. Then I set to work. Neither of us mentioned it again."

The father, Jonathan, who was tutor and goad to his son John, was born in 1805 to a family that emigrated from Virginia to rich farmland outside Nashville, Tennessee. Jonathan Browning was the sixth of seven children raised on a homestead at Brushy Farm along Bledsoe Creek, a four-mile-long tributary feeding the Cumberland River. Early on, Jonathan decided he'd rather hammer on an anvil than walk behind a plow and at nineteen years of age apprenticed himself to a Nashville rifle maker. He returned to Bledsoe Creek to open his own shop in 1826, and in November of that year, at age twenty-one, married a local woman, Elizabeth Stalcup. She was twenty-three, the only child of a widowed mother. When Jonathan's parents and several brothers moved west to Quincy, Illinois, a newly settled town on the Mississippi River, Jonathan and Elizabeth followed. In

1834 they moved to the village of La Prairie. It was the start of a decade-long trek westward as they added children at the rate of one infant per year.[3]

The extended Browning family in Illinois included a cousin, Orville, a politically ambitious attorney who boasted that frontier rarity, a college education. Orville practiced real estate law, and so, along with gunsmithing, Jonathan began purchasing land in the surrounding counties, often at sheriff sales, and holding the parcels for eventual resale. While Orville persuaded Jonathan to run for justice of the peace, it was gunsmithing that produced a lucrative income for his growing family. In addition to a steady flow of repairs, Jonathan designed a repeating rifle that used the same mechanism found in Samuel Colt's new six-shooter pistol: a metal cylinder with six cylindrical chambers, each loaded with a lead ball and gunpowder, which would be ignited by a percussion cap. Colt's gun was the first practical repeating firearm. Jonathan produced a rifle-sized version and crafted a trigger, stock, and barrel. A surviving example shows an exquisite level of craftsmanship, but it required time and effort that Jonathan found unsustainable.[4]

While Jonathan was inventing, cousin Orville was elected to the state legislature, where he befriended another young lawyer, a tall, thin man with a distinctive jaw named Abraham Lincoln.[5] The men were of similar age and background. Both grew up in Kentucky, served in the state militia, and had similar politics— they were opposed to the expansion of slavery—which eventually led them to join the new Republican Party. The two legislators became friends, and Browning family oral history says that at Orville's behest Jonathan and Elizabeth, who enjoyed a relatively spacious home on account of their ever-expanding family, played host to Orville's friends or clients in need of lodging. On two occasions young lawyer Lincoln was the guest. So the story goes, anyway. Research by a Browning descendant comparing the dates and locations in family lore with the available records of Lincoln's travels wasn't definitive but suggests the family lore is "likely" grounded in fact. One story does have a strong whiff of verisimilitude. At an evening meal with Lincoln, probably around 1840, Jonathan remarked how earlier that day he'd set a neighbor's broken arm, a skill learned after trading a gun for a "doctor book."

"Fact is, that's the way I got my first Bible, traded a gun for it."

Lincoln said that reminded him of "the saying about turning swords into plowshares—or was it pruning hooks?"

"Plowshares," Jonathan replied.

"Well, that's what you did, in a way turned a gun into a Bible. But the other fellow—he canceled you out by turning a Bible into a gun. Looks like the trade left the world about where it was."

The men chuckled; then Jonathan admitted "there was something else funny" about the transaction. "To tell the truth, the mainspring in that old gun was pretty weak, and some other things . . ."

"You mean to admit that you cheated in a trade for a Bible—a Bible!" Lincoln exclaimed.

Jonathan said that the artful deal making went both ways. "When I got to looking through the Bible at home, I found that about half the New Testament was missing."

Mending, be it bones or guns, was the evening's favored metaphor. "The United States are to become the greatest country on earth. But what if the hotheads break it in two, right down the middle? That would be a welding job!" Lincoln declared. "It would need the fires of the infernal for the forge. And where was the anvil? Where is the hammer? Where was the blacksmith?" That blacksmith turned out to be Lincoln, and the fires four years of bloody civil war. Cousin Orville became an advisor to President Lincoln, though the better-educated man believed himself worthier and was privately envious of the rougher, self-educated Lincoln.[6]

Of greater significance for the Browning family was Jonathan and Elizabeth's introduction to another man, the charismatic Joseph Smith, who in 1823 declared that he'd found a new holy gospel written on golden tablets discovered buried in a New York hillside, and so was inspired to found a new religion. Most of his neighbors considered it a blasphemous cult. Smith called it the Church of Jesus Christ of Latter-day Saints, or the Mormons. Forced to flee Missouri in 1839, Smith and his followers trekked to Illinois and founded the town of Nauvoo, a name drawn from Hebrew for "they are beautiful." An earlier stop in Missouri led to that state issuing an extradition warrant for "overt acts of treason," but Jonathan's cousin Orville got the warrant thrown out by an Illinois court. That didn't end Smith's problems, as rumors circulated about his "plural marriages," an affront to the law and social mores. Yet the new faith expanded. Unlike most other sects born during the spiritual revival of the mid-1800s, Smith's religion provided a cohesive community and economic security, a "theocratic-democracy" that offered structure "for lives beset by unpredictability, disorder and change" amid the uncertainties, isolation, and insecurity of the frontier.

In 1840 a proselytizing Mormon in need of a gun repair introduced Jonathan to the faith and, after a lengthy conversation in the shop, the customer called at his home and presented Jonathan with the Book of Mormon. Jonathan wasn't economically insecure—his business dealings were thriving. Though uneducated in any traditional sense, he was an ambitious, curious man who may have seen the church as an alternative to the many warring Protestant sects. It offered the promise of salvation and a comprehensive social network that was rooted in a patriarchal family structure. "He seemed to perceive a clearly marked road to salvation, a map in effect, to guide man through the wilderness of life to the gates of heaven," his grandson Jack wrote a century later.

Jonathan was baptized into the church, moved to Nauvoo with his family, and briefly became owner of a two-story home and gun shop. In 1844 the first and only edition of a Nauvoo newspaper, the *Expositor*, published an editorial that bitterly criticized Smith for serving in the dual role of mayor and church leader. Smith declared the newspaper a public nuisance and ordered the town marshal to destroy the printing press, an ill-considered decision that led to criminal charges of riot and "treason against the state." Smith was jailed and on June 27, 1844, a mob stormed his cell. A gun battle broke out and Smith was killed.

It was around this time that Jonathan designed a second firearm, soon much sought after by his Mormon brethren. It was an ingenious device called the slide bar repeating rifle, colloquially named a harmonica rifle, since a vital part indeed bore a resemblance to the musical instrument. A brief description of how a firearm works is helpful to understand not only that rifle but John Browning's later work.

As Browning reached manhood in the 1870s the basic architecture of the modern firearm was cemented into place. Any pistol, rifle, shotgun, or machine gun, no matter how complex or powerful, has the same essential components: a hollow steel barrel, with an opening at one end called the muzzle, where the bullet emerges, and a hole at the other end, called the breech, where the barrel is bored out to create the loading chamber. When a gun is loaded, the "cartridge"—a brass case with a pinch of explosive primer at its base followed by gunpowder and topped by a lead projectile—is inserted into the chamber. Then the chamber is sealed by a "breechblock" so that the hot gas produced by fast-burning[7] propellant is directed forward, out of the muzzle, and not backward (into the shooter's face).

The breechblock is also sometimes simply called the block or the bolt. Thanks to the English language's many borrowed words, and a history of firearm development dating to the 1200s, a single component can have a variety of names. "Bullet" is from the French word for "small ball" and technically only refers to a lead projectile, but it's also used to describe what is otherwise called the cartridge, a word with roots in medieval Latin. A cartridge is also called a round, from the original round musket balls. "Ammunition" refers to one or more cartridges.

Whatever the name, ammunition in a modern firearm is loaded through the breech, rather than down the muzzle. That advance came when inventors in the nineteenth century figured out how to design breechblock mechanisms that could quickly open and close while withstanding the force of exploding gunpowder. Reduced to its most basic element, a modern firearm design begins with selecting—or inventing—the breechblock. As John Browning later wrote, "With me, the breech closure is the initial point, everything else is designed to conform to it."[8]

In Jonathan's harmonica gun the sliding bar was drilled to hold five charges that could be fired in quick succession. The loaded bar slid sideways into the rifle and was locked in place by a lever. With a pull of the trigger the hammer snapped forward, struck a percussion cap, and ignited the powder.

To reload, the lever was released, the bar was slid over, and the next chamber was aligned with the barrel. About four hundred of the rifles were built over the next decade as the family traveled west, pausing in Iowa before setting out for Utah with a family of eleven children and seven wagons of supplies and equipment, and carrying a respectable $600 in savings. They arrived in Salt Lake Valley on October 2, 1852, midway through the great Mormon migration west.

By then Jonathan was forty-seven years old and had lived more than half his life. Nevertheless, he marked his arrival in Mormon Utah by starting two new families, permitted by the Mormon doctrine of plural marriage. In 1854 he married his second wife, a thirty-seven-year-old native Virginian, Elizabeth C. Clark. She had two daughters named Mary and Nancy from a previous marriage in Illinois—a marriage Jonathan had in fact presided over nine years earlier as a justice of the peace. Clark and that husband made the trek to Utah and settled in Ogden, where they divorced and she became reacquainted with Jonathan. What the first Elizabeth thought is unclear, though some family accounts say displeasure prompted her to find separate living quarters.

The second Elizabeth and Jonathan had three more children. The first was John Moses, who arrived in 1855, followed by a sister who died as an infant in 1857. Two years later Elizabeth gave birth to Matthew Sandefur, his middle name the maiden name of Elizabeth's mother. John Moses became the inventor and Matthew the financial wizard behind what eventually became a joint enterprise called the Browning Bros. They grew up in an adobe home Jonathan built for Elizabeth and her children at what is now the corner of Twenty-Seventh Street and Adams Avenue in Ogden, some ten or twenty yards from his crude blacksmith shop. Hastily erected soon after his arrival in Utah, it was built of green, freshly cut timber boards with the bark still attached. Jonathan installed an anvil, hearth, bellows, and foot-driven lathe carried all the way from Illinois.

Jonathan wed for a third time in 1858, marrying Ann Emmett, twenty-eight, an emigrant from the United Kingdom with a two-year-old daughter, Sarah, who died before she reached adulthood. It's unclear whether Ann was ever married to Sarah's biological father.[9]

Jonathan was now the patriarch responsible for three families. That fact must have hit home with particular force when his second wife, Elizabeth, gave birth to Matthew on October 27, 1859, just ten months after his third wife, Ann, gave birth to her first son, Jonathan Edward Browning, nicknamed Ed. Six more children followed for a total of twenty-two among Jonathan's three wives. They lived a simple, difficult frontier existence, in three different homes. One of Ann's sons, T. Samuel, recalled their adobe home had only two rooms, two windows, and a dirt floor. "Mother made all of our clothes," he said. "She would wash and card the wool, spin and weave it, and cut it and sew it." The ubiquitous sagebrush was used as fuel for heating and cooking, and Jonathan "usually killed a beef, put it into brine and then hung it high above the fireplace to dry. We could just slice it off and I remember how good it tasted." Unruly children were disciplined with "a strap on the seat of our pants."[10]

The grown children from Jonathan's first marriage never developed the close family ties established by their younger half siblings. The children of second wife Elizabeth Clark—who'd nurse her husband's first wife in her old age—and third wife Ann generally considered themselves members of a single family.

Jonathan branched out into new business endeavors, including a brickyard, a leather tannery, and a sawmill, though none brought prosperity. He held positions in the church and served in the state legislature. He proved to be a "rough and ready" engineer, skills that put him in wide demand, but despite his popularity, and a reputation for honesty and skill, economic security eluded him. Grandson Jack described Jonathan with this carefully written paragraph:

> Thus, versatile in imagination and mechanical skills, generous, never thrifty, obeying more wholeheartedly than most the admonition to "love thy neighbor as thyself" and, let it be admitted, gullible, Jonathan soon saw his shop turned into a kind of community first-aid station. He made a good deal of money, but always, as it came in a new project was waiting for it—or the outstretched hand of a borrower. If he had possessed a moderate talent for business management, he could have become wealthy. As it was, no man in the community worked harder, accomplished more, and had less to show for it. He lived in confusion, and seems to have been only mildly troubled by it.[11]

The business failings of the father were not to be repeated by John and Matt.

Ogden's isolated character abruptly changed in 1869 with the completion of the Transcontinental Railroad, 1,933 miles long and connecting Omaha, Nebraska, to a wharf on San Francisco Bay, with a major hub in Ogden. Chinese and Irish emigrants had built the line by hand, forty-foot rail by forty-foot rail, installing each with a choreographed display of hard labor. Divided into crews of a dozen men, the first laid down wooden crossties, atop which another crew laid one-thousand-pound iron rails. Lever men moved each rail into place, bolters connected it to the previous rail, and spikers pounded in ten spikes per rail. Then it was all repeated again, and again, and again. The Union Pacific crew working westward arrived in Ogden on March 8, 1869, to find the entire town gathered for a celebration. At 2:30 p.m. the coal-fired locomotive *Black Hawk* steamed into view, slowly rolling in on the newly laid tracks.[12]

"A number of us boys had heard that it was coming," Samuel said. "So we went out to the south end of town and climbed over a bank and heard it whistle." He was nine years old and had never seen a train or heard an earsplitting steam whistle and found, "It frightened us very much." The track crews worked into the center of town, and "when the train came into Ogden, and whistled, people were so frightened they ran in all directions." Children fell into a muddy trench in their panic.

After the *Black Hawk* ground to a halt, a band played, artillery fired a salute, and a celebration lasted into the night. Track work resumed the next day, and on May 10, after another fifty-seven miles of rail were laid, a Union Pacific train met a Central Pacific train at Promontory, Utah. The moment was recorded in the famous photograph of two locomotives head-to-head on a single track, surrounded by workingmen and dignitaries posing motionless for the camera.

Never profitable, and plagued by corruption, the railroad nevertheless changed the national concept of time. A trip from Washington, D.C., to San Francisco, which previously took months, cost $1,000, and required either a voyage around Cape Horn or a trek across the disease-ridden Isthmus of Panama, was reduced to seven days, including stops. Within a year, $65 purchased a seat in "immigrant" class—on a bench—and a trip from one coast to the other. Equally important, freight no longer moved at the pace of an ox or horse, and the telegraph, paralleling the rails, joined cities and towns in near-instant communication. When John Browning began designing his firearms he ordered supplies directly from the large wholesalers in New York City, communicating with them by letter in a matter of days. If the need was urgent, a telegram arrived in hours.

The quality of life in Ogden also changed. Some Mormons worried that an influx of railroaders and non-Mormons would undermine the Latter-day Saints' strict prohibitions against drinking, swearing, premarital sex, and gambling, and there was, inevitably, an influx of "Gentiles" and their less-than-Mormon practices. The wickedness reached its apogee at a transient "hell on wheels" labor camp in Promontory. Workers lived in box-cars surrounded by tents serving as hotels, restaurants, saloons, gambling dens, and brothels. There were con men, assorted criminals, and one fellow called Behind the Rock Johnny, said to have bushwhacked five people. Ogden's population grew to ten thousand and it acquired the nickname Junction City, along with a red-light district of national repute.[13] Each year, tens of thousands of passengers traveling east or west stopped in Ogden to change trains and entertain themselves along Twenty-Fifth Street, a broad avenue a few blocks over from Browning's home, extending from the station into the center of town and lined with hotels, bars, and, discreetly, bordellos.

The year of the railroad's arrival also marked the end of John's formal education. At age fifteen, he had completed the equiva-lent of eighth grade. His few teachers had only modest educations themselves, and one is said to have told John he'd exhausted his instructors' store of knowledge. Life outside the classroom con-tinued to offer an education of its own.

For nearly a decade, starting in the 1860s and ending in the early 1870s, a Native American—his tribe is unknown—appeared at the Browning homestead twice a year. He dropped a ragged bundle of possessions in the barn, set himself down at the base of an apple tree, and began constructing moccasins. "He never spoke, never even nodded; the lot might still have belonged to his people so did he make himself at home," Jack wrote. Once or twice a day Elizabeth sent John out with a meal. In the first years the young Browning delivered the food and wandered away, until one day he delivered an extra ration of food and asked the In-dian to show him how to cut and sew the deerskin into footwear. "Although there was no exchange of words, there was doubtless a spiritual confabulation between the two creative artists. John was permitted to pick up this or that piece for close examination, to slip a hand into a finished moccasin, and trace every seam," Jack wrote. Years later Browning came across a display of Native American handiwork and showed his children the little tricks of construction taught to him as a child.

He also built himself a bow and carved and fletched his own arrows, becoming sufficiently skilled to trade his handiwork to siblings and neighbors' children in return for their labor. "He could get his chores done for a week for a bow and a couple of arrows." Of course, the buyer would soon need additional arrows, which John traded for eggs, potatoes, and the occasional nickel. When he wanted material for his own moccasin making, John staged a demonstration for a local Native American youth and traded a bow and arrow for tanned deerskin.

By 1869 Browning possessed a range of metalworking skills. He could saw, file, weld—hammering strips of metal into a larger, stronger piece—and use a hearth and bellows to forge and shape iron and steel. That spring a freight wagon driver arrived with a finely made but now badly damaged single barrel shotgun. It had been crushed when a wooden cargo box fell on the stock and metal parts—the trigger, springs, hammer, and levers that comprise a firearm's "action." The barrel was intact, but the warped and twisted action made the cost of repair exorbitant. The customer was both in a hurry and drunk, the story went, so he purchased one of Jonathan's reconditioned guns with a $10 gold piece. On his way out he handed the seemingly useless shotgun to a surprised and pleased young John.

Unconstrained by time or the need to turn a profit, Browning saw an opportunity, as the expensive barrel was the one part Jonathan's shop couldn't replicate. He laid the damaged gun parts out on the bench for a close inspection and felt his confidence vanish. John had no idea what, exactly, to do. Where to begin? How was he to convert this mashed-up collection of metal and wood into a functioning firearm? Frustrated, stewing in a potent mix of youthful anger and pride, with the chance to own the best shotgun in town disappearing before his eyes, John burst out with a curse. "Damn it to hell!"[14]

On the other side of the shop Jonathan was shaping metal parts for a sawmill, his latest entrepreneurial effort. He looked up and pointed a big steel file at his son. "John Moses, don't you know that everything you say and do is recorded?" And jabbed the tool skyward.

For young John it was a moment of sublime exasperation, followed by the discovery that the unconscious mind, stimulated by stress, can solve the previously insoluble. Spurred by his irritation, Browning's mind spit out an idea, and he hit on the thought process that underlay his work for the next six decades.

"A good idea starts a celebration of the mind, and every nerve in the body seems to crowd up to see the fireworks," he said years later. "It was a good idea, one of the best I ever had, and so simple it made me ashamed of myself."

"Boy-like—and very often man-like too—I had been trying to do the job all at once, with some kind of magic," Jack wrote in the 1950s, quoting the story told by his father decades earlier. Browning at that young age taught himself how to solve mechanical problems by first discovering where to start—importantly the *correct* place to start—and then proceeding in a strict sequence. "The oldest 'step at a time method,'" he called it. "The idea was no great shakes itself," but as he correctly observed, "It requires a lot of patience and a good many men get discouraged and quit."

The years already spent in his father's shop also proved their value. "It seemed as though every haphazard bit of knowledge I picked up playing in the shop, watching Pappy, doing little jobs for him, and every knack I'd learned they all bunched together and focused like a lot of little lights. In the aggregate to make quite an illumination. I learned right there how to use your brain."

The next morning he spread the parts across the workbench and, as he examined each piece, saw "that there wasn't one I couldn't make if I had to."

John rebuilt the shotgun in two months, finding time between chores and work in the shop. The quality of his final product was on par with the high-end barrel, though Jonathan couldn't quite come out and say so. Instead, he offered a thick plank of expensive walnut for the shotgun's new stock.

As Jonathan spent more time attending to his outside business ventures, he left John to run the shop, overseen by his mother, Elizabeth. With his father's attention already spread thin among his many children and three wives, John became accustomed to running his life pretty much as he pleased, which clashed with Jonathan's prime principle of child raising—at least with boys—to never allow an idle moment for fear trouble would ensue. Jonathan became infamous for concocting make-work jobs. John became skilled at evading them. As the oldest among Jonathan's second and third broods, he also became the de facto leader.

One anecdote from the early 1870s illustrates John's role as intermediary between older father and youthful children. In advance of a summertime three-day trip to Salt Lake City Jonathan called together John, Matthew, and the four boys of his third wife—George, Samuel, Ken, and Tom—and announced that during his absence they were to busy themselves digging a cellar hole for a supposed addition to the homestead, notwithstanding that it meant three days sweating in the July sun. Once Jonathan departed, however, John cobbled together an escape from the unpleasant task. First, a customer dropped off a repair job, and John pointedly negotiated the price up from $2 to $2.50, sure to please his father. That gave John an excuse to remain indoors. Then an uncle on his way to repair an irrigation ditch arrived with a bent shovel. John negotiated a deal. In return for fixing the shovel the uncle would put the boys to work on the ditch in the mornings, and let them swim in the canal in the afternoons. That pleased the four boys. When Jonathan returned there was no hole in the ground, but John showed him $2.50 in gold and described the ditch repair. Jonathan took $2 and gave John 50 cents for ammunition. No more was heard of the cellar project.

John increasingly forsook work for hunting, riding into the mountains in pursuit of majestic elk, which could reach seven hundred pounds and sport a massive rack of antlers. In summers the animals roamed above six thousand feet on aspen-covered mountainsides, moving downhill as winter approached. Years later—while eating by himself in a Hartford hotel—Browning was approached by young magazine writer Lucian Clay. Browning refused to discuss his firearms work but eagerly recalled his youthful hunting adventures. "He went on to tell me of the year when he lived on elk steaks for weeks at a time—elk steaks for breakfast, elk steak sandwiches for lunch while hunting, and steaks for supper."[15] Those mountain journeys were almost certainly in the mid-1870s, when John was in his late teens or early twenties and trying to figure out his future.

Browning knew a life spent repairing old muzzle-loaders offered only terrible boredom. It would have taken an exceedingly dim mind not to be inflamed with curiosity and restlessness by the strangers crowding Ogden streets, borne back and forth across the continent by locomotives moving east and west at all hours of the day and night. Browning could have pursued other work—the railroad would have welcomed a talented mechanic—but he never did so: "I couldn't bring myself to ask anybody for a job. It seemed to me that by the act of asking a man for a job I admitted my inferiority to him." Browning added, "The fact is, I was lazy." If so, it was laziness only by Browning's definition: "The only shop work I liked was gun work." But by his early twenties he'd been hammering, filing, and fitting the same parts for more than a decade. There was little more to learn from fixing guns.

Browning was freed from that drudgery by the scientific advancements that transformed America in the later decades of the nineteenth century. Had John lived just ten or twenty years earlier he would have been stymied by crude materials and unsophisticated technology. Browning's genius lay in imagining new machines—which is what a firearm is—and the guns he created grew from chemical, metallurgical, and manufacturing advances. As Browning acknowledged to family members later in life, those discoveries matched his talents and took him from small-town repairman to international inventor.

• • •

Two new technologies in particular laid the foundation of Browning's career, developments he followed from behind his workbench in Ogden. Most important was the advent of metallic ammunition, which meant that by the early 1870s muzzle-loaders were rapidly supplanted by breech-loading rifles. No longer did powder and ball have to be poured down the barrel and then compressed with a ramrod. These new rounds were called rim-fire cartridges because a pressure-sensitive explosive was layered inside the rim of a thin copper base easily crushed by a gun's hammer. A drawback, however, was that soft copper limited rim-fire cartridges to small, low-pressure charges. Otherwise, the car-tridge could rupture and jam the firearm.

Rimfire cartridges were soon supplanted by sturdier center-fire ammunition, with the explosive primer contained in a small metal cup pressed into the cartridge base. Because the base didn't have to flex, the ammunition maker could use a thick shell of brass, a robust alloy of copper and zinc.

This was a big deal. The size and power of a bullet was now only limited by the strength of the steel barrel and action. In response the Winchester Repeating Arms Company in New Haven, Connecticut, upgraded its existing rimfire lever-action rifle and gave it a new name, the Model 1873. Readers will know it by a marketing slogan: "The gun that won the West." It was, indeed, sought after by settlers, cowboys, and Native Americans, too, as George Armstrong Custer learned to his regret in 1876. His troops were armed with U.S. Army issue single-shot carbines while some 25 percent of the Lakota, Cheyenne, and Arapaho warriors carried lever-action repeaters.

The Model 1873 fit easily in a saddle scabbard, held fifteen rounds, and could fire as quickly as a shooter could work the lever and pull the trigger. It also had its own significant limita-tion. The internal mechanism that loaded, fired, and ejected the ammunition—called the action—couldn't withstand the high pressure generated by long-range cartridges. It limited the rifle to low-powered revolver rounds, also designed and produced by

Winchester. While sufficient for short-range hunting and self-defense, it was unsuitable for the military. The Army wanted a cartridge that traveled farther and hit harder and for its sturdier single-shot rifles adopted the powerful .45-70 cartridge. The first number describes a bullet nearly a half inch in diameter, the second the weight of black powder in grains, in this case about equivalent to a modern nickel.[16] Combined with a brass cartridge the round was 2.55 inches long. The .45-70 could kill a deer, or slay an Indian, at twice the range of Winchester's revolver ammunition. Widely available at a reasonable cost, the .45-70 cartridge became a favorite among hunters and target shooters, leaving Winchester at an increasing competitive disadvantage.

The year 1873 also saw a near catastrophe in the Browning household. Jonathan was heavily invested in real estate while unable—or unwilling—to collect on debts owed to him by fellow townspeople. With cash tight, Jonathan purchased a cut-rate load of wet coal and carelessly tossed a shovelful into the shop's open hearth. Moisture in the coal flashed into steam and turned the black nuggets into incendiary bombs that scattered burning embers across the wood floor. An otherwise small accident developed into a near disaster because the workshop floor was only swept twice a year. Feeding on dry wood shavings and other debris, the smattering of small conflagrations began merging into a single, large one. Elizabeth rushed in with a bucket to help fight the blaze. It was touch-and-go, but father, wife, and son quenched the flames, after which Jonathan's second wife unloaded on her husband's lackadaisical attitude toward neatness, cleanliness, and organization.

"Good thing if this rubbish heap burned down long ago," she said. "What do you reckon people say when they pass here?" Her condemnation took in the exterior walls, unpainted and still shedding bark, and the sign, which hung by a single nail and was so weathered as to be near unreadable. "I wouldn't keep pigs in this place," she said.

The eighteen-year-old John Browning knew his mother was

correct on all counts. Jonathan had thrown the shop together twenty years earlier, and it had received little maintenance since. If the shop was to remain a going concern the family patriarch would have to confront reality. That task fell to John, who dreaded a confrontation with the old man. Jonathan had abandoned the religion of his parents to embrace a controversial new faith, sired three families, and crossed the Great Plains to Ogden, where his vigorous work helped secure the town's future. Taking on his father would be like taking on Goliath, John said. When the time came, John found his father sitting with one foot wrapped around the anvil, and a different mythical figure came to mind, the ancient Roman god of fire:

> When I came in and saw Pappy sitting on the anvil, he looked, somehow, like Vulcan himself. I was so used to seeing a giant of a man, shaped by a rough and rugged life. Seated on the anvil, one heel hooked on the block, the sledgehammers and tong sprawled about him, he took a picture that hasn't faded in all these years.

But there was no fight in the old man.

Jonathan sold the property where his shop and home were located—the southeast corner of Twenty-Seventh Street and Adams Avenue in Ogden—"together with all the improvements" to John and Matt for $500 on January 7, 1879.[17] The exterior was refurbished with new siding and the interior was painted. Matt joined John full-time in the shop, and their daily chatter about repairs included a running critique of each malfunctioning firearm. The extent of John's skill was still unclear. The brothers "ridiculed some of the guns we fixed, and I damned some of them when Pappy wasn't there, but it never occurred to us to make better ones. He was too old, and I was too young," said John. His life remained unformed until, the story goes, a particularly frustrating repair job moved him to declare the defective firearm a "freak." He invited his father over to take a look.

Jonathan's eyesight was failing, and he leaned in close as John said, "I can make a better gun than that myself." Jonathan, now seventy-two and knowing his end was far closer than his beginning, looked up. "I know you could, John Mose. And I wish you'd get at it. I'd like to live to see you doing it."

CHAPTER TWO

LAND OF INVENTION

In 1875, after twenty-four years of painful excavation through New England limestone, a railroad tunnel opened that connected Massachusetts to the farms and burgeoning industrial centers west of Albany, New York. At nearly five miles it was the second-longest tunnel in the world, exceeded only by an eight-and-a-half-mile excavation through the French Alps. Engineering firsts included the use of pneumatic drills, which performed admirably, and a tunnel-boring machine, which failed after ten feet. Better luck was had with nitroglycerin and new electronic detonators, though accidents claimed the lives of 193 workers.[1]

Fatalities aside, the central engineering challenge was ensuring that the teams digging from opposite sides of the Berkshire Mountains met head-on underground. The solution was to erect six stone guide towers linked by a cable laid out exactly above the planned route. Each day surveyors inside the tunnel took careful plots and compared them to the data from above ground. Much checking and rechecking was required, but the system was nevertheless simple and elegant. The tunnels met exactly as planned.

The nation cheered, and as the first trains chugged under the mountain, Boston's *Atlantic* magazine extolled the surveyors' skill with a sports analogy written in torturous nineteenth-century prose: "No Creedmoor rifle needs to be aimed so nicely in order to hit the bulls-eye. No allowances for wind to swerve, or the power of gravitation to draw down the ball from its proper course, render the marksman's problem so difficult to solution as the engineers' in this case."

No American should be surprised by the sporting reference, though twenty-first-century *Atlantic* readers will likely be taken aback to realize that the magazine's nineteenth-century, upper-crust Yankee subscribers not only knew what a Creedmoor rifle was—a type, not a specific manufacturer—but also the ins and outs of long-range ballistics.

Creedmoor was the name of a village, now part of the New York City borough of Queens, where in 1871 America was introduced to long-distance target shooting by a new association of Civil War veterans and National Guard officers. They were aiming to solve a persistent problem: City-bred recruits were lousy shots. "Soldiers who could not shoot straight were of little value," retired general George W. Wingate wrote in rank understatement. Wingate's new organization, the National Rifle Association, intended to fix that. A Gettysburg veteran and attorney who managed construction of Brooklyn's first elevated railway, Wingate believed shooting wasn't just a necessary military skill but a builder of character. Competition with a dangerous weapon, he declared, "develops coolness of nerve under excitement, powers of observation and rapid judgment."[2]

Wingate's new organization constructed a firing range and shooters began practicing just as the Irish national sharpshooting team, fresh from happily beating the British in 1873, issued a challenge "to the riflemen of America." There was no existing national American team, so Wingate and his local club recruited eight men, a combination of veterans and professional gunsmiths. The contest became a national sensation, and on the warm Saturday afternoon of September 26, 1874, between eight thousand and ten thousand spectators overwhelmed the local train line. Flanking the line of riflemen, the audience watched each team member fire fifteen shots at targets set out at eight hundred, nine hundred, and one thousand yards, at which distance the bull's-eye was nearly invisible to the naked eye.

The Americans used two types of single-shot, black-powder,

breech-loading rifles.[3] One was based on an 1848 design by the Sharps Rifle Company, updated but still showing its pre–Civil War roots. The second was produced by E. Remington & Sons, a firm equally well-known for its manufacture of an invention called the typewriter. The makers of both rifles saw a marketing opportunity, so Sharps and Remington provided firearms optimized with select barrels and sophisticated sights inscribed with minute gradations for exact shot placement. A factory expert from each manufacturer was on the team.

The Irish used custom muzzle-loaders from a prestigious Dublin firm, Rigby & Son. It, too, had a factory rep on the firing line—John Rigby, a descendant of the founder. Long-range shooting was a well-established sport in the United Kingdom, and the Rigby muzzle-loaders ranked among the best firearms, though they had to be charged the old-fashioned way, with powder and lead ball loaded into the top of the barrel and pushed down with a rod. Some purists believed it would prove the more accurate device.

The purists were almost right. After a morning and afternoon of loud booms and sulfurous smoke, the Irish won the eight-hundred-yard shoot, the Americans the nine hundred. The crowd swelled through the day; one fantastic estimate said there were forty thousand spectators by late afternoon for the one-thousand-yard match, which came down to the last cartridge fired by Col. John Bodine of New Jersey. The Americans' best marksman, Bodine was six feet tall and sported bushy muttonchop sideburns. Unlike his teammates, he grew no mustache, and at forty-eight he'd already turned gray. On this day a thirsty Bodine grabbed for a bottle of ginger ale before his last shot only to have the glass burst and slice his shooting hand.[4]

Bodine was renowned for his coolness under pressure, and now he proved it. A cloth appeared, was wrapped around the wound, and Bodine stretched out on the ground in prone position, his Remington rifle hard against his shoulder and his left hand—his good hand—supporting the fore end. He slowly took aim (perhaps clouds were passing over, shadowing the distant target) and squeezed the trigger. Nearly four seconds passed before the bullet struck home. For another moment the result was a mystery. Then the target was carried forward and the New Yorkers burst into cheers, for Bodine had scored a bull's-eye on the final shot of the match.[5] The Americans won 934 to 931. It was the lead story in the next day's *New York Times*. "A Victory for America" read the headline. "Their success is the reward of steady and well-attested prowess," the *Times* declared.

There was no news story in Ogden, but nineteen-year-old John Browning most certainly read the *Salt Lake Herald*, published thirty-five miles to the south, which ran a detailed story headlined: "The American Team Wins." The Irish were said to have borne defeat well, and the Lord Mayor of Dublin accompanied them to competitions in Washington, D.C., New Orleans, Louisville, Philadelphia, and Chicago, where they met President Ulysses S. Grant. Shooting clubs popped up around the country. Such excitement must have rankled Browning, who found himself stuck, mentally and physically, in his father's shop, living and working in a state of "barely controlled exasperation."

He was growing up, indeed was an adult by frontier standards, and feared ending up like Jonathan—a jack-of-all-mechanical-trades, conscripted to solve all manner of problems inflicting Ogden's machines while remaining cash-poor and forever teetering near financial ruin. Browning believed his father had squandered his talent and feared falling into the same rut.

So he faced the difficult task of judging himself. How was Browning to understand his abilities? Who, or what, was he to measure himself against? Around this time, an exact year is unknown, Browning began reading *Scientific American*, the weekly chronicle of discoveries and inventions bursting forth from the world's leading industrial society. It cost $3.20 a year for a subscription, postage included, for often exhaustive articles and finely detailed illustrations. Each issue featured an "Index of Inventions," columns of tiny six-point type listing the latest patents by type, name, and number. Already there were more than one hundred thousand new ideas on file with the government. The discovering and inventing, however, was mostly east of the Mississippi River, a reality that intimidated the young Browning.

How did one invent? "Did he learn how in college?" Jack Browning wrote, quoting his father from memory. "He must have a fine shop. Nobody could do any inventing in our shack, that was certain. I actually wished that I lived back east, where I could snoop around and find out how guns were invented. Every now and then, in repairing a gun, I'd see what looked like a better way to perform an operation, and even make a rough sketch." Into his early twenties Browning didn't yet comprehend that invention's primary requirement was a mind, not a tool bench. "I was still wishing I was back east where all the inventing was done. Inventing was still beyond the mountains, mysterious."

By then virtually every model of firearm had crossed the Brownings' workbench, thanks to Ogden's role as a railroad terminus. Innumerable firearms, new, used, and military surplus, of every caliber and design, were shipped west by wholesalers or carried by settlers—rifles and pistols, single shots and repeaters, each with its attendant faults and failures caused by design, accident, or wear.[6] For an aspiring inventor, it was a graduate-level course in what worked and what didn't, and a smart student saw how disparate mechanisms that failed in one application could be redesigned, repurposed, and reimagined.

Browning was twenty-three years old in 1878 when his father's admonition to invent overcame his self-doubt. But what, exactly, would he build?

The history of firearm design is as much a history of failure as success, and inventing a reliable, affordable firearm in mid-nineteenth-century America was a far more difficult task than one might imagine in a nation now awash with modern weapons. During the Civil War at least eighteen different manufacturers produced some version of a repeating handgun, but none lasted much past 1865, except for two firms whose superior designs and manufacturing talent made them household names: Colt and Smith & Wesson. A similar winnowing out occurred among the many new rifle makers, as the advent of metallic cartridges made feasible reliable repeating rifles. At least a dozen inventors, motivated by varying combinations of patriotism, money, fame, and simple mechanical curiosity, presented rifles to the Army's Ordnance Department. Its officers resisted, claiming soldiers armed with repeaters would merely waste ammunition, but eventually Union cavalry received seven-shot Spencer carbines. Infantry units with troops from the better-off classes purchased repeaters on their own. Some ten different rifle designs saw action, though most were troubled by one flaw or another. The best was the fifteen-shot Henry rifle, which became the basis for Winchester's famous models 1866 and 1873 lever-action arms.

Jack Browning's manuscript suggests his father considered, and rejected, building a repeating rifle of his own design. His creative insecurity no doubt played a role, though the primary constraint was not his imagination but his tools. Browning lacked the steam- and water-powered cutting and shaping machines that were used to form steel by industries back east. In his shop, parts for repairs were sourced from the corner junk piles and hardened steel was scrounged from wrecked train axles, abundant at the Union Pacific depot. The metal was chopped into smaller pieces with chisel and hammer, heated and forged on the blacksmith's anvil, and finally shaped with files, drills, or the foot-powered lathe that Jonathan had carried to Utah from the Midwest. So Browning set out to invent a single-shot rifle with the strengths of the Sharps or Remington, but none of their weaknesses. It had to be a unique gun, since a firearm that merely mimicked those designs, with a few frills added to sidestep their patents, would find no market in the West, where a rifle provided food, income, and protection. He needed a new idea. Browning found it as he devised the firearm's most important part, called the breechblock, around which all else was designed.

Browning borrowed an idea from the Sharps rifle, designed in 1848 by New Jersey–born Christian Sharps, who made the first commercially successful rifle loaded from the breech, the back end of the barrel, rather than by jamming a bullet and powder down the muzzle. A cartridge inserted into the Sharps's barrel entered the "chamber," which as noted earlier must be sealed so high-pressure gas from the gunpowder goes in only one direction—out the barrel. Sharps's idea was to use a movable chunk of steel called a falling block. It was controlled by a lever and traveled up and down in metal grooves cut into the rifle's interior sides. Raising the lever lifted the block and sealed the chamber. When the trigger was pulled the pressure from exploding powder pressed the block into the receiver together so they behaved as a single piece of steel and directed exploding gas down the barrel and out the muzzle, propelling the bullet to its target.

A downward pull on the lever lowered the block and ejected the spent cartridge and the rifle was ready to be reloaded. It was speedy, compared with a muzzle-loader. The high quality of their manufacture made Sharps rifles particularly accurate and expensive, at three times the cost of an ordinary muzzle-loader. In the Civil War, only eleven thousand were purchased by the Army for use by dedicated sharpshooting units.

Out in the Wild West, the Sharps became the rifle of choice for hunters who were achieving the seemingly impossible feat of destroying America's 20 million bison. The "unlimited supply of new and marvelously accurate breech loading rifles" allowed the slaughter to proceed swiftly, wrote William T. Hornaday, the chief taxidermist at the Smithsonian Institution.[7] Hornaday led an expedition west to discern the why and how of the buffalo's virtual extermination and also to kill, skin, and stuff some of the few remaining animals for specimens in a Smithsonian exhibit.

Hornaday watched the "hide hunters" in action. Dismounting from their horses, they crawled to within two hundred or three hundred yards of a herd before opening fire. "The oldest cow is always supposed to be the leader, and she is the one to kill first. The noise startles the buffaloes, they stare at the little cloud of white smoke and feel inclined to run, but seeing the leader hesitate, they wait for her. She, when struck, gives a violent start forward, but soon stops and the blood begins to run from her nostrils in two bright crimson streams. In a couple of minutes her body sways unsteadily, she staggers, tries hard to keep her feet, but soon gives a lurch sideways and falls."

To Hornaday's surprise, he discovered that the buffalo didn't flee at the sound of rifle fire, and concluded that the "phenomenal stupidity of the animals themselves" numbered among the reasons for their near extinction. As hunters dropped one buffalo after another, "they cluster around the fallen ones, sniff at the warm-blood, bawl aloud in wonderment, and do everything but run away."

Despite the Sharps's lethality, its drawbacks were evident. It had a large, awkward hammer and reloading required five separate movements.[8] Browning's competition also included a second popular rifle, the Remington Rolling Block, which as its name suggests, had a steel block and a hammer, each rotating on a thick steel pin.[9]

The Sharps, with its large external hammer, was clearly obsolete. The Remington was a design dead end, as a rolling block and a hammer of similar size was fundamentally duplicative. Better to combine them into a single unit. Even better would be a design that reduced the number of movements necessary to load, fire, and eject a cartridge. Both rifles were robust, so Browning's action—block, lever, trigger, hammer, and associated parts—had to shrug off the high pressure of a government military cartridge and safely handle the even more powerful buffalo ammunition. It also had to sell at a competitive price, which meant $30 or less, depending on caliber, options, and accessories.

In the Ogden workshop there was much trial and error, filing and hammering, as Browning never suffered from a paucity of ideas. "As soon as I started to make the gun I found my head so full of parts that my greatest difficulty was sorting them out." He cut templates from tin sheets or thick paper to check the shapes and interplay, running through one version after another and discussing each with his father. Jonathan spent his days ensconced on a box "mostly bossing Matt," who handled repairs and sales. Once a part seemed correct it was forged—pounded into shape, one hammer blow at a time—on the shop's anvil and then shaped by chisels and files. Browning did all the work by hand.

The important receiver, the metal frame that contains the trigger, block, springs, and hammer, was cut from a block of steel. John excavated the interior with hand drills and then used chisels and files to cut channels on each side to guide the block. Pin and screw holes were carefully drilled to place each moving part in its exact spot. With his crude tools Browning worked in thousandths of an inch or better. One or two swipes of a file could mean the difference between parts sticking and jamming and parts smoothly meshing.

He started work in 1878 and finished his first rifle in 1879. His design used a falling-block action like the Sharps, but there the similarity ended. In Browning's rifle, the block and the hammer moved together, turning what were multiple parts in the Sharps and Remington into a single unit controlled by the lever. A retracting firing pin was integrated into the block, thereby preventing accidental discharges. Loading and unloading was simple: Move the lever down, a spent cartridge was ejected. Load a new cartridge, move the lever up, and the rifle was ready to fire. That was it. Lever up, lever down. On May 12, 1879, Browning filed his first patent application. It described a rifle with a small, compact action, strong and elegant inside and out, touchstones that marked his future work.

To the modern reader surrounded by airplanes and automobiles Browning's rifle is an exceedingly simple machine, but attaining simplicity is itself a difficult achievement, and in 1879 his rifle was a notable advance in firearm design. Browning had made what the world would acknowledge as an ideal single-shot rifle, with an action of enormous strength despite its size. With minimal formal education, Browning had designed and forged a receiver, hammer, and block so robust that for decades Winchester used the 1885 rifle as its test bed for new ammunition.

● ● ●

The prospect of marriage must have added impetus to Browning's work. On Ogden's Main Street was the W.G. Child & Son dry-goods store, owned by Warren G. Child Sr., an impatient, ambitious man who'd survived the difficult early years at Ogden to prosper in construction before moving into retail. "Clothing, carpets, Gent's furnishing goods, silks, satins, hats and caps, boots and shoes, ladies underwear, etc.," said one advertisement for his shop.[10] His customers included John Browning, who met and began courting Child's daughter, Rachel, then sixteen years old. While she didn't discourage John's attentions, her father was ambivalent toward a prospective son-in-law who toiled away in a ramshackle shop with no certain prospect of improvement.

But John was handsome, hardworking, and ambitious and neither drank nor smoked. The couple were married on April 10, 1879, as two thousand miles away in New York City an attorney prepared the patent application for Browning's single-shot rifle—four illustrations on the first page followed by two pages of closely spaced text. Rachel's father gave the new couple a cookstove, a bedroom set, a cow, and a small organ for their new home.

Jonathan lived long enough to attend the wedding. He died on June 21, 1879, at age seventy-three and was buried with this eulogy: "The life, character and public and private example of Brother Browning have been such as to compel the bitterest foes of his religion to speak well of him as man." He left behind three wives, eighteen of his twenty-two sons and daughters still living, ninety-one grandchildren, and "12 or 15" great-grandchildren. Jonathan's property holdings weren't insignificant, but he died more than $5,000 in debt. He left no will, so his estate was overseen by a probate court judge.[11] He owned a seventy-eight-acre farm, heavily mortgaged, plus eleven acres with fourteen thousand bricks from his short-lived brickmaking endeavor. There were three items from the gunsmithing shop included in his estate: the foot-driven lathe, the anvil, and the bellows that blew pressurized air across the burning coals, increasing the oxygen flow and pushing temperatures to 2,500 degrees Fahrenheit, hot enough to melt steel.

They were important tools, which John believed he already owned. The January 1879 sales agreement, which Jonathan painstakingly wrote out in his own hand, encompassed not only the land on Twenty-Seventh Street but also "all the improvements and privaleges [*sic*] belonging to the same." That included the house where the brothers grew up and the gunsmithing shop, so John was surprised and upset when he learned those tools were to be auctioned off at an estate sale.

An auction put to risk the very business that not only supported John, Matthew, and their mother but also helped provide for Jonathan's third wife and her six living children. Particularly infuriating to John was that the executors of the estate were part of the family: a son by Jonathan's first wife, and the husband of one of his daughters. Nevertheless, on Saturday, November 8, 1879, at 10:00 a.m., the equipment went up for sale. John bought back the lathe for $20, the anvil for $5.25, and the bellows for $6.50.[12] He never forgave his half brother and brother-in-law.[13]

By then Rachel was pregnant with their first child, and Browning had become the nominal head of his father's second and third families. Inventing a gun was all well and good, but he had to make a living. As did Matt. They posted signs advertising firearm repairs and supplies along major thoroughfares and suddenly the shop had more business than the two men could handle. At the end of that year their half brother Ed, the offspring of Jonathan Browning's third marriage, left his job in the railroad freight yard and began what would be a lifelong career constructing the dozens of John Browning prototypes to come.

But that was the future. In 1879 all that Browning had was a single design. The question was what to do with it. He could sell the patent to a manufacturer, but he dreaded traveling east to knock on the doors of strangers. So far, the longest train ride he'd taken was to Salt Lake City. Increasing mechanization in the years leading up to the Civil War was relegating the local rifle maker to a rifle repairman, a transition all but completed when the government's Springfield Armory in Massachusetts began churning out one hundred thousand rifles a year between 1861 and 1865. The American arms makers were in and around New England, where Browning was a stranger. He didn't want to present himself and his rifle to those famed industrialists only to become a laughingstock. Yet making his rifle by himself, rifle by rifle, was a slow, burdensome, and boring future that risked turning his life into a near duplicate of his father's. What Browning *did* have was Matt, already demonstrating a bright sense of business, and their many half brothers. So John and Matt decided they would build a factory, modest as it would be, and go into the gun-making business.

By the next year, 1880, with their repair business flourishing, the Browning brothers purchased the essential machinery: a used steam engine to power the lathe, and a "mill"—a sort of drill that makes precision cuts up and down or sideways—used to turn raw steel into parts. Browning didn't make the barrels. They were produced to his specifications by those well-equipped factories back east, including by the well-known arms maker Remington, and shipped to Ogden. A copy of the receiver, the heavy metal shell into which all the other parts were fit, was dispatched to a steel fabricator who manufactured rough forgings that Browning and his brothers finished in the Ogden shop. To construct their one-story factory and retail storefront—Matt wanted to sell sporting goods—the Brownings used leftover material from the brick kiln once operated by their father.

Ogden residents didn't know quite what to think of John's factory but were impressed that a local boy had obtained a patent from the government in Washington, D.C. Doubts about his product were banished by those who saw the handmade prototypes. The gun's admirers included one man called Split Nose Barlow, whose nose, literally split down the middle, reportedly by a shard of steel from an exploding stove, had healed in two separate pieces.

Barlow trapped and hunted in the mountains with a Sharps rifle repaired by John. He was intrigued by the young Browning's invention and was said to have been particularly "tickled" when he saw that closing the lever automatically cocked the hammer. He pulled out a gold piece and offered it as payment for the first rifle from the Brownings' factory. John refused, since organizing the manufacturing process was proving a struggle. Browning was stymied until, at a serendipitous moment, came the unannounced appearance of a short, arrogant British gunsmith.

He was Frank Rushton, and he needed a job. A convert to Mormonism, Rushton was trained at Britain's sprawling Birmingham firearms factories and insisted to a dubious Browning that he could lead the brothers through the process of setting up their machinery and organizing production. A photo taken that year shows the Brownings and Rushton standing in front of the shop with rifles in hand, the six-foot-tall Browning brothers towering over Rushton, who at barely five feet looked suspiciously like a bearded child.

"For the first hour I was a little irritated by his strutting, but he was just compensating for his size, I suppose," Browning recalled. "We were a hulking lot of overgrown youngsters, yet Frank could see in no time that he knew more about setting up that machinery than all of us put together . . . Pretty soon he didn't look so short to me." In Jack's account, Browning describes Rushton as an answer to unspoken prayers. "He looked more like one of the angels Pappy thought might drop in at any time." As the days passed, Browning realized the true depth of Rushton's skill. "I learned more [from] Frank than from any other man I met, except Pappy." Nevertheless, before long Browning was improving on Rushton's methods. That impressed his brother Ed, who said John "figured out new ways, short cuts, that made Frank blink."[14]

The plan was to make twenty-five rifles as proof that the Browning gun factory was a reality. Ed did the milling work; Rushton fitted sights onto each barrel and fashioned jigs that Browning half brothers Sam and George used to drill and tap holes for pins and screws. Matt carved the wooden stocks, a skill his older brother had taught him as a child. By now the brothers' partnership was illustrated by the signs out front. One read: "John M. Browning's & Bro." The second, placed above the first, said: "Browning Bros." The sign also spelled "ammunition" with one *m*, a fact only realized when Browning's former schoolteacher passed by.

The parts were probably not interchangeable, and final assembly of each rifle required careful filing and shaping, particularly of the sear, a small but crucial part of hardened steel. It rotated on a pin and acted like a gear to control the hammer. When the rifle was cocked the sear gripped a groove cut into the base of the hammer. Spring tension held the parts together until the trigger was pulled, which allowed the sear to move, freeing the hammer to snap forward and fire the cartridge. Anything short of an exact fit made the rifle dangerous (if the sear slipped, the rifle could accidentally fire) or useless (if the sear didn't release) or both, if the sear worked erratically. Browning did that work himself.

To the Brownings' pleasant surprise, the first twenty-five rifles sold in a week for $25 each, along with necessary accessories like powder, bullets, cartridges, and "wiping sticks" to clear black-powder residue, raising the final sale price to $30, enough for John to present his brothers, and Frank, with a $5 gold-piece bonus. Within three months they made and sold one hundred, and suddenly there was money for store-bought clothes for Browning's wife and children and an occasional dinner of roast beef or canned oysters. Demand for the rifle didn't slump once the Ogden-area orders were filled. Browning's gun, it seemed, had acquired a reputation. Success, however, came with a significant downside.

Browning discovered that overseeing and producing the same firearm, time after time, was tiresome to the extreme. The magic of gunsmithing was in the inventing, not the grind of manufacturing. The sameness of repair after repair already "had become a great bore." After months spent setting up a production line, all the while keeping up with the daily inflow of repairs, he discovered that making rifle after rifle, each nearly identical to the other, was merely drudgery of a different sort. New firearm designs were taking shape in his head, and time spent producing the single shot was time not spent turning those ideas into metal.

• • •

Browning was saved from his self-inflicted manufacturing misery by Thomas G. Bennett, officially Winchester's vice president but practically speaking its chief executive. Cynics might say his rise to the top was begun the old-fashioned way, by marrying the boss's daughter, which is what Bennett did in 1872 when he wed Hannah Jane Winchester.[15] She was founder Oliver Winchester's youngest child, and while tongues wagged in New Haven social circles, the marriage proved a success for both the couple and the company.

Born in 1845, Bennett was sent to an elite private school in his native New Haven, intended to prepare students for nearby Yale College or the West Point Military Academy. When the Civil War broke out Bennett, then only sixteen, was named a second lieutenant in the Twenty-Eighth Regiment of Connecticut Volunteers—a unit of about one thousand men—and in January 1863 he was deployed to New Orleans. For the next six months the regiment moved slowly eastward along the Gulf Coast until it reached Fort Barrancas on the western end of the Florida Panhandle. In 1864, Bennett was promoted to first lieutenant and given command of Company C of Connecticut's Twenty-Ninth Regiment of Colored Volunteers.[16] From Annapolis, Maryland, the unit traveled south to join the federal siege around Richmond, Virginia, and in September were among 26,000 Union troops who assaulted rebel fortifications in the Battle of Chaffin's Farm. The two-day clash ended in a Union victory that left 691 soldiers dead and some 5,400 wounded, Bennett among them.

An African-American sergeant in Bennett's Twenty-Ninth, Alexander H. Newton, later a minister in the AME Church, described the encounter as a "slaughter pen."[17] As the regiment's commissary sergeant, Newton was responsible for supplying troops with food and water. Moving from company to company gave him a comprehensive view of the fighting. "The wounded and dying scattered over the battlefield thick," he wrote in a postwar memoir, "The explosion of bombs, the whizzing of bullets, the cracking of rifle; you would have thought that the very forces of hell had been let loose. And, indeed, it was a hell, the horrors of which no one could ever forget."

In his diary, Bennett described the black troops jeering at the enemy in the midst of combat. "You could hear the men taunting the Reb. cannoneers," he wrote. "'Why don't you load your old gun?'" the troops yelled at the Confederates. When enemy shots missed they taunted, "You ain't killing niggers as much as you was."

As the battle progressed, the Twenty-Ninth was ambushed by Confederate troops. Newton recounted that "we finally retreated under the cover of cavalry. The colored troops were the first to enter the field and the last to fall back."[18]

Newton's reference to Union cavalry raises a fascinating question. Were the Twenty-Ninth and their commander protected by cavalry armed with early lever-action repeating rifles? Quite possibly. Spencer repeating carbines were coming into wide use among Union horse soldiers, and one cavalry unit at the battle, the First District of Columbia Cavalry, was armed with the more advanced Henry repeater.[19] So the firsthand detail in Newton's memoir may be proof of a story that otherwise was too good to be true: that Bennett, the champion of the lever-action rifle, may have owed his life or liberty to one of the first breech-loading lever-action repeaters.

With the war over, Bennett returned to New Haven, graduated from Yale with a degree in engineering, and in 1870 joined Winchester. The company survived the industry's postwar contraction by upgrading the Civil War–era Henry rifle into the rimfire Winchester Model 1866, the first lever-action rifle with ammunition loaded through a gate in the side of the receiver, as viewers saw in countless movie Westerns. Foreign customers were pursued, and the sale of rifles and ammunition to Mexico, Chile, France, and Turkey kept the factory profitable.

Winchester's great success came with its next rifle, the famous Model 1873, derived from another improvement to the original Henry design. This rifle used the new center-fire cartridge, as described earlier. It was a relatively short-range pistol-caliber round, but with a magazine holding fifteen rounds there was no other rifle like it on the market. Newly minted celebrity William F. "Buffalo Bill" Cody wrote from Nebraska to declare: "I have been using and have thoroughly tested your latest improvement rifle. . . . I've tried and used every kind of gun made in the states for general hunting, or Indian fighting, pronounce your improved Winchester the boss." Sales took off, and by 1880 Winchester was the nation's third-largest civilian arms maker.

An influential segment of the firearms market, however, remained out of Winchester's grasp: the hunters and target shooters who wanted to use the long-range .45-70 military round. Its power, range, and ubiquity made it the cartridge against which all others were judged, yet Winchester made no rifle—single shot or lever action—capable of withstanding its breech pressure of 31,900 pounds per square inch at each shot. The blast dissipated in an instant—but that instant could blow apart Winchester's outdated toggle-link design.

The model 1873's price was lowered from $50 in 1874 to $28 in 1880 and Winchester introduced a version called the Model 1876 that used the same toggle-link action enlarged in length, width, and, unfortunately, weight. Yet the heavy, unwieldy result was still unable to handle the government cartridge's size and power. Competition appeared to ease in 1881, when Sharps went out of business, the victim of an ill-considered expansion that pushed the company into bankruptcy. More than filling that void was the new Marlin Firearms Co., which unveiled a .45-70 lever-action rifle that was aimed, pun intended, at the gaping hole in the Winchester product line. Adding to Winchester's woes, news arose that Colt, widely respected for its revolvers, was planning to enter the rifle business.

Amid those challenges, company founder Oliver Winchester died, followed only months later by his successor and son, William, who perished of tuberculosis. Bennett was elevated to the post of vice president with orders to solve Winchester's existential problem—its failure of imagination. None of the engineers or gunsmiths in its New Haven factory succeeded at conceiving a fresh design to replace the obsolete Henry toggle mechanism. That failure couldn't stand. Lever-action rifles were the core of Winchester's business and the basis for its reputation. It could not be an also-ran.

Bennett thought he found his solution by hiring away a top Colt engineer, William Mason, who with another colleague had designed Colt's .45-caliber revolver—competitor for the title of "gun that won the West" and later the favorite handgun of Western films. Mason joined Winchester in 1882 and designed two lever-action rifles, both failures.[20] One was prone to jamming and the other to excessive wear. The talented Mason thereby demonstrated the difficulty of inventing a machine packed with moving parts yet able to withstand heat, pressure, corrosion, the friction of metal-on-metal contact, and exploding gunpowder not once, but thousands of times. In a long career, Mason invented a variety of new manufacturing tools and obtained ninety-two patents, many for shepherding a better inventor's rifle and shotgun designs into mass production. That other inventor was John Moses Browning.

So unlikely was Winchester's discovery of a frontier genius, educated in a one-room schoolhouse and living in what amounted to a glorified western train stop, that versions of the story have been retold and debated for decades. A Winchester salesman based in Montana gets the credit. Or maybe Winchester was tipped off by Browning's New York City parts supplier. Or maybe it was a company representative in Utah who spotted the rifle and sent it east to Bennett. He, of course, immediately jumped on a train west to purchase the rights. So maybe Bennett presented Browning with his momentous first contract—the contract that freed him forever from manufacturing drudgery—in the spring of 1883. Or maybe it wasn't until December, after Winchester tried to copy Browning's rifle but failed to find a patent workaround.

The best-known account is in Jack Browning's book, written sixty-five years after the fact. It's dramatic but omits important details that are undoubtedly true, like the Browning brothers' infringement on a Winchester patent.

According to Jack's version, a Winchester representative in Montana, one Andrew McAusland, came upon a used Browning rifle and shipped it east to Bennett, who instantly realized it solved one part of his .45-70 problem—here was a single-shot rifle that filled the gap left by Sharps's demise, was easily capable of handling the powerful cartridge, and was better designed than any other single-shot rifle on the market. In this version Bennett—who was running the entire Winchester enterprise with its one thousand employees—received the rifle and within a week took a train west and walked unannounced into the Ogden shop. The eastern arms magnate saw a handful of young men, almost boys, working at various tasks. Matt approached him. Bennett noted he was a very young person and asked to speak to a Browning brother. Matt said he was one, to which the nonplussed Bennett replied, "You have an older brother?"

That's him, Matt said, and pointed at John, in rough clothes at the workbench. Negotiations were completed in a few hours. Browning asked for $10,000, later explaining that he couldn't imagine a higher number. Bennett offered $8,000 and the right to purchase Winchester products at a discount for resale in the Brownings' store. He gave Browning a check for $1,000, the balance to be paid in thirty days. Importantly, Browning is said to have convinced Bennett he was near completing a totally new lever-action rifle, sturdier and stronger than any sold in America.

The terms were written down in pen and ink—no doubt reviewed by Matt, the finance expert of the two brothers—signed, and Bennett took a train home the very same day.

That's the story in the Browning book.

The real story, or at least the version most likely true, is the one laid out in part by the late eminent firearms historian Herbert G. Houze. It begins not with Browning's rifle but with Winchester's patent for an ingenious pocket-sized reloading tool simply called the cartridge implement. Much like a modern multi-tool, it had two handles hinged at one end and contained all the tools needed to reload a brass cartridge. The "implement" could punch out a spent priming cap, press in a new one, re-form the cartridge, and press in a new bullet. The Brownings made and sold the implement without asking or obtaining permission from Winchester, a company notoriously vengeful toward such malefactors.

Browning's sin was spotted by Charles Benton, a Winchester salesman who visited the Ogden storefront in early 1883. Benton was smart enough to get his priorities straight, and while he reported the violation to his bosses in New Haven, he also sent a Browning rifle. Bennett, of course, realized it solved a problem that stymied Winchester's own designers. But business was business. Rather than spend what would be a significant sum to buy the patent, Bennett asked Mason to design a rifle that incorporated Browning's ideas but didn't violate his patent. Mason worked on the project for months, and only when he came up dry did Bennett stoop to open his checkbook.

That's essentially Houze's version. In fact, Bennett did travel to Utah as Browning family members recall in Jack's book, but not until late that year. In the Connecticut State Archives are two letters Bennett wrote to his wife after arriving in Ogden on December 10, 1883, one in the morning and one in the evening. After weeks spent traveling across America on business Bennett was left distinctly unimpressed. In the morning letter he wrote: "Our country is, I regret to write, a hollow sham gilded at its outer edges with a few places like N.H. and N.Y. and perhaps San Fran on the other side and with-in a vast plain of mud and rocks completely indescribable in its unattractiveness."[21]

"The Rockies are a sham," he continued, perhaps not realizing that the peaks beginning a few hundred yards west of his hotel were technically not the Rockies but the Wasatch Mountains. Nevertheless, he conceded that in Utah "the country commences to be inviting." He extolled the climate, saying that "the air is so clear that you see with great distinctness at long distances and miscalculate them greatly." He pointedly noted that he'd spotted no wildlife, no bison or antelope, "only one small wolf."

And it's empty compared to Connecticut. "There are no houses or people for hundreds of miles." Bennett told his wife he expected to spend one night in Ogden, as he had a meeting scheduled later that day. "I hope to go on to San Fran tomorrow, though it's too early to say with certainty as I have not yet seen my man." The man is not named, but the only person living in Ogden who mattered to Bennett was John Browning. That evening Bennett penned his second letter. "My Dear Girl, Since writing you this morning I have finished [indecipherable] my business here and am now sure to go to S.F. tomorrow."[22]

The deal was done. Browning was plucked from obscurity. One more step cementing the Browning-Winchester relationship was to come the following year, but as Bennett boarded his train out of Ogden he must have hoped he'd found his inventor. As for the "implement," Bennett had already allowed the Brownings to sell off their existing stock of 125 tools. As punishment for their patent infringement, the brothers paid Winchester $1.

CHAPTER THREE

CONQUERING THE EAST

John Browning was amused, Matthew less so. They were heading east to the Winchester factory in Connecticut, the very heart of the land of invention. The brothers told and retold the story of this trip throughout their lives, as it marked their entry into the world outside of Utah. John was twenty-nine years old, and Matthew, soon to turn twenty-five, was about to lose his lunch.

They boarded a Union Pacific train in October 1884, one of three that departed daily from Ogden's two-story wooden train station. It chugged along at 20 or 30 mph on a route straight across the prairie to Laramie, Wyoming, where the track took a brief turn before heading east again and crossing Nebraska to Omaha and the Mississippi River. From there it was up to Chicago and across the Midwest to New York, where they planned a one-day stop to meet their parts supplier. The final leg was to New Haven and the Winchester Repeating Arms Company, where the brothers intended to sell their new gun. It was a lever-action rifle nearly four feet long and weighing about nine pounds, carefully wrapped in heavy brown paper and twine. If Browning was correct it would prove him to be more than a one-gun wonder.

The cross-country train journey would take nearly a week, presuming no adventures or calamities. Bridges were known to collapse, trains did collide, and there was the occasional robbery. Passengers on the first long leg had to carry their own food or else disembark at station stops for meals of indeterminate qual-

49

ity, often wolfed down, usually while standing. That ill-served the nation's fastest mode of transportation, so dining car service was added. Those opulent rolling eateries served food of a quality and variety equal to the decor. A Pennsylvania Railroad menu from January 1884 offered passengers soup, broiled cod with oyster sauce, roast beef, turkey, ribs of beef with brown potatoes, and pork with applesauce. Side dishes included corn, peas, potatoes, turnips, stewed tomatoes, and baked sweet potatoes. For dessert there was pastry, ice cream, cake, or fruit. It cost one dollar. Seconds were unlimited.[1]

Matthew found the cornucopia irresistible and ate to the point of illness, forcing him into an involuntary fast for the next two days. In Browning's humorous retelling Matthew was compensating for a frontier childhood that had always left him "a little hungry." The story also illustrated John Browning's lifelong frugality, along with a dry, practical sense of humor. "He kept it down," Browning said of his brother's ultimate digestive success, "and at a dollar a meal he was money ahead."

They reached Chicago three days out of Ogden, switched rail companies, and spent the next eight hundred miles passing through the freshly harvested fields and industrial centers of the Midwest. Six days after leaving behind the mountains, high plains, and Ogden's eight thousand people, they disembarked shortly after dawn at New York's Grand Central Depot, the largest railroad station in the world, in a city of 2 million people. They were unashamedly astonished. Greeting them was a familiar face, a traveling salesman for the parts wholesaler Schuyler, Hartley & Graham, who served the Browning Bros. shop in Utah. He now led them south through Manhattan to the company's offices on Maiden Lane near the Federal Reserve Bank and New York Stock Exchange. A few minutes east was the world's first steel-wire suspension bridge, completed a year earlier, linking Manhattan to Brooklyn. A short stroll farther south was the nation's first commercial electric-generating station, operating in a collection of otherwise nondescript four-story buildings. It was the creation of Thomas A. Edison, already recognized as

America's greatest inventor, and it supplied power to some five hundred surrounding buildings fitted out with another Edison invention, the incandescent electric light.

Schuyler was a full-service company, selling new and surplus guns and firearm parts, outfitting pioneers heading west and exporting Civil War–era rifles overseas, so the brothers likely gawked at its stock of arms before walking to Battery Park on the tip of Manhattan at the conjunction of the Hudson and East rivers. It was one of the city's great public spaces, dominated by an eighteenth-century stone fort turned into the disembarkation point for European emigrants. It was eventually replaced by Ellis Island, but in 1884 the brothers strolled along streets filled with foreigners conversing in incomprehensible languages and clothed in garments never seen in Ogden.

They rented a hotel room for one night, and that evening the Schuyler guide escorted them into the ornate first-floor saloon. The Brownings watched, fascinated, as the bartender mixed juices and spices into alcoholic concoctions neither man had ever seen or tasted. Now they did both, Mormon prohibitions notwithstanding. From there they moved into the dining room for a meal that "made the dining car look like the summer kitchens back home," as Jack was later told. Perhaps there was wine with the meal, as afterward, "in the most pleasant state of mind imaginable," they headed off to a theater performance.

At evening's end they were back in the hotel lobby, to the consternation of the company salesman. Management had given him $10 to show the brothers a good time and here he had $2 left. What should they do? If Matthew was intoxicated with the day's adventures, John remained focused on their purpose. He saw an opportunity to scratch a worry nagging at him for months, so he asked the Schuyler man if he'd care to look at a gun.

The rifle was the final version of the repeater Bennett was teased with the previous December. As Browning promised, it was sturdy enough to handle not only the government cartridge but most any other black-powder round irrespective of explosive power. Its mechanism was unlike any other rifle, or at least any rifle Browning knew about. But what might he not know? What if Winchester or a competitor had leapfrogged his imagination with an even more advanced design?

"I don't want to hit Bennett for more money than there is in Ogden and have him tell me that somebody else, maybe Winchester, is ahead of me," he told Matt. The Schuyler salesman, John figured, would know the industry gossip and could provide a warning.

John unwrapped the package and watched the man, his name lost to history, make a close inspection, working the lever action and peering at the interior mechanism as the breechblock slid back and forth. He saw that Browning used the falling-block concept in a new way that turned the various parts of the action into a virtual steel block.

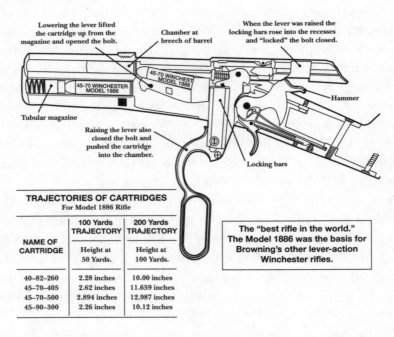

Lowering the lever lifted the cartridge up from the magazine and opened the bolt.

Chamber at breech of barrel

When the lever was raised the locking bars rose into the recesses and "locked" the bolt closed.

45-70 WINCHESTER MODEL 1886

45-70 WINCHESTER MODEL 1886

Hammer

Tubular magazine

Raising the lever also closed the bolt and pushed the cartridge into the chamber.

Locking bars

TRAJECTORIES OF CARTRIDGES For Model 1886 Rifle		
NAME OF CARTRIDGE	100 Yards TRAJECTORY Height at 50 Yards.	200 Yards TRAJECTORY Height at 100 Yards.
40–82–260	2.28 inches	10.00 inches
45–70–405	2.62 inches	11.659 inches
45–70–500	2.894 inches	12.987 inches
45–90–300	2.26 inches	10.12 inches

The "best rifle in the world." The Model 1886 was the basis for Browning's other lever-action Winchester rifles.

Lowering the lever caused five events to occur nearly instantaneously: Two thick steel bars on either side of the receiver slid down. The rectangular block moved backward. The spent cartridge was ejected out the top. The hammer was cocked. A fresh cartridge was lifted out of the tubular magazine under the barrel. Then a flick of the lever upward performed another three actions: the block moved forward, the cartridge was pushed into the chamber, and the steel bars slid upward. With a soft clunk the lever locked the bars, block, and receiver together. When the cartridge was fired, the explosive energy didn't try to force the action open, as in existing Winchesters, but instead pressed the moving parts together into a solid unit.

It was an enormously strong mechanism like nothing else on the market and would entrance anyone who depended on a rifle for food or protection. It was compact, worked smoothly, and like all of Browning's work it was mechanically elegant.

The salesman finished his examination and said, "It isn't necessary to tell you that you have, right here, in this hotel room, the best rifle in the world."

The next day when the brothers traveled their final eighty miles to New Haven, they arrived at the southernmost end of nineteenth-century America's Silicon Valley.[2] Beginning in the 1790s, a cadre of mechanics and inventors in arms factories stretching north along the Connecticut River into central Vermont invented the tools and techniques that enabled mass production of interchangeable parts. Winchester, Marlin, and Remington were in New Haven; Colt was in Hartford; and Smith & Wesson in Springfield. Lesser names filled other brick factories north to Windsor, Vermont. What they created was a modern system of industrial manufacturing originally called the armory system and later renamed the American system.[3] When the Browning brothers arrived in New Haven, Winchester was one of its leading practitioners.

The factory complex was a short carriage ride from the waterfront train station. Its central three-story brick building stretched eight hundred feet with another half-dozen buildings in the rear, and rising over all was the smokestack from Winchester's power plant, a steam engine that transmitted power via rotating wheels and gears that turned drive shafts running along the factory ceilings. Power was transmitted the final ten or fifteen feet via thick leather belts that connected the drive shafts to pulleys on each machine. Hundreds of metal cutting, shaping, and drilling machines filled the factory's halls, all lined up in rows, each with a dedicated operator.

The workforce of one thousand men and women had doubled in the past decade, driven by demand for the Model 1873 lever-action rifle. Winchester's lucrative ammunition business, which employed many women from nearby New Haven neighborhoods, was an important profit center. While firearms sales fluctuated, there was always a need for cartridges for hunting, target practice, peacetime stockpiles, or wartime consumption. A recently completed mill rolled out brass sheets for rifle and pistol cartridges—Winchester's catalogue offered ninety-eight different cartridges, each optimized for a specific use and a specific firearm. There were small .22-caliber rimfire cartridges, less than a quarter inch in diameter and used for shooting galleries or hunting rabbits and squirrels, up to rounds like the .50-90 Sharps Special, 3.2 inches long and a half inch wide, intended for buffalo, grizzly bears, or African game.

But the heart of the business was the row upon row of specialized metalworking machines, each built to perform a specific step in the manufacturing process. They were the American system. Its "European System" competitor, a creation of the United Kingdom, relied on highly skilled workers. The Americans relied on an ever-increasing variety of highly engineered machines. By necessity there were dozens of each type, including identical rifle-boring machines, "copy lathes" to shape wooden stocks, slab mills to flatten steel, turret mills to cut a variety of shapes and grooves, drill presses for screw holes, taps to cut screw threads, and machines to polish the finished products.

The goal was to produce interchangeable parts so if a firearm part broke high in the Rockies it could be repaired by installing an identical spare with no adjustment or filing needed to make it fit. In the early nineteenth century interchangeability was considered by many to be "an irrational pursuit because it continually flew in the face of experience, which had borne out time and again that the system could not survive practical application," wrote historian David A. Hounshell. If a single person can claim to have proven otherwise it may be Simeon North, a Connecticut man contracted to build twenty thousand flintlock pistols for the federal government. Instead of having each worker build a complete pistol from scratch, North had a single employee produce a single part, over and over. It may have been boring for the worker, but it sped production for finished guns as the parts were more accurate and required less fitting for final assembly. Hounshell aptly described North's system as an "intellectual leap" of historic importance.

Practical application of North's idea was ahead of its time, however, and he abandoned interchangeability after a few hundred pistols.[4] He soon had another idea, though. Around 1816 he is believed to have devised the first milling machine, a device capable of repeatedly cutting identical parts. No longer was precision metal production dependent on a skilled worker and a metal file. North's developments traveled rapidly. At the government's Harpers Ferry Arsenal in Virginia, another New Englander, transplanted Maine native John H. Hall, improved upon North's work and made mass production of near identical firearms a reality. Hall invented three new milling machines and developed an extensive system of gauges. Hall also devised "fixtures" that allowed the same part to be moved from milling machine to milling machine—each machine performed a specific cut on a single part—while remaining oriented to the exact same spot, eliminating the risk of cumulative errors.

By 1824 Hall had fulfilled a contract to produce one thousand interchangeable rifles and described his achievement in a letter to the secretary of war: "I have succeeded in establishing methods for fabricating arms exactly alike, & with economy, by the hands of common workmen."

Practically speaking, it would be decades before handfitting was largely eliminated, but nevertheless the inventions of North, Hall, and other Americans led the United States to supplant Britain as the world's leading industrial innovator.

• • •

By 1884 Winchester was selling thirty thousand Model 1873 rifles a year, requiring its workers to roll, shape, bore, and cut rifling grooves to produce six hundred gun barrels a week.[5] Each step in that process required a specific machine. Likewise, to produce the hollow steel frame of the receiver, a solid steel block was milled, drilled, and shaped on a variety of machines. Other workers manufactured countless springs, screws, hammers, and triggers.

It was Bennett who managed Winchester's adoption of large-scale, fully interchangeable manufacturing, a daunting task. Setting up a production line was enormously costly and a single mistake was expensive. "It takes considerable nerve when you find you have run an order of, say, 10,000 receivers and that one cut is slightly off," wrote Edwin Pugsley, a twentieth-century Winchester executive.[6] "The receivers could be salvaged by making a corresponding change in the bolt or other operating components, which of course would destroy interchangeability with former production. Bennett had the nerve never to compromise and if parts were wrong they were scrapped and interchangeability rigidly maintained."

When the Brownings arrived in October 1884, they found the company's master mechanic, Mason, tooling up the factory for production of their single-shot rifle. Handcrafted examples were produced for testing and in the process Mason revised Browning's design, including cosmetic touches made affordable with Winchester's advanced machinery. Most obvious was the elegant S-curved lever handle—a frill Browning had originally included only to eliminate due to cost. The plain vertical interface between the steel receiver and wooden stock was replaced by a concave curve, more difficult to manufacture but stronger and with greater visual appeal. The receiver's exterior was given a slimmer appearance, another change that made the rifle look less like a frontier tool. There were also three notable mechanical differences: To make loading easier the block was tilted five degrees off vertical so closing the lever not only pushed the block up but also pushed the cartridge forward into the chamber as the block locked into place.[7] The firing pin mechanism was simplified and a safety feature called "half-cock" was added so that the hammer didn't rest on a live cartridge.[8]

Winchester's attitude toward its previously unknown inventor and his weapon was apparently marked by ambivalence. Or perhaps a touch of wounded pride. In an 1885 letter to the commander of the Navy's ordnance proving ground, a Winchester official, quite possibly Bennett, explained: "We're going to put it out as a cheap and well-made single-shot sporting rifle," and said Winchester's mechanics "have changed considerably" the original design.[9] It's unlikely Winchester would have described an in-house design as "cheap," and the latter claim of significant revisions is simply untrue. The rifle was fundamentally as Browning designed it. As for cheap, it sold for $15, compared to $18 for the base 1873 lever-action repeater, mechanically a far more complicated gun. If Bennett wrote that letter he may well have already understood, and perhaps resented, that his company risked becoming dependent on the man from Utah, for at their meeting in October 1884 to negotiate the purchase of Browning's new rifle the inventor did ask for "pretty much all the money in Ogden" and Bennett did pay it.

The price was $50,000. It's an after-the-fact estimate, but never denied by any member of the Browning family. Converting that sum to current dollars is a risky endeavor. Using the Consumer Price Index, Winchester's payment in current dollars was $1.4 million, but the CPI calculations for that era are unreliable. Determining value according to changes in wages and income between 1884 and 2017 places the Winchester payment at around $14 million—probably too high, though Winchester could afford it. The company had no debt, and profits in 1884 were $491,000, or $137 million based on a wages and income estimate. In either case, Bennett gave up 10 percent of one year's profits for a valuable new rifle and the promise of more Browning designs. It was a good deal.

• • •

When Browning's single shot reached the market it was officially named the Winchester Model 1885. Nowhere on it was the name of its inventor. Browning and his brothers had produced five hundred of the rifles before selling the patent to Winchester, which manufactured 44,042 in the next five years. Competitors offered other single-shot rifles, and while each had its negatives, positives, and a cadre of loyal users, history has endorsed the Browning gun. Ned H. Roberts, a New Hampshire hunting writer born in 1866, shot them all and declared that "the Winchester single shot hunting rifle . . . is regarded by many as being the most reliable, strongest, most symmetrical, and altogether best single shot rifle ever produced. It is doubtless stronger than the old Sharps rifle, is better designed, made of better materials, and is of better appearance than that famous arm."[10]

The single-shot rifle was quickly adopted by professional hunters. In 1888 *Forest and Stream*, a popular sporting magazine of that era, published a lengthy account of a bear hunt in the Kashmir region of the Himalayas.[11] The author, a professional guide, carried Browning's single shot chambered for the massively powerful "express" cartridge, which, at 3.6 inches in length, was the longest American rifle cartridge on the market. It had a tremendous kick, and firing more than a few rounds could turn a shooter's shoulder black-and-blue.

The guide's employers, a couple identified only as a man, "S," accompanied by his wife, carried a British double-barreled hunting rifle, while native Indian hunters attached to the group were armed with shotguns.

The hunters, guide, and their forty bearers and servants climbed above eight thousand feet searching for what the writer said were oak tree "nests" where Himalayan bears sat eating acorns high above the ground. After some fruitless days afoot, the hunters' luck changed when they camped near a local village whose residents arrived one evening to announce that "they were much troubled by bears as their . . . crops were all spoilt." They directed the hunters to a large patch of jungle alongside a stream where the guide and "S" set up shooting positions and a line of beaters created a hullabaloo to spook the bears into the open. What happened next testifies to how hard it was for a shooter, tense and excited in the field rather than relaxed at a range, to hit even a slow-moving target with even the best nineteenth-century weapon. Though the author doesn't say, the hunters may have been shooting "offhand," standing without a support to steady their aim.

"Soon after the beat began, a large bear came trotting along the boulders at the bottom of the stream, and as soon as he was about 120 yards off I fired, but without effect, and the bushes immediately afterward hid him from my view." He heard "S" on the other side of the stream open fire, followed by the sound of shotguns. "S" had also missed. "In the meantime another bear broke opposite me to my left and ran down the hill past me. I fired a shot at 40 yards with the Winchester 45 Express and to my delight he rolled over stone dead, falling some 30 or 40 feet down into the ravine. The bullet entered the right side of the neck and came up behind the left shoulder."

Shot after shot sounded from where "S" was stationed. The high-end British rifle and shotguns loaded with solid slugs finally killed what the writer called a "monster he-bear."

"It took eighteen coolies to drag him out of the jungle into the rice field, where he, together with the smaller bear, was skinned."

More prosaically, a Colorado hunter, identified only as A. S. Sage, wrote to his local newspaper that in September 1890 he'd spotted four bears and killed two with one shot from Browning's rifle. "One was a black, and the other a brown bear. They were standing broadside, one beyond the other, at about 100 yards distance. The ball passed through the shoulders of the first one and broke the back of the second. The black bear was full-grown weighing about 300 pounds. The brown one was about half grown, likely a yearling. I used a single-shot Winchester."[12]

Browning's second model for Winchester, the lever-action Model 1886, went on the market later that year, as the Statue of Liberty was dedicated, and was equally well received. One of the first reviews came from the nation's best-known big-game hunter, Theodore Roosevelt Jr., a member of New York's upper crust whose childhood asthma had led him to pursue what he famously called "the strenuous life." After he graduated from Harvard University, an inheritance gave him the wherewithal to invest in a North Dakota cattle ranch where he delighted in cowboying and hunting. Active in New York politics when not out west, Roosevelt had a keen eye for publicity, and a widely reproduced photograph from that era shows him in western buckskins holding a pre-Browning Winchester rifle, the Model 1876, which he earlier praised as the "best." Roosevelt changed his mind after shooting Browning's invention. In a letter to *Forest and Stream*, Roosevelt declared the new Model 1886 provided "a lower trajectory, a stronger breech action, is absolutely accurate for any range at which game can be killed with the least certainty, and is as handy and capable of standing rough work as the old gun." He ordered his rifle in one of Winchester's most powerful cartridges—the .45-90—and praised Browning's invention for easily handling the high-powered load. "The most satisfactory rifle I've ever yet come across for the wilder kinds of hunting in the United States," he wrote.

A base model of the Browning's 1886 rifle was only 15 percent more expensive than the popular Model 1873 but nevertheless remained a specialized weapon that filled out the prestige end of the Winchester line. It fended off competitors but never matched sales of the smaller-caliber rifles: Forty-four thousand of the heavy 1886 rifles were sold in the five years from 1886 through 1890 versus 166,000 of the pistol-caliber models. Ammunition for the 1873 rifle was less expensive for the average settler or farmer, and the effective range of one hundred to two hundred yards was sufficient for self-defense or hunting deer or elk.

The 1886 rifle was a different beast and became the favorite of people who depended on a firearm for their living—or lives: professional hunters, lawmen, and outlaws.

Browning's 1886 rifle featured prominently in two shootouts that numbered among the last famous western gunfights. Both occurred in 1892, the first in April when the Wyoming Stock Growers Association—cattle barons, in other words—hired fifty gunmen, half from Texas and the rest recruited from among local ranch foremen. They were paid $5 a day and promised $50 a body to eliminate what the cattlemen denounced as a collection of rustlers pillaging their herds. The supposed rustlers considered themselves homesteaders and the cattle barons land hogs.

The gunmen, who had the explicit or implicit support of the Wyoming governor and both U.S. senators, were fitted out with new Winchesters and dispatched north to the town of Buffalo in Johnson County. Among their leaders was Frank M. Canton, a former Johnson County sheriff and bounty hunter who in his memoir called the 1886 "the best rifle we had."[13] The expedition didn't turn out well. The gunslingers were delayed by a late-season snowstorm and then made a decisively bad tactical decision. They paused to lay siege to a log cabin whose defender, cowboy Nate Champion, held off the gunmen for ten hours. Even large-caliber rifle fire couldn't penetrate the cabin's heavy timbers. After wasting much ammunition from Browning's 1886 and other rifles, the invaders switched tactics and converted a wagon into a fortified handcart impervious to Champion's return fire. From behind that shelter they set the cabin afire and shot Champion dead as he tried to escape. It was a fruitless murder. The delay gave the Johnson County residents time to organize, and a day later the gunmen were trapped at an isolated ranch.

The two sides traded shots for three days while the settlers prepared for an all-out assault. The invaders were outnumbered five to one and faced extermination until Wyoming's senators in Washington, D.C., received a last-minute telegram begging for help. At 11:00 p.m. they raced to the White House and woke up President Benjamin Harrison. He ordered a U.S. Cavalry regiment to saddle up and ride out and separate the warring sides, and the next morning troopers arrived with their trumpets blaring, ending the major episode in what history knows as the Johnson County War. The gunmen were taken into custody and surrendered forty-four rifles, thirty-eight of them Winchesters and seventeen of those the Model 1886.

A savvy Wyoming lawyer, Willis Van Devanter, ensured that no gunman, politician, or rancher was ever punished, and in 1910 he was named to the U.S. Supreme Court. A statue honoring Nate Champion now stands in Johnson County, and in 1980 the incident inspired the legendary but flawed film *Heaven's Gate.*

The second shootout of 1892 is famously illustrated by a photograph of four dead bodies laid out in Coffeyville, Kansas. In the background a small boy peers through a fence at the scrawny, unshaven remains of the Dalton brothers' gang, who a few hours earlier had staged two simultaneous bank robberies. Or tried to. Lying atop the corpses, and occupying the center of the photograph, is a Winchester 1886.[14]

The ambitious scheme was the brainchild of Bob Dalton, an infamous outlaw whose goal was to "beat anything Jesse James ever did—rob two banks at once, in broad daylight." The central flaw to Bob's plan was that he and brothers Emmett and Grat had once lived in Coffeyville. They tried to thwart recognition with wigs and fake beards, but as they walked out of an alley a passerby recognized one of the brothers. They picked up the pace and split into two groups. Grat Dalton carried his Winchester 1886 and with accomplices Bill Power and Dick Broadwell stormed the C. M. Condon and Company Bank.

Bob and Emmett Dalton dashed into the First National Bank. Meanwhile, shouts arose. "The bank is being robbed!" Local townspeople—it was *their* money in the banks—loaded their personal firearms and a hardware store proprietor passed out extra rifles and shotguns. In minutes townspeople were ready to shoot.

Inside the Condon bank, Grat's plan was thrown into disarray when a teller insisted the bank's cash reserves were in a vault sealed by a time lock. As Grat fumed, townspeople behind wagons and improvised breastworks opened up on the bank building, piercing the exterior plate-glass windows. The bandits gave up on the vault, grabbed cash from the teller drawers, and tried to flee out the front door, only to be driven back by volleys of gunfire.

Across the street at the First National, Bob and Emmett filled a sack with $20,000 and tried to run the three hundred feet to their horses in the alley, but gunfire forced them back inside, too. They found a rear exit. Apparently, there was none at the Condon bank, where Grat, Bill, and Dick steeled themselves for a second attempt to dash out the front door. As they emerged, townspeople fired. "The dust was seen to fly from their clothes" as bullets struck home. The three stumbled, wounded, toward the alley and their horses as Marshal Charles Connelly ran across a vacant lot toward the mounts. Once there he looked left, where the horses were tied up, while unseen to his right was Grat, badly wounded, his vest stuffed with cash spilling onto the ground. Grat lifted his Winchester 1886 and shot the marshal in the back. He fell, fatally wounded.

When the shooting stopped, three other townspeople were dead. Of the Dalton Gang only Emmett Dalton was alive, despite being hit twenty-three times by buckshot and rifle rounds. He lived to serve fourteen years in prison, win a pardon, move to California, and try his hand at acting. He also went into real estate and wrote two books, *Beyond the Law* and *When the Daltons Rode*. There was even a movie. He died in bed at age sixty-six. Grat's 1886 Winchester can be seen today at the Dalton Defenders Museum in Coffeyville, a short ride north on the interstate from Tulsa, Oklahoma.[15]

But all that was yet to come. When Browning and his brother returned to Ogden in late 1884, their relationship with Winchester seemed secure—not only had Bennett purchased the new rifle, but he'd also commissioned the design of a shotgun. Disappointingly for Browning, Bennett wanted a lever-action shotgun, which by its very nature would be large, heavy, and inelegant. Shotgun shells were as thick as a cigar and almost three inches long, forcing Browning to design an equally large receiver capable of transporting the shells from the tubular magazine up into the chamber. It was exactly the sort of gun Browning would never design on his own, as demonstrated by his single-shot and 1886 lever-action guns, both models of compact efficiency.

Bennett could have manufactured one of the modern pump-action guns Browning was already developing, but that was too adventurous for the conservative Bennett. Lever actions were Winchester's trademark, so lever action was what Browning delivered. Winchester had it in stores by 1887, but the gun was barely profitable, selling only 78,355 over its manufacturing life. Its relative failure probably persuaded Bennett to take a second look at Browning's sleek pump-action guns. He was particularly amenable to Browning's idea of a small pump-action rifle that fired low-powered .22-caliber rounds to serve a new market, Americans living in populated towns where a traditional hunting rifle was impractical.

By early 1887 Browning was at work on the design. Then the Mormon Church intervened, and Browning was dispatched across the country to spend two years walking the dirt roads of Georgia.

CHAPTER FOUR

TREKKING THROUGH GEORGIA

It's unknown whether Richard Barnett was tall and thin or short and round, but he was a farmer in North Georgia hill country, so thin is likely. As for religion, evidence suggests he was a freethinker, wed to no particular Christian sect. He was illiterate, as was his wife, Rhoda Emily, and signed county land records with a single letter X.[1] They had eight children and owned 150 acres of land near the village of Wahoo, its name a corruption of the original Cherokee. Barnett was a tough old man of seventy-three when in 1887, armed only with an axe, he chased off a gun-wielding mob and thereby saved John Moses Browning from a whipping, or worse.

Browning hadn't planned to imperil his well-being in rural Georgia. He was thirty-two, Winchester was beginning production of his lever-action shotgun, he was developing a unique .22-caliber pump-action rifle, and his fourth child with Rachel, a girl named Louie after a maternal relative, had survived past her first birthday, a happy consolation following the deaths of two previous infants. Louie went on to enjoy another eighty-six years of life, but for the next two years she and her brother, Jack, were without a father and Rachel was without a husband, for Browning was two thousand miles away proselytizing for the Mormon Church.[2]

Missionary work was central to the purpose and survival of Latter-day Saints, as it was through relentless proselytizing that it grew from six people in 1830 to nearly two hundred thousand in 1887. Mormon missions were multi-year journeys undertaken by male church members judged "worthy" by church authorities, meaning they demonstrated strict adherence to Mormon tenets and biblical knowledge combined with a sociable countenance. A missionary also needed strong legs and mental fortitude. As they walked from house to house and town to town they were supposed to travel without "purse or scrip," carrying only a small valise, little money, and few personal items other than a Bible.[3] It meant depending on the charity of strangers for food and lodging, a prospect that Browning, who'd been too proud to ask a stranger for a job, must have greeted with dread.[4]

Missionary work was a prerequisite to church leadership and either by dint of his own faith or his father's stature in the church—like many early converts Jonathan Browning had personal relationships with Joseph Smith and Brigham Young—the younger Browning was ascending the complex church hierarchy. He was an "elder" in the "Melchizedek priesthood," the higher of two priesthood categories. He taught Sunday school and held the office of "Seventy," a required precursor to missionary work, which led him to be "set apart" for the mission by Lorenzo Snow, an early convert and influential church leader with nine wives.[5]

Antipathy toward the Mormon's polygamy was why Browning is said to have carried a rifle[6] when he left Utah for Georgia, probably a "take-down" model that disassembled to separate the barrel from the receiver and stock and so fit into an innocuous bag or box. While the Mormons' embrace of a "new" Gospel was heresy to other Christian faiths, it was their open practice of marrying one husband to multiple wives that generated a nationwide storm of denunciation. In 1856 the newly formed Republican Party compared polygamy to slavery and denounced both as "the twin relics of barbarism." As Utah was still a territory under federal jurisdiction, Congress passed its first anti-polygamy law in 1862 as the Civil War raged. Mormon protestations that the legislation intruded on freedom of religion failed after a tortuous legal challenge decided by the Supreme Court in 1879, which ruled that banning polygamy was not an infringement upon the free exercise of religion. During the 1880s some thirteen hundred Mormon men were jailed for living with more than one woman, and for a time resistance and noncompliance to that law were features of Mormon society. Newspaper accounts report that Matt Browning posted bail for Mormons charged with cohabitation, an act of communal charity the church would've expected from a member with Browning's financial resources.[7] While John Browning's commitment to the church over the course of his life is doubtful—in later years he was uninvolved—as a young man he bore no aversion to polygamy.

How common it was remains disputed. Estimates for polygamous Mormon families in the nineteenth century range from a low of 2 or 3 percent to a high of 25 percent. Ten to 20 percent seems most likely. Plural marriage was apparently concentrated among church leaders, who saw it as a commitment to their faith, though more earthly instincts were likely at work, too. One or the other motive, or both plus the example of his father, prompted Browning to seek a second wife of his own.

Rachel firmly squelched that notion. She was the fourth of ten children from her father Warren Child's first marriage in 1853. He married a second time in 1858, adding twelve more children to his brood. A third marriage and three more children followed in 1870. Child's journal records his fury at the federal law that made his family life illegal. "What do the wicked world and especially the wicked hounds want?" Child wrote in April 1886. "They ask us to be like them but God forbid, we would sooner spend our lives in the pen and know we are serving God than serve the devil and be like the rest of them." Child was arrested for illegal cohabitation but said he "escaped with only a fine of three hundred dollars" and court costs of $92.10, "which was paid and I discharged." Why he didn't receive a prison sentence was, Child wrote, "a dream totally wrapped in mystery to me."[8]

By then Rachel had put the plural marriage question to rest in her household. Photographs of her show a woman of ordinary appearance, hair pulled back, and wearing conservative, high-bodice dresses. She was short—at least twelve inches less than her husband—and some found her foreboding on first meeting. A young female cousin said "she was terrified of her." Yet that cousin's first reaction was unreflective of who Rachel was: "Everyone that knew her said she was the kindest, sweetest most wonderful person in the whole wide world," said Browning's granddaughter Judith Browning Jones. "When John Browning was in town every morning she put his collar studs in for him. Now, she was all of five feet tall . . . so it must have been quite a sight."

But Rachel's sweetness and accommodation had its limits. Mormon rules governing plural marriage required at least tacit agreement from the first wife. How that worked out in practice no doubt varied from family to family, but when Browning raised the proposition to Rachel the family's oral history reports that he was firmly checked.

"Over your dead body," she said.[9]

The weekend before Browning's departure to Georgia, his fellow Sunday school teachers threw a going-away party at the family home. "They spent an enjoyable evening singing and speeches were indulged in, all expressing esteem and appreciation of his labors in the Sunday School and in the (church) ward," Rachel's father wrote in his diary. The entry ends with: "John M. Browning starts to the southern states on a mission on the 29th of March 1887."

Browning would have reached Georgia after stopping in a regional mission office in Chattanooga, Tennessee, where his rifle was likely confiscated by church officials. There is no record of him carrying it in Georgia, and mission rules strictly forbid a weapon, even though the physical threat to missionaries was real. Georgia was part of the church's Southern States Mission, as the church called its work in the former Confederacy, and accounts of threats, beatings, whippings, the occasional tar and feathering, and, in the worst case, murder were reported by missionaries posted throughout the region. "Save me from that horrible place. Any place on earth but the Southern states," wrote one of Browning's contemporaries.[10] Unloved in much of the Union,

Mormons were greeted in the South with a particular fierceness. They were reputedly "out to destroy marriages, steal wives, perform nude baptisms, and smuggle women to Utah." A missionary was killed in Tennessee in 1879, followed in 1884 by the "Cane Creek Massacre" in that state, which left two missionaries, two potential converts, and the leader of the attacking mob dead. Southern codes of honor and manhood, the insular nature of rural society, and the challenge to local religious authorities all contributed to the violence. Missionaries faced "particular wrath" from Methodist and Baptist preachers who considered their spot in the southern social hierarchy threatened by the Mormon interlopers. The particular fury over plural marriage puzzled some Mormon missionaries, who noted the large number of children in the South who were obviously the result of extramarital interracial sex. How could married southern white men consort with black women yet condemn Mormons with multiple wives?

Hostility was not ever present, of course, as the dozens of missionaries dispersed across the southern states needed food and shelter from local citizens to survive their backroad travels. "The elders received extraordinary kindness, apathy and indifference, and rank, reprehensible brutality, each in varying degrees," wrote one historian. On the worst days even the weather was an enemy. Missionaries raised on Utah's high, dry plains discovered that trudging along humid, hot, buggy, and sometimes disease-ridden dirt roads could be traumatic in its own right.

Old Richard Barnett's courage was described in a letter from Browning's partner, Jedediah Ballantyne. At age nineteen, he was unusually young for a missionary of that era, but the team proved persuasive at least once when a Wahoo-area couple, William R. Evans and his wife, she was unnamed in Ballantyne's letter, accepted the new faith and so on Saturday, August 13, provoked the mob.

"From 25 to 50 men waited on us and gave us notice to be out of the county before the next Monday night," Ballantyne wrote.[11] "They could find nothing against our character, but they did not want our doctrine taught to their children. We tried to reason with them, but it was like trying to talk to a lot of angry wolves." The two Mormons placated the mob by agreeing to "think about leaving, and if we felt like it we would go, but if not we felt like trusting the consequences to a Superior Power." Which they did. By Monday night news that they remained circulated through the area and the mob descended on the home of farmer Barnett, who'd befriended Ballantyne and Browning and "where we had been accustomed to stop part of the time."

The angry crowd surrounded Barnett's home "and began beating the house and asking if we were there.

"The old gentleman, 73 years of age, told them that was for him to know and them to find out, and invited them to come in and see. They refused to do this and still kept beating the house. When our friend thought they had hammered long enough, he ran out with the axe and told them to hold on and he would help them: as soon as they saw him coming they began to scatter.

"After emptying their guns," apparently up into the air, "nothing more was heard of them." Buoyed by Barnett's successful defiance, the two missionaries remained in the area, and although the mob returned three days later, they milled about outside Barnett's home but made no hostile moves.

A later article in the Lumpkin County newspaper, the *Dahlonega Signal*, offered the backstory, explaining that the missionaries' stubborn persistence had led "60 of the best citizens of the district" to organize and prepare "to inflict sufficient punishment." The writer was working on secondhand information and wrote: "It is not known exactly what was the intention of the citizens unless it was to give the Mormons a good whipping if they persisted in remaining in the district . . . These apostles of bigamy will probably soon learn that they cannot carry on the infamous work in as intelligent a section as Wahoo."[12]

The *Signal* correctly predicted the missionaries would find few followers and, indeed, Ballantyne eventually reported that only two convert families were moving west to Utah that fall. During the years of Browning's mission, church records show there were thirty-one converts in all of Georgia in 1887 and another seventy-two in 1888. But Georgia was never prioritized as a missionary destination; between 1877 and 1898 it hosted only fifty-seven missionaries while the church concentrated its southern proselytizing in Tennessee, Alabama, North Carolina, and Virginia.

One more glimpse into Browning's work in Georgia is an October 1888 letter describing him as among the leaders of a two-day missionary conference convened near Augusta. Selecting as his topic a line from the Bible about believers confronting the unbelieving, the inventor turned temporary missionary was reported to have given "an interesting discourse upon how the mission of Christ and His apostles was received in their day, and how the mission of the servants of God is received today; showing conclusively that the people of the world have lost sight of the gospel in its purity."[13]

Browning's southern sojourn raises the question of what happened to the Browning Bros. business, as John was supposed to be out-of-state for the entire two years. Newspaper advertisements show that activity at the retail shop continued apace under Matt's leadership, and patent records show the gun-designing business continued, too. On December 13, 1887, after Browning should have spent the previous nine months on the other side of the continent, a patent application for his new .22-caliber pump-action rifle was filed under the ususal name of "J.M. & M.S. Browning." It was one of four Browning patents filed during the two years he was away, strongly suggesting that Browning was granted an exemption to leave his mission for some part of his two-year assignment. Once produced the .22-caliber rifle became one of the best-selling Winchester rifles ever manufactured.[14]

It wasn't a military arm and wasn't even primarily intended for hunting. It was invented to eliminate pests in barns and fields, and it was also used for fun, as public shooting galleries were an important market for the .22 pump-action rifles. Inconceivable in twenty-first-century America, shooting galleries were common entertainment from the late nineteenth through the mid-twentieth century, which should be no surprise given the extraordinary success of video shooter games. Any passerby could walk in, plunk down a nickel or dime, pick up a .22-caliber rifle, and bang away at steel targets shaped and painted to mimic chickens, sheep, cowboys, ducks, and cows. Shooting galleries were commonplace in cities, beachfront arcades, and amusement parks—themselves a late-nineteenth-century innovation to entertain city dwellers and factory workers. There was even a gallery at Disneyland in the 1950s. In the United Kingdom, the galleries were called Winchester Rifle Ranges, testament to at least one reason for Browning's success in civilian arms—he'd teamed up with a manufacturer that invested in sales as well as tools.

Perhaps because of the rifle's diminutive size—it's light and slim and, for a rifle, almost cute—the .22 pump-action model has received scant attention from the many aficionados of Browning firearms, despite the unique circumstances of its creation. It's the only known instance of Browning, or his brothers Ed and Matt, providing Winchester with paper drawings rather than a working model.

In his book, Jack Browning glides over the gun's genesis. "John had been busy when Winchester asked him to make this gun and, contrary to his usual practice, to save time he sent detailed drawings of the proposed model rather than making and sending the model itself." That would have been in late 1887 or early 1888, when Browning was supposed to be busy proselytizing. So who made the drawings—indeed, who invented the gun—if John was in Georgia? Matt was busy expanding the sporting-goods store and investing in new Utah industries. Thirty-five of Browning's 128 patents included Matt as a co-inventor, and while he certainly offered advice and often helped out in the shop, he was increasingly occupied by the retail business and other investments. Half brother Ed, an excellent machinist and eventually a holder of patents in his own name, would likely have produced a model rather than drawings and in any case never claimed credit for the design. He also never worked on a Browning prototype without his brother's presence. It must have been John Browning himself, on leave from Georgia, who did the work. Or perhaps he sketched when not proselytizing? He may have temporarily returned because nine months after Browning departed Rachel gave birth to another daughter, Carrie, the third of their living children.

In any event, Winchester was not enamored with the paper drawings. Winchester engineers examined the plans and replied that the gun "could not possibly work." Suggesting a Browning gun didn't work was an affront to the inventor, who at some point cobbled together a steel prototype and sent it east with a note declaring: "You said it wouldn't work, but it seems to shoot pretty fair to me."

That rifle became the Model 1890 and was the first repeating rifle to reliably load, fire, and eject the cheap and popular .22 short cartridge, a tiny round little more than a half inch long. For gallery shooting the solid lead bullet could be replaced by a tip of sintered metal that fragmented on impact. There were also very short-range versions in which the only charge was the primer. Later models were revised to shoot longer, more powerful .22 rounds, but no matter the cartridge there was little to no discernible recoil. Working the pump-action rifle mechanism yielded a solid, satisfying feel, and firing it offered the enjoyment of operating a quality machine. Throw the rifle to your shoulder—it weighs only a few pounds—pull the trigger, and there is a sharp but not painful "pop" as the cartridge fires. Slide the pump-action handle back about two inches and before your eyes the bolt retracts, the top of the gun opens up, and a small bright object is ejected out to the right. A short push forward closes the rifle and loads another round. The motions are accompanied by soft but solid "clicks" and "thunks." An electronic rendition of that satisfying "click" of metal on metal is heard every time the button on an iPhone is pressed to lock the screen.

Shooting galleries vanished in the wake of World War II. The Disneyland gallery closed, while others hung on by switching to air-powered rifles. Liability laws and social pressure forced their demise, unsurprising in a litigious age, since there was always an element of danger when handing a stranger a loaded rifle. Making galleries even more problematic was that the customers who lined up to use them were increasingly unfamiliar with guns, a dangerous fact when combined with the Model 90's resemblance to a toy. So every few years headlines like this appeared: "Joker Shoots Young Woman; Shooting Gallery Man Thought the Rifle Was Empty" or "New Yorker Shot by Friend; Accident in Pittsburgh" and "Shot in a Shooting Gallery. Young Woman Employed at It Probably Mortally Injured," though that last incident may have been a workplace dispute, since a co-worker at the Revere Beach arcade in Massachusetts was arrested.

The Model 1890 remained in production, essentially unchanged, until 1958. There were 2.1 million sold.

After he officially returned from the Mormon mission in 1889, Browning quickly resumed inventing. Matt was devoting more time to Ogden politics as well as business.[15] The brothers emerged as major community benefactors when they helped finance construction of a professional opera house and theater.

Ogden had an active amateur theater community, a recreational pastime endorsed as healthy family entertainment by Joseph Smith and Brigham Young. By the 1880s, the Ogden theater scene had outgrown an existing small, run-down stage, and led by the Chamber of Commerce, the city intended to erect a "Grand Opera House" capable of serving local troupes and hosting national touring companies. When that effort faltered for lack of financing it was rescued by four of Ogden's affluent "capitalists," as they were admiringly called. They were John Browning, his brother Matt, David Eccles, an early business partner of Matt Browning's and perhaps the richest man in northern Utah, and prominent businessman Joseph Clarke. They would pay, and seek no financial return.[16] The *Ogden Daily Standard* explained that they'd give the city "what it has craved for the past 10 years."

The goal was to erect the finest opera house between the Pacific Ocean and the Mississippi River and a close duplicate of the much-acclaimed California State Theater in San Francisco.

The result was a stone and brick building five stories tall, with offices and apartments on the top floors, and the front topped by an elaborate onion-shaped dome flanked by smaller ones on either corner, evoking that era's fascination for all things "Oriental."

When Browning returned to his workbench in 1889, he found that the science undergirding firearms technology had undergone a monumental shift. After much experimentation a French scientist, Paul Vieille, had discovered a replacement for traditional black powder. That ancient combination of charcoal, sulfur, and saltpeter was essentially unchanged since its discovery in China one thousand years earlier. Other than by increasing or decreasing the size of the powder granules—big for cannon and small for handheld firearms—the mixture's explosive properties couldn't be altered. The formula was the formula. But it easily absorbed moisture from the atmosphere, rendering it inert, and produced a plume of acrid smoke. One shot tagged a soldier's position, and when hundreds or thousands of troops in massed combat fired round after round—Waterloo, Gettysburg, or any major battle in the black-powder era—soldiers were enveloped by clouds of dense, white smoke. On windless days, a few volleys from a defensive line of infantry could inadvertently provide cover for attacking troops.

Plus, in even the best-designed nineteenth-century firearm, half the powder in each charge didn't go out the barrel as hot gas but instead turned into a black ash that coated the interior. Infantry firing volley after volley were said to urinate down the barrel to clear out the residue.

The development of smokeless powder began with the discovery that the nitrogen in the saltpeter was the primary explosive component, and by the 1840s chemists produced "gun cotton," a propellant made by combining cotton—essentially pure cellulose—with nitric acid to produce nitrocellulose. Attempts to mass-produce it were less than successful. Between 1847 and 1873, four gun-cotton factories in England and Austria blew up, leaving behind dozens of dead and wounded employees.[17] Gun cotton was easily ignited and acted more like a genuine explosive than a propellant. An explosive changes from a solid to a gas in an instant, while a propellant might seem to explode but in fact burns, or "deflagrates." Development languished until 1884 when Vieille figured out that a mixture of nitrocellulose, alcohol, ether, and paraffin could be combined and rolled into thin sheets, then cut up into small flakes. The complete process took weeks, compared to a day or two to mix black powder. But Vieille's powder was stable and deflagrated instead of exploding. By 1887, the French put it into production, designed a new cartridge and bullet, and began making the first smokeless military rifle, the bolt-action Lebel. Firearms were never the same.

Not just cleaner, the new propellant was three times more powerful than black powder. A small amount in a small cartridge propelled a rifle bullet at a far higher velocity—2,500 feet per second rather than the 1,100 typical of black powder—producing a flat trajectory unlike the curved flight path of a black-powder charge.[18] A Creedmoor contestant using black powder, for example, had to compensate for a large "bullet drop," the effect of gravity and air resistance on a low-velocity projectile. Their rifles were tilted up, not aimed straight ahead, as bullet drop over one thousand yards was measured in feet. Smokeless powder rounds still dropped, but their relatively flat flight path meant that for the first time an ordinary trooper stood a good chance of hitting a target past one hundred yards.

Also important was that 99 percent of a smokeless powder charge went out the muzzle as gas. There was no built-up grit and little corrosion. It was safer, cleaner, and easier to use, so for the first time firearms inventors and manufacturers could take advantage of the close tolerances and complex mechanisms enabled by late-nineteenth-century machine tools and manufacturing. A critical mass in firearms development had arrived that changed warfare, hunting, and self-defense forever, and Brown-

ing would make full use of it, beginning immediately on his return to Utah.

Given Browning's regret, expressed late in life, at not having
begun design work at nineteen rather than twenty-three, it's fair
to suggest the two years more or less "lost" in Georgia now drove
a burst of creativity that propelled him to international prominence.

CHAPTER FIVE

THINKING IN THREE DIMENSIONS

The sun was set and the stars were out when a newspaper reporter entered the Browning Bros. storefront on a December evening in 1889. He departed a few hours later, stepping out into the dark western night convinced he'd borne witness to a mechanism worth a small fortune—he estimated a hundred thousand dollars—that would "change modern warfare."[1] His first prediction was an underestimation. Not so the second.

For weeks anyone venturing near the Browning shop on Main Street had their ears battered by a sharp, cracking noise never before heard in the city, in Utah, or, it could be plausibly argued, anywhere else in the world. It wasn't the bang of a single-shot rifle or the bang, bang, bang of a lever-action repeater, sounds familiar to any westerner. This seemed like fifteen or twenty shots fired in three or four seconds, far faster than anyone could work a lever-action rifle. The explosive chatter was heard again and again, day after day. Within a few weeks, a close listener would realize there was now a steady twenty-five shots in a row, a near-instantaneous bang-bang-bang-bang-bang-bang. . . .

Ogden learned what it was on the morning of December 4. "A reporter of *The Standard* happened into the shop last evening while they were trying the new invention and what he saw there astonished him to the greatest degree," began the newspaper article, the only firsthand account of Browning in his workshop known to exist.

"The boys said, 'Just stay here a moment and see what we have

79

to show you.' He did so, and John M., the genius of the firm, lightly touched the trigger on a piece of machinery fastened in a vice and in an instant, too quick to be counted, 15 shots were fired into a box of sand placed to receive the bullets. The invention is what may be termed an automatic rifle."

Without the intervention of a human hand except for the first pull of the trigger, Browning's crude prototype fired, reloaded, cocked, and fired again and again until the ammunition was exhausted. The energy driving his automated rifle was the high-pressure gas generated by the burning gunpowder.[2]

The idea of such a mechanism wasn't new, but Browning was the first to prove that a gas-powered gun could actually work.

It wasn't the world's first machine gun—that had been invented in London five years earlier by expatriate American Hiram Maxim. For energy to drive his mechanism, Maxim had tapped the "kick" from his gun's recoil, an effective solution with the drawbacks of weight and complexity. Browning's gas operation needed fewer moving parts and so was simpler and lighter. Gas-powered firearms—which were adapted and improved by a host of later inventors, Browning included—would eventually become the standard-issue weapons for every soldier, freedom fighter, and terrorist: what are now commonly called assault rifles.

Browning's inspiration had come only a month earlier, at an Ogden shooting range where he found himself watching a patch of sweet clover sway back and forth. It's a common, spindly plant, valued in the nineteenth century as "green manure," a nitrogen-rich growth plowed back into the land for fertilizer. Significantly, it also grows to a height of five feet.

The Browning brothers had established the Ogden Rifle Club a decade earlier along the Weber River as a smart way to promote their first rifle while competing with friends and family. The club had little in the way of facilities. The range was simply a couple hundred yards of open ground with a backstop to catch the bullets. A match consisted of ten shots fired by each contestant, with the results printed in the *Ogden Standard.* John or Matt often took first place.

During the 1880s participation grew commensurately with the Brownings' success. On one occasion Browning competed against "celebrated rifle shot" W. Milton Farrow of Massachusetts, who was in Ogden to demonstrate rifle-maker Marlin's newest lever-action firearm. Combining showmanship with business, Farrow and Browning agreed to a test of skill. Each man fired ten shots, with Farrell scoring 48 out of 50 points and Browning only 45. The new Marlin was for sale at the brothers' successful sporting-goods store—it was indeed a business, and Matt made sure he stocked a complete line of firearms, not just Winchester arms—so perhaps Browning was only being businesslike and polite. It would be unseemly to beat his guest.

The brothers' simple shack and the sign hanging from a single nail were long gone. "Browning Bros. Armory" was painted on the storefront windows, and to eliminate any doubt as to the shop's purpose, a ten-foot-long model of Browning's first rifle, muzzle pointing skyward, hung above the entrance. Inside was what the brothers believed to be the longest rifle rack in the West. Shelves were stocked with revolvers, ammunition, and more pacific sporting goods: roller skates, ice skates, boxing gloves, dumbbells, telescopes, knives, and razors. The newly invented "safety bicycles"—with both wheels the same size—were also big sellers. Matt opened a branch in Salt Lake City, appointing half brother Sam as manager. The brothers could now be counted among Ogden's more prominent residents. Matt invested the brothers' profits in a successful land development venture and joined a select group of businessmen who provided the capital for Ogden's new bank, the Utah Loan and Trust Company.[3]

John was at work on a variety of new rifle and shotgun concepts, among them a whimsical lever-action rifle with five cartridges held vertically—the bullets faced the ground—rather than horizontally. The entire box magazine full of cartridges swung up and down with a lever. The design was completely impractical; it was invented for fun, a joke told in steel, and a device showing off Browning's imagination, a gun Browning knew would never be produced, even if Bennett felt obliged to purchase it. Any Browning design could contain a germ of an idea that a competitor could exploit.

The local shooting range, however, remained a crude affair, laid out on a field covered by a thick growth of grass and weeds. Aisles were likely scythed through the greenery, leaving plants on either side. At a club match on October 25, 1889, Browning tied for fourth. Coming in last at eleventh place was an old friend, Will Wright, a small man not much taller than his rifle was long, who leaned backward to balance the heavy Browning single shot.[4] The grass and weeds had grown tall on either side of the firing lanes, and at each shot the vegetation shook as it was blasted by the hot gas that emerged behind each bullet. When it was Wright's turn, his short stature amplified the movement so that a clump of sweet clover, ten feet ahead and off to the left, got a particular shake.

This was not new. Every time a gun was fired a blast of hot air—gas—followed the bullet out the barrel, and over the years many shooters had wondered if that energy could be tapped. It was now Browning's turn. He watched as gangly "sweet clover" was blown down and popped back up at Wright's every shot. The account of what happened next was reconstructed sixty years later by Jack Browning, who heard versions of the story from his father, his uncle Matt, and his uncle Ed, who were all present when John insisted the three men pile into Matt's buggy and return to the shop. He had an idea.

Back on Main Street, John took an old Winchester .44-caliber lever-action rifle, wired it to a wooden plank, and nailed that to the floor. In a block of wood he drilled a hole ever so slightly larger than the lead bullet's diameter, placed it in front of the muzzle, and carefully aligned the hole so the bullet would pass through and leave the block untouched. He told his brothers to find some sort of backstop to catch the bullet. He attached a wire to the trigger and predicted "that block will go hell winding." Then John yanked the wire. The rifle fired and as he predicted the block of wood flew down the impromptu indoor range, bouncing around the workshop and ricocheting off one surface or another. The block was driven by gas from the combusting powder moving at the speed of the bullet it drove out of the barrel.

According to Jack Browning's account, his father stood silent for a moment before he turned to Matt and Ed and said, "It looks as though we've stumbled onto something new," and told Ed they would start work on a fully automatic gas-operated gun the next morning.

"Figure on having it done by noon?" Ed asked. This was a joke. "Hardly," John replied. "About four p.m. I'd guess." Which was about right. By the next afternoon, John had contrived an odd-looking but workable "proof of concept." In front of the muzzle was a ping-pong paddle-like device, but made of metal with a hole in the middle. The handle was connected to the rifle by a bracket. A rod ran from the paddle backward to a modified trigger and lever. When John pulled the trigger—just once—the first bullet flew out of the barrel and through the hole in the paddle. At the same instant the expanding gas pushed the paddle forward, which pulled the rod along with it. As the rod moved, it pulled the lever, which, as in a hand-operated rifle, ejected the spent cartridge and cocked the hammer. The paddle was snapped back by a spring, which pushed the rod backward. That closed the lever and pressed the trigger, firing the gun and repeating the process. An entire magazine of fifteen rounds was discharged in a few seconds.

John, with assistance from brothers Ed and Matt, had built a functioning automatic weapon in one day. By no means was it ready for production—it was crude, ungainly, and almost certainly unreliable—but it was the first gas-operated firearm ever made and as such was the forerunner of firearm designs that ultimately led to the modern gas-operated "assault rifles" like the M-16 and AK-47.

Throughout November, bursts of rifle fire reverberated along Main Street as the brothers shot off magazine after magazine to test, revise, and retest the mechanism. It was this unique sound that likely brought the *Standard* reporter to the shop. Perhaps his status as a customer or a friend of a Browning brother granted him entry. "It is not possible to describe the works of the gun so as to make it clear to the reader how it operates, but this much can be said," the reporter wrote, and went on to give a cogent description. "By this means all a man has to do is hold the trigger and the whole magazine is fired quicker than one can possibly count." A shooter could also fire one bullet at a time, as "the machinery then only doing the work of loading."

"John M. Browning has worked on this invention about a month, and now that the machine has been almost perfected the firm has applied for a patent. In his labors on this machine John found the greatest trouble in feeding the gun quickly enough," the newspaper explained. "Now a narrow tin box is placed on the top of the works. . . . In this can be placed 25 cartridges. The rapidity with which this can be fired cannot be understood except by actually seeing it work." Finally, the newspaper declared, "The invention is one of the greatest, and in fact the greatest which has been made by the firm and of its kind the greatest in the United States."

Browning was already at work on an improved version. The ordinary rifle barrel was replaced by a heavier, larger diameter version to better absorb the heat generated by hundreds of bullets a minute running down its length. As Browning developed the firearm, it morphed from a rifle into a more conventional tripod-mounted machine gun, a decision perhaps influenced by Maxim—Browning wanted to sell his guns, and Maxim's machine gun was a commercial success. While John worked on the gun, Matt went looking for a customer. Winchester was out of the question. Bennett's conservative approach to Winchester's product line would never countenance a machine gun; even producing one of Browning's pump-action shotgun designs was originally too innovative for Bennett. The alternative was Colt's Patent Firearms Manufacturing Company in Hartford, which along with the famous six-shot revolver manufactured the Gatling gun, a multi-barreled, hand-cranked weapon invented during the Civil War, a reliable, if human-powered, eventually

capable of firing some 500 shots per minute. The U.S. Army purchased a few hundred but never bothered to incorporate the
weapons into its tactical doctrine. The guns were heavy, awkward,
and required a team of horses to transport and a team of men to
set up and operate.

After ten months of off-and-on work, Browning's gas gun
weighed in at a relatively modest forty pounds and could be fired
by a single man. In November 1890, Matt mailed off a handwritten letter on Browning Bros. stationery—its elaborate letterhead
engraved with scenes of hunting, fishing, and bicycling—that
opened with "Dear Sirs," as neither man knew anyone at the Colt
company.[5]

"We have just completed our new automatic machine gun
and thought we would write to you to see if you're interested in
that kind of a gun. We have been at work on this gun for some
time and have got it in good shape." Matt explained their latest
model fired a .45-70 government cartridge six times a second, or
360 rounds a minute. "It is entirely automatic and can be made
as cheaply as a common sporting rifle," which was more than a
bit of marketing exaggeration. "If you're interested in this kind
of gun we would be pleased to show you what it is and how it
works as we are intending to take it down your way before long.
Kindly let us hear from you in relation to it at once."

The letter is signed: "Yours Very Truly, Browning brothers."

John wondered if the Browning name meant anything to
Colt, located in faraway Hartford a hundred miles north of New
Haven. The Browning name appeared nowhere on Winchester's
firearms or in the pages of its twice-annual catalogue, but it
turned out Colt knew exactly who John Browning was. In the
small world of Connecticut, arms-making ideas and employees
moved back and forth between the various firearms makers, and
Colt's reply praised the 1886 Model rifle as "a masterpiece of the
gun making art." John thought that was very polite, while also
observing that the Browning Bros. wholesale and retail operations sold a great many Colt revolvers. Colt certainly would think
it worth a few hours of company time to humor an important

distributor who was also an inventor—if the brothers arrived in Connecticut at their own expense.

A month later, after a visit to Winchester, Browning unveiled a mechanism that didn't look like any gun anyone at Colt had ever seen. It was sort of triangular. The long leg on what looked like the top—it was hard to be sure—was the thick, heat-absorbing gun barrel. The short leg contained the flapper mechanism, and the long third side contained the moving control rod, which led to an improved firing mechanism. There was also something that looked like a handle. The entire mechanism looked as handmade as it was, with shop-forged metal parts scarred by hammer blows and the metalwork burned black from test firing.

John, in fact, was suddenly embarrassed when he cast fresh eyes on his crude prototype erected in Colt's test-firing tunnel. The company president, John Hall, took a look and squelched a smirk. Nevertheless, Browning loaded the first of four ammunition belts, each holding fifty cartridges secured by canvas loops. He pulled the trigger, and in a minute or so the demonstration was done. "I ran the 200 through so fast nobody could think. We smoked up the Colt factory with those .45-70s and waked echoes clear back to the Colonel himself," referring to deceased founder Col. Samuel Colt. Browning noted Hall was no longer suppressing a smile. "The changed expressions on the faces of Hall and his men put a pound of fat on my ribs."

Browning explained he'd built the machine in seven or eight months, a speed that surprised Hall. Matt, ever the salesman, added that his brother had completed a pump-action shotgun sold to Winchester just the day before. The increased popularity of shotgun sports was finally forcing Bennett to expand Winchester's line. Hall was suitably impressed but worried that Browning's machine gun—the first machine gun he'd ever seen—would elicit little interest from an army content with its relatively few Gatlings and with spending constrained by a peacetime budget. Hall nevertheless sounded out his military contacts and two U.S. Navy ordnance officers eventually responded, intrigued because the Browning gun was one-fifth the weight of the Gatling gun, which was too large and too awkward to be muscled ashore by a Marine landing party. The officers said they'd attend a demonstration, in an unofficial capacity, provided the prototype could sustain three minutes of continuous fire at six hundred rounds a minute.

Matt and Ed considered that an extraordinary demand, while John hired an Ogden tentmaker to sew ten canvas belts with two hundred cartridge loops each. Then the three brothers carefully inserted each cartridge by hand, as a misaligned round would jam the feed mechanism. The gun and ammunition belts were shipped to Hartford. John was the only brother who came east. The gun was his idea, and whether he met with success or failure, it was going to be a brief demonstration. Each ammunition belt was folded into a wooden box designed to hang off the gun's side and feed directly into the loading mechanism. John offered the two naval officers cotton balls for their ears, as the aural pounding from eighteen hundred cartridges in three minutes would stun them into temporary deafness. He lined up the ammunition boxes in a row and sat down on a seat attached to the sturdy tripod supporting the gun. He grabbed a belt, fed its brass endpiece through the mechanism until the first cartridge snapped into place, then pulled the charging lever under the barrel and let it spring forward. The gun was now cocked and loaded. He pulled the trigger and was enveloped by a cloud of noise and white smoke as two hundred rounds fired flawlessly in twenty seconds. Browning loaded the next belt, and the next, and as his world focused on the sound and feel of the mechanism he watched the barrel change color as it heated up. First it turned a dull red, then a bright red. Spent brass casings extracted after each shot were flung out the side and piled up at his feet. A faint mist began blowing out the barrel, which turned out to be tiny molten-lead droplets stripped off the speeding bullets. The flapper, swinging back and forth six hundred times a minute, blew them back onto Browning's hands. By the third minute the barrel had turned blue and the intense heat was radiating back into the action's chattering metal parts. Browning loaded the last belt, pulled the trigger, and waited for something to break. When the gun finally stopped he thought the extractor had failed, jamming the gun with a spent shell. But the test was merely complete. The gun had fired all eighteen hundred rounds without a single problem.

In a letter home Browning observed the two naval officers exhibited the "hysteria of excitement." One man with a weapon a third of the size of the Gatling gun had fired more rounds than could fifty Marines banging away at a furious pace with their standard-issue single-shot breechloaders. "Nobody can be a close observer of the machine gun through three minutes of continuous fire without getting excited," Browning said. At a celebratory dinner the next evening Browning sipped his first-ever glass of champagne, which he knew was about all the profit he'd likely see from his invention. While the naval officers were amazed by his technological achievement, there was no money to buy the gun, the largest likely customer, the Army, was uninterested, and in any case much work remained to change it from an ungainly triangle into something sleeker and more portable.

There was also a fundamental problem Browning couldn't overcome. Heat. Unlike the Maxim gun, which surrounded the barrel with a tubular, water-filled sleeve, Browning's gun only had its thick barrel. It had to cease firing and cool down after a few hundred rounds, a drawback in an era when machine guns were expected to lay down long barrages of sustained fire. Browning's gun couldn't do that. Nevertheless, Colt was impressed and offered him a contract, which the inventor declined. He would take his crude prototype back to Ogden and continue refining it, according to his own schedule, rather than Colt's, as he pursued other ideas sparked by the gas-operated gun. He preferred the civilian market in any case, with its more certain income and no military bureaucracy to wear him down with questions and demands. Perhaps there was a market for a gas-operated pistol? Or an autoloading rifle or shotgun?

• • •

The exact combination of skill, mental acuity, ambition, imagination, and mere curiosity that enabled Browning's long creativity streak is inevitably a matter of speculation. He possessed all those characteristics to one degree or another, but also one unique talent in excess of the norm: Browning thought in three dimensions. He was able to visualize a three-dimensional object—or multiple objects—and manipulate them in his mind, enabling him to go from "mind to metal" with no blueprints in between. To him, objects were ideas.

"I got to figuring a lot, running the mechanisms of guns through my mind till I could have hammered one out from memory. I developed the knack of visualizing parts and seeing them in operation. And while I was doing that, I didn't realize that I was practicing the first requisite of inventing, concentrating," Browning told his son. The long years spent repairing firearms in his father's shop, starting as a young boy, no doubt honed those skills. In a written anecdote Matt recalled John's rapid production of toy guns as child:

> One time and another John made me dozens of guns. I'd lose my gun or trade it off, and then find a likely board and get him to whack me out another. Whack is the word, and he's been whacking out guns ever since. To this day, he may drop in the office in the morning, talk things over for half an hour, then jump up suddenly put on his hat, saying, "I've got to go to the shop."
>
> "Ed," he will say, "is picking up the material I will need." And by the next evening at quitting time he and Ed, bending over the old milling machine, will have whacked out the rough frame. . . . No blueprints. For the most part he makes his sketches as he goes along. They look pretty crude but the measurements are carefully noted. After all, though, his drawings are in his head. He will stand by the miller or lathe with a ruler or caliber, "hold on a second Jonathan," he'll say, and make measurement, stare a moment at a blueprint in his mind then say, "That slot ought to be little deeper. At 32nd, I think will be about right."[6]

Most people practice a simple form of "spatial thinking" every day. At the most rudimentary, it's used every time someone looks at a map and applies what's on paper to the real world, or when packing for a trip one folds and arranges each item to fit in the smallest possible space. A mechanic with good spatial skills can easily take a mechanism apart and put it back together by visualizing how each part interacts with the other. James Watt, the inventor who turned the steam engine into a practical power plant for ships and trains, visualized his complex creation during a Sunday-afternoon walk through a Glasgow park in 1765. "I was thinking upon the engine at the time, and had gone as far as the herder's house, when the idea came," he wrote. "I had not walked farther than the golf house when the whole thing was arranged in my mind."[7]

Albert Einstein explained that he thought in images, writing in 1945 that "the words or the language, as they are written and spoken, do not seem to play any role in my mechanism of thought. The physical entities which seem to serve as elements in thought are certain signs and more or less clear images which can be 'voluntarily' reproduced and combined." Einstein said he struggled to describe his mental process in words. Only after the elements in his mind took shape in "visual and some of a muscular type" could he find the language to explain his idea.[8]

Research into spatial visualization skills began in the 1920s, but the debate over what it was and how to characterize it continued for decades. There are key elements. One is called mental rotation: the ability to imagine three-dimensional objects and rotate them left and right or up or down. Imagine a cube, each side a different color, and rotating it in your mind to choose which color faces which direction. A second element, "spatial realization," involves "multi-step manipulations" of the objects in your mind. Imagine two identical cubes, each with the same color scheme, and manipulate each individually at the same time. If you want the blue side of one cube to face the yellow side of the other cube, you can watch the cubes turning in your head. Now add a third cube. Or a fourth.[9]

The late Bruce W. Browning, John Browning's grandson and an accomplished designer of both firearms and an innovative bicycle drive system, experienced three-dimensional visualization but found that the skill vanished after he started using computerized design programs. Yet at age ninety he recalled those early experiences with enthusiasm. "You watch the stream of ideas go by . . . that sort of a chaotic thing that goes on in your mind, and you have to have the ability to spot that one good one amongst all the other." Browning said those moments materialized like this: "When thinking about something like . . . a gun or bicycle or whatever, I think about it really very intently and focused, and then I just let go. . . . Your mind keeps working on it, and especially when it's a little bit relaxed, and injects all sorts of funny things into it. Pretty soon, enough things line up." The chaos becomes organized.[10]

Browning's granddaughter, artist Judith Jones, experienced similar thought processes when she found herself imagining a drawing in three dimensions. "It's otherworldly in a funny way, because you don't know you're doing it until you're done. I was trying to get the perspective in depth on something, and I saw—literally saw it—it was there. . . . I thought, 'You never thought like that before in your life! What went on?' It was just amazing."[11]

Browning remained wedded to Winchester even after his machine-gun demonstration to Colt. Winchester purchased every rifle and shotgun prototype that he designed and Ed built—by now the younger man was doing most of the machining to turn Browning's ideas into metal—and those guns were a major source of income. The brothers joked that every trip to New Haven with a prototype wrapped in paper was a "raid" on the Winchester treasury. As Jack wrote, the inventor's brothers "bantered him about the ruthless way he was blackmailing Winchester, compelling the company in self-defense to buy more guns than all the factories in the country could manufacture."[12]

Bennett may well have resented Browning's twice-yearly trips to New Haven—Winchester would eventually purchase the patents to thirty-four guns it never made, at a cost of about $10,000 per gun. It was a practical, if costly, business decision, as it gave Winchester a monopoly on the best ideas from the best inventor. Bennett was buying roadblocks to impede his competitors.[13]

Exactly how much Browning was worth to Winchester can be discerned from a meeting the inventor had with Bennett in 1890. By that decade the West was no longer the frontier. Sitting Bull, the legendary Sioux chief, was shot and killed that year, and in December hundreds of Lakota Sioux were massacred at Wounded Knee, South Dakota, ending the decades of war between white settlers and Native Americans. Fewer western settlers needed a rifle for self-defense, and Winchester faced competition from new manufacturers, so Bennett decided to replace Winchester's very obsolete lever gun, the Model 1873 rifle. Ideally, a new design would combine the mechanical elements and elegance of the heavy-duty 1886 rifle, but in a simpler, less expensive design for lower-power cartridges.

Matt provided an account of what followed. Bennett offered a financial incentive to speed Browning's efforts. He'd pay $10,000 if John delivered a design in three months, and if he did it in two months Winchester would up that to $15,000.

John stared at a calendar and spoke. "Let's see. It takes five or six days between here and Ogden. Say we call it twelve days for me to get home and for the rifle to get to you by express. I'll have the rifle in your hands in thirty days for twenty thousand dollars or give it to you." Bennett considered the offer preposterous, but Browning insisted. A contract was drawn up in which Bennett agreed to pay the $20,000 if Browning made the one-month deadline, but, to Bennett's credit, he declined to demand the new gun *gratis* if Browning ran late.

John later explained to his brother, "I felt all at once that it would be worth ten dollars or fifteen thousand dollars to change the expression on Bennett's face. In all the years I've known him, since he came out to Ogden, he has hidden behind that heavy beard, and you can never guess what he is thinking. But I made him jump that time."[14]

On the train ride home he worked through the new design in his head, telling Matt there were a few "snags" to solve. They reached Ogden on an early-morning train, and by the afternoon he and Ed were roughing out a receiver—the steel frame around which a rifle's action is built. John had already designed the gun in his head. In two weeks, the new rifle was being test-fired. The prototype made it to New Haven within the thirty-day window. A $20,000 check followed, and the rifle became the Model 1892, which eventually sold 1 million copies. It was as Bennett asked—a simplified version of the 1886 rifle, cheaper to make and firing smaller cartridges with more manageable recoil.

The following year Winchester finally began selling Browning's pump-action shotgun. Neither Browning nor his brother Matt may have yet realized it, but by 1890 Browning had embarked on a decade-long stretch of mechanical creativity that encompassed every type of firearm. His inventions between 1890 and 1900 changed how hunters hunted, how armies fought, how people protected themselves, how crimes were committed, what laws were passed, and how people were killed, the innocent and guilty both.

CHAPTER SIX

AMERICA'S DEER RIFLE

With Winchester's cash and Matthew's business acumen, hunting wildfowl became a sport rather than a necessity for Browning, who shot for the challenge and the camaraderie rather than the frying pan. Finding birds to hunt was another matter, however. Grouse were no longer pecking the dirt a few minutes from his front door, as throughout the West settlements pushed wildlife farther out into the plains and mountains. In the 1890s Browning and shooting companion Alex Brewer traveled by horse and buggy into the hills south of Ogden where, for a time, game remained abundant. "We could often shoot 25 or 30 prairie chickens in an evening," Brewer recalled.[1]

The shotgun Browning used bore little resemblance to the crude implement he'd built as a child. Throughout the 1880s Browning had devised a variety of pump-action shotguns, an expression of his confidence and ambition, as no commercially viable pump-action gun was yet on the market. Details of his shotguns varied, but each held shells in a tubular magazine partly encircled by a moving handgrip. Sliding the grip backward opened the breech and ejected the spent shell as a new round emerged from the magazine. Push the grip forward and the gun was loaded and ready to fire. By 1890 he had patented four distinctive pump-action designs and used those concepts as the basis for another three prototypes.[2]

Each firearm was created in the usual manner—mostly in John's head. "My brother does not make working drawings,"

Matt said. John began working in steel after thinking through a concept for days, weeks, or months. In the evenings he sat holding his head in the palm of his hand, slowly tapping his fingers on his bare scalp, oblivious to his surroundings, as he thought through his latest mechanical concept. The tapping was like a metronome. "It would drive my mother crazy," Browning's granddaughter Judith Jones said.[3] Then he sketched out the parts on paper, just rough lines with no dimensions, and once he was satisfied made sheet-metal templates to test the interaction.

With any new firearm Browning began by conceiving the breech mechanism and then inserted it into the frame, or receiver. He cut flat, one-dimensional parts from a thin steel plate. "Then he drills holes and cuts grooves and rivets pieces on this plate, then makes the breech parts in a skeleton form, so he can see how the breech parts co-act with one another. This is after he has made sketches and has got the shape of the parts in his mind," Matt said in a description of his brother's work. "The receivers are then milled to the shape of this plate, also the other parts." That work was usually done by Ed, sometimes with Matt's help. John stood next to Ed as the parts took shape. "He always being present tells how wide to make the cuts and how thick to make the parts. He can tell about what he wants from the sketches, but no one could work from them," Matt said.[4] A U.S. Army officer who worked with John and Ed said they all but read each other's minds. "Both had told me how the one got an idea and the other put into metal the thoughts of the other."[5]

Using the flat, sheet steel parts as templates the brothers produced a fully operational prototype. The prototypes didn't sit idle. Financial success allowed Browning to test each step of a design by firing hundreds or thousands of shells while watching and listening for a hiccup or a pause that signaled a faulty part or dimensional error. Friends and shooting partners took their turn with the rifles and shotguns, the latter used for trapshooting, a newly popular sport sweeping the country. Each contestant fired at a set number of targets, and whoever scored the most hits—sometimes on clay discs or glass balls, but ideally on live pigeons—was the winner. It was good practice for hunting grouse or waterfowl in the wild.

Browning's favorite duck-hunting spot was where the Bear River fed the marshland on the edge of the Great Salt Lake, where an exclusive camp for Utah's wealthiest businessmen was eventually erected, with John and Matt among the founding members. Utah's duck-hunting season at that time ran from September through March, but there were no bag limits, so a hunter with a sturdy shoulder, good aim, and lots of ammunition could spend a day and depart with dozens of birds. In October 1891, Browning was interviewed by the *Ogden Daily Standard* in advance of a hunting trip. The one-paragraph account was said to be "as clear an exposition of John's oratory as cold type can make it without illustrations."

"We leave this evening for Corinne," John told the newspaper, referring to a small town twenty-five miles north of Ogden. "There a team awaits to take us direct to the lake. A tent is already pitched at that picturesque spot. We repose our weary limbs for rest and at early dawn arise and begin the work of annihilation. The slaughter continues all day. We finish at night, pile up our ducks in the wagon, fold our tent, steal away to Corinne, there put up at the finest hotel in the city and feast after our arduous labors. Having refreshed ourselves with the bounties which Corinne alone affords we return to Ogden to resume our daily routine of life and to eat our ducks."

It's very likely Browning was having fun at the reporter's expense. "Picturesque," "repose," and "annihilation" weren't words Browning threw around in the shop. His remark on the "slaughter" piled up in the wagon sounds purposefully over-the-top. A final clue came when he referred to Corinne's "bounties," likely a reference to the town's history, not long in the past, as a red-light district for railroad workers.

Wielding his own pump-action shotguns, Browning would have cut a large swath through the waterfowl. He wouldn't have wasted the game, as the ducks weren't killed for cash but eaten by family and friends. Not every hunter with a modern firearm was as considerate, however. The buffalo were gone, and now deer, bear, elk, along with ducks and grouse, were shrinking in number.

It was an old problem grown worse. The first game laws—to protect the deer population—dated to mid-seventeenth-century colonial New England but met with little success. By the 1890s, there was a new urgency, thanks to technically advanced, easy-to-use, and aesthetically appealing rifles and shotguns, the best of which were designed by Browning and manufactured by Winchester. Thanks to Browning's work, Winchester was poised to dominate the domestic firearms market—provided there were animals left to hunt.

A nationwide debate over the future of hunting—and so the civilian firearms business—was ignited in the late nineteenth century by naturalist and editor George Bird Grinnell, a child of America's narrowest social stratum. His ancestors arrived on the *Mayflower* and his grandfather served ten terms in Congress. In 1894, after the country paid tribute to Columbus's 1492 voyage to the New World, Grinnell published a biting editorial on the front page of his influential sporting magazine, *Forest and Stream*, denouncing greedy hunters and their profligate use of firearms

"We have just been celebrating the four-hundredth anniversary of the coming to this continent of men equipped with firearms . . . We have been killing and marketing game, destroying it as rapidly and as thoroughly as we knew how," the editorial declared. "For the most part the game has been blotted out from wide areas, and today, after 400 years of wanton wastefulness, we are just beginning to ask one another how we preserve what remains for ourselves and our children."

Grinnell was not opposed to firearms or hunting—it was a question of degree and intent. His specific enemy were commercial "market hunters" who killed wildlife in an "unrelenting pursuit" of profit. Grinnell was aghast at market hunters' mass slaughter, the practice of a mere one or two hunters with modern weapons killing hundreds of ducks or dozens of deer in a day to feed the bellies of indolent city people. "The game paucity today is due to the skin hunter, the meat killer, the market shooter," he wrote. As everyone knew, market hunters were little-educated, rough-hewn blue-collar workers of the day, while Grinnell's and Roosevelt's peers called themselves sportsmen, who hunted not for money or food, but to develop inner fortitude and character. They were not the problem. "The work of the sportsman, who hunts for the sake of hunting, has had an effect so trivial that in comparison with that of the market hunters need not be taken into consideration."

While the new movement demonized market hunters—and they were indeed driving game to extinction—they also numbered among Browning's friends. But he was too astute a businessman not to recognize that the success of Grinnell's campaign, and the push to preserve open space to sustain and then increase wildlife, also preserved and expanded the market for Browning's rifles and shotguns.

Browning's friend Brewer followed the fate of wild game populations because, in addition to a successful canning business, he ran a "commission house" that paid hunters for deer, ducks, and grouse that he then shipped east in newly invented refrigerator railcars. Years later Brewer recalled that "when it was legal to buy and sell wild game I used to handle the kill from 25 hunters. I have shipped out as many as 500 dozen wild ducks in one shipment to Omaha, Kansas City and St. Louis."

In 1894, he recalled, "Some ranchers came in and offered to sell a box carload of deer." They agreed on a price, "big and little, at $0.50 per head." The hunt began south of the aptly named town of Huntsville, in the hilly country east of Ogden where mule deer—virtually identical to eastern white-tailed deer, except for bigger ears and black tips on their tails—feasted upon abundant sagebrush. "Wagons followed the hunters on horseback," and a Union Pacific railcar was stationed on a branch line about thirty-two miles distant. "The hunters brought in wagonloads of deer and we hung them as closely as possible in that car and I shipped it to St. Louis." A buck weighed 150 pounds, a doe about 125, and after skinning and butchering each produced 50 to 70 pounds of boneless venison, which in Chicago could fetch 20 cents a pound. It was a profitable day, but an unsustainable venture. "After a time, the deer disappeared," Brewer said.[6]

Market hunting was a practice as old as the country, and devastating to wildlife. In 1646 the town of Portsmouth, Rhode Island, limited deer hunting to six months a year. Connecticut followed, as did Massachusetts, which along with steep fines added an additional penalty: If miscreants didn't pay, the offenders were sentenced to two months of forced labor. Despite sporadic enforcement of game laws, the rolling extinction of edible wildlife moved west along with the nation. Even before Grinnell published his scathing editorial, the undeniable fact of vanishing game led to the first stirrings of a conservation movement in the 1840s and 1850s, led by middle- and upper-class hunters repulsed by the mass slaughter and fearful that the seemingly endless parade of wildlife would prove finite. It was often a fruitless effort. Americans moving from the farm to the city took with them a taste for wild game, which was suddenly available and affordable—at least to the better off. Hundreds of branch rail lines linking out-of-the-way towns to trunk lines and the rapidly expanding fleet of refrigerated railcars put wild game on restaurant menus and kitchen tables.

It wasn't just out west. In 1889 Pittsburgh, Pennsylvania, businessman John M. Phillips set off on a winter hunting trip and for three days followed the tracks of a deer through six inches of fallen snow. Phillips and a companion camped on the trail for two nights until the cold weather forced them to spend an evening inside at the small western Pennsylvania hamlet of Brockwayville. "In the morning we took up the trail again and succeeded in tracking and killing the buck," Phillips wrote. "During all that long chase, we didn't cross another deer track. I said to my friend, 'I am done—I think I've killed the last deer in Pennsylvania.'"[7] By the early 1890s, there were few, if any, deer in most states east of the Rockies. Rhode Island, Connecticut,

Pennsylvania, Maryland, West Virginia, New Jersey, Ohio, Kentucky, Tennessee, Illinois, Iowa, Kansas, Missouri, and Nebraska all counted their whitetail herds at near zero. In 1893 Indiana officials announced the state's "last deer" was shot.

It didn't seem the best time to launch a new hunting rifle, but launch it Winchester did in 1894, which coincided with the start of a five-year economic depression sparked by a collapse in international commodity prices and a run on the banks. However inauspicious a moment, the new rifle nevertheless became the best-selling hunting rifle in American history—Browning's legendary Model 1894, aka the ".30-30 Winchester," eventually nicknamed America's deer rifle. That the white-tailed deer survived to repopulate the nation's forest was thanks to the conservation movement Grinnell inspired, making the survival of American wildlife and the success of Browning's rifles and shotguns thoroughly intertwined.

After graduating from Yale University in 1870 at age twenty, Grinnell joined a fossil-hunting expedition at Fort McPherson, Nebraska, carrying a Henry repeating rifle, a revolver, a large store of ammunition, and a Bowie knife. On the first day, Sioux attacked a party of white antelope hunters. One hunter was wounded, one Indian was shot, and a troop of cavalry set out in pursuit, guided by scout William F. Cody, aka Buffalo Bill. They returned with the body of an Indian discovered dead on a hilltop and wrapped in a buffalo robe. Grinnell found none of this discouraging and two years later leapt to accept a Pawnee invitation to participate in what is believed to be the last great Native American buffalo hunt. His account was a best seller. "There were 800 warriors, stark naked, and mounted on naked animals," Grinnell wrote. "Among all these men there was not a gun nor pistol nor any indication that they had ever met with the white men. They were armed with bows and arrows. . . . Here was barbarism pure and simple. Here was nature." In 1874 he joined George Armstrong Custer and his Seventh Cavalry on a peaceful scouting expedition into the Black Hills. The two men hit it off, and Custer invited Grinnell to accompany his 1876 expedition, which Grinnell presciently declined, as it ended abruptly at the Little Big Horn.

Grinnell also befriended a fellow upper-class denizen of the West, Theodore Roosevelt, and together they became leaders in the campaign for national parks, game laws, and wildlife preserves. Both men wanted wild game preserved so that an increasingly urban, immigrant America could still fashion what was termed the "American Native"—very different from a Native American. This new American was a self-assured hunter, explorer, and family man, armed with his rifle, independent and self-reliant, at one with nature.

As the periodical *The American Sportsman* put it, the ideal hunter "pursues his game for pleasure, makes no profit of his success, giving to his friends more than he retains, shoots invariably upon the wing and never takes a mean advantage of bird or man. It is his pride to kill what he does kill elegantly, scientifically and metrically. Quantity is not his ambition; he never slays more than he can use."[8]

Sport hunting was not always so favored. In the Revolutionary War era the better classes considered it an endeavor more suited to "savage" Indians that encouraged bad behavior in whites. Dr. Benjamin Rush, a signer of the Declaration of Independence, surgeon general of the Continental Army, opponent of slavery, and early student of mental illness, was a loud voice opposed to hunting. He listed six objections, including that it "hardens the heart, by inflicting unnecessary pain and death upon the animals." Hunting was also a time waster, created "habits of idleness," led to "low, bad company," which in turn led to intemperance, and, finally, risked accidental injury or death. He wasn't opposed to eating meat, only against wasting time trekking through the woods when it could be obtained easily and cleanly by butchering domesticated animals.[9]

By the late nineteenth century, the sport hunter's reputation underwent an upgrade. As historian Daniel Justin Herman wrote, the hunter had been remade from repulsive near savage to hardy individualist; hunting connected increasingly urbanized Americans to their tougher, more resourceful, more noble pre-industrial heritage. Or, as *The American Sportsman* unpleasantly put it, "provided an antidote to the noise and dirt and moral degradation incident to large towns."

A growing middle and upper class embraced the new hunting ethos and the new weapons as strict new laws banned market hunting and states hired game wardens to enforce the rules. What arose was the uniquely American phenomenon of the weekend hunter, trapshooter, or target shooter, the city or suburban man, or woman, who shouldered a shotgun or rifle for a week during deer season or for a weekend of duck or pheasant hunting. State tax dollars financed game preserves for the public, and game commissions to manage wildlife. Deer were successfully reintroduced in almost every state, often by importing animals from Maine, Vermont, or Wisconsin. In Pennsylvania restocking began in 1900 and was spectacularly successful. By the 1920s, the deer population reached an unmanageable size and game laws were relaxed to reduce the herd.[10]

All that hunting, of course, was done with guns, and the best-selling rifles and shotguns in the nation were John Browning's designs, built and sold by Winchester and bearing Winchester's name only.

The Model 1894 was a particular revelation. To the untrained eye, it resembled Browning's previous two rifles, though in fact it was smaller in every dimension and significantly lighter. The carbine version weighed 6.6 pounds, about 2 pounds less than the larger Model 1886, an advantage to a rider on horseback or a hunter on foot.

During the first year of production Winchester chambered the rifle for black-powder rounds, a stopgap measure as William Mason, the engineer who adapted Browning's prototypes for mass production, struggled to drill lengthwise through twenty-six-inch rifle barrels made from hardened nickel steel, necessary to withstand the powerful smokeless cartridges. Once Mason

succeeded, the upgraded barrel, able to handle the smokeless
.30-.30 ammunition,[11] reached gun owners in 1895. Browning's
design needed no improvement to withstand the new ammunition, and the combination stunned experienced hunters.

Compared to their black-powder predecessors the new round
propelled a bullet twice as fast, with a longer range and a flatter
trajectory. As previously noted, that meant the average hunter
didn't have to compensate for "bullet drop," the curved trajectory of a black-powder round, which required aiming above the
intended point of impact. Since most deer hunters took their
shot at a range of 150 yards or less, they could now just point and
shoot.

Traditionalists resisted the newfangled arm. They clung to
the .45-70 black-powder cartridge and insisted "the heavy bullet
has more killing power." But experience prompted quick conver-
sions, and jokes. One Alaskan hunter said "the boys" objected to
the new ammunition "because it kills game so far away the meat
spoils before they can get to the animal to clean it."

More seriously, A. A. Haynes from Montana said that after
hunting with the 1894 for a year he concluded, "This gun suits
me better than anything I have yet used. There is no disagree-
able recoil as with a .45-70, .45-90 or .50 caliber, while in my opinion it is superior to them in ranging and killing power."

"I killed five mountain sheep, two elk, and a bear with this
gun," wrote another correspondent to an outdoors magazine.
"Four of the sheep were each hit once and were killed almost instantly, the bullets passing clear through their bodies. One of the
five was about 400 yards away." He added that "it was the gun that
did this and not I, for had I been using a .45-90," the large black-
powder cartridge, "I would never have touched him." Reflective
of the new hunting ethos, he went on to add he was hunting to
provide food. "None of this meat was wasted."

Outdoors writer F. Chatfield Taylor praised the rifle as the
ideal saddle gun, and indeed it was soon everywhere throughout
the West. With its slim shape and light weight, the Model 1894 fit
into a saddle scabbard without encumbering the rider or horse.

There was no protruding cocking knob, as with a bolt-action rifle, to snag a rope or bush, and the front sight was protected by an optional steel shroud. It was quick to bring on target, accurate at any reasonable range, and powerful enough to take down any wild creature likely to be encountered on the plains or in the mountains—even a bear, if the need arose. "There were only a few rifles which can meet all these requirements. There are the lever actions—Winchester, Marlin, Savage . . . Of these the Winchester is far and away the most popular," wrote Taylor.

All combined to make the 1894 the best-selling lever-action rifle, and the best-selling hunting rifle, in the nation's history. By the end of the twentieth century, more than 6.5 million were sold, though in 2006 the New Haven Factory was closed and production moved to Japan.

That was only a single rifle, however, and Winchester needed to expand its product line, which also meant increasing its dependence on Browning's designs. Mason and other engineers were expert at the small revisions needed to turn a Browning prototype into a mass-produced weapon, but they designed no firearms of their own. When the specter of competition finally moved Bennett to produce a pump-action shotgun for wildfowl hunting and trapshooting, he chose a Browning design dating to 1890. It was introduced in 1894 and called the Model 1893.

The result of Winchester's first venture into pump-action shotguns was dismal. Either because of a design error by Browning or a miscalculation by Winchester, the firearm became the only Browning-designed gun ever to be, effectively, recalled and replaced by its manufacturer.

There were two problems. In 1890 Browning designed his gun for low-pressure black powder, just before it was supplanted by safer, cleaner, and more powerful smokeless powder. While Browning's rifle designs withstood the switch to smokeless powder, the Model 1893 shotgun didn't. A hunter who erroneously loaded a smokeless cartridge could blow up his gun, or himself if he was particularly unlucky. The firearm also suffered from a design flaw. Under rare circumstances, the bolt could prematurely blow open, exposing the shooter to injury from burning powder ejected backward into the face and eyes.[12]

In a yellow-lined pocket notebook, Winchester engineer T. C. Johnson tersely described encountering just such an unhappy customer by the name of Frank Willard of Brooklyn, New York. "He was out hunting" Johnson wrote, "and while shooting the bolt blew back & stuck in its rearmost position—some of the powder blew back into his eye. He said he would not shoot the gun anymore and would make us a present of it."[13]

Willard provided samples of his ammunition, and after examining the shells Johnson wrote that they were indeed blackpowder rounds. The gun, not a careless shooter, was at fault, so Winchester provided a free replacement, the redesigned version issued as the Model 1897.

Other notebook entries hint at legal action over the firearm. Johnson lists the names and addresses of twelve owners, the serial numbers of their firearms, and describes them as "witnesses who have used the model 1893." So thorough was the replacement that few 1893 guns exist today.

Browning's reaction is unrecorded, but Winchester was left to design the fixes on its own even as Browning arrived with new shotgun prototypes that Bennett felt obliged to purchase. Winchester paid for shotguns in 1892, 1894, 1895, and 1896. Some were variations on Browning's previous work, others were distinctly original, but a new design was exactly what Bennett didn't want. Tooling up a production line was expensive and time-consuming, and Winchester saw no reason to abandon what was a fundamentally solid design. Indeed, the Model 1893 "established a framework" for modern shotguns, "the fundamentals of which remained in use for well over a century," observed firearms writer Dennis Adler.[14] But Bennett was stuck. If he didn't purchase the patents there was nothing to stop Browning from offering his designs to a competitor.

So Winchester's machinists and engineers went to work incorporating ten major or minor revisions in the Model 1893. The "new" Model 1897 became so successful it was often, and incorrectly, considered the first pump-action shotgun. It remained in production until 1957, selling 1.24 million copies.

Why Browning didn't assist with the design changes is uncertain, but the succession of alternative shotgun designs he presented Winchester suggests he was simply busy with new ideas. His enormously inventive mind had already moved on. Why bother with an old concept when he had a new one? It was a phenomenon his brothers noted; once John was finished experimenting with a particular component, he'd incorporate it into a prototype for patenting or else toss it and move on to his next idea. Days were spent standing with Ed, machining, fiddling, and filing with experimental versions of whichever firearm was under development. If John encountered a dead end it would be sent to a junk pile where a part might lie forever or be fished out for a new purpose. He didn't look backward and never worked on just one design at a time. While he was knocking out shotgun prototype after shotgun prototype Browning completed his first pistol prototype, a mechanism that dominated the next decade of his career. In 1895 Winchester also introduced the last Browning lever-action gun to reach the market. It was not the last lever action Browning designed—Winchester kept buying prototypes, which remained only that—though this final production gun was famously used on the plains of Africa by Theodore Roosevelt and by the army of Czarist Russia.

With that Model 1895, Browning abandoned the loading tube for a metallic box magazine that held six horizontally stacked cartridges. Since the rounds didn't have to be lifted up and out of the tube, the action was smoother than preceding Browning lever actions, though the "throw" of the lever was long. The recoil was harsh, as the rifle was designed specifically for large game. That soon included outlaws, as the rifle was adopted by western sheriffs, Texas Rangers, and the posse hired to hunt down Butch Cassidy and the Wild Bunch. The Model 1895 also became a favorite of Winchester's best-known customer, Theodore Roosevelt, cowboy, hunter, outdoorsman, amateur naturalist, and president. His love for the "strenuous life" included a near-obsessive affection for firearms and hunting, and his many books and articles recounted his cowboy and hunting adventures and his history with Browning's rifles. This latest was capable of handling the new, sharp-pointed bullets, and Roosevelt carried one with him to Cuba during the Spanish-American War, where he presented it to a fellow Rough Rider. Roosevelt's many letters to Winchester show him to be a demanding customer. His protests about the seemingly minute difference in the length of a rifle stock, for example—in an exchange of letters he complains of a quarter-inch error—were the demands of a professional hunter. Like a golf pro whose competitor's clubs could throw off a swing, deviating from his specifications could throw off Roosevelt's aim, wasting decades spent burning the best position for arms, head, shoulders, and legs into his muscle memory. A change that might not matter on the target range could mean everything hunting a lion, as Roosevelt set out to do in his famous—or, to some, infamous—1909 expedition to Africa.

Accompanied by his son Kermit, Roosevelt embarked on a yearlong expedition partially underwritten by the Smithsonian Institution. They began in Kenya, worked their way west to what was then the Belgian Congo, then to the Nile, which they followed north to Khartoum in the Sudan. Roosevelt dispatched fourteen hundred specimens to the Smithsonian Institution and other American museums, including the skins of hundreds of "large mammals" and along with "small mammals" taken mostly with his collection of Winchesters. Along with at least three Model 1895s, chambered in either the massive .405-caliber round or the military .30-40 cartridge,[15] Roosevelt carried an English double-barreled Holland rifle, the sort of rifle called an elephant gun for both its intended prey and the size of its bullet.[16] The guns were in constant use. The expedition claimed 17 lions, 11 elephants, 20 rhinoceros, 19 zebras, and dozens of animals from lesser-known species. The grand total was 512 big-game animals, which subjected Roosevelt to intense criticism from erstwhile allies in the conservation movement. In a robust defense Roosevelt insisted, "I am not in the least a game butcher. I like to do a certain amount of hunting," clearly an understatement, "but my real and main interest is the interest of a faunal naturalist." He wasn't trophy hunting, Roosevelt insisted, and said the game was meant as specimens for natural history museums. The resulting meat was consumed by the expedition's large army of porters or was distributed to local villages.

The former president was particularly pleased with his Model 1895, chambered for the .405 cartridge, 3.2 inches long. "At least for me, personally," he wrote, the rifle was his "medicine gun" for lion hunting. The big cats were considered pests and Roosevelt's party didn't feel any need to restrict their take. In his best-selling book *African Game Trails*, Roosevelt vividly describes stalking one lion after another, and records his son Kermit's encounter with a pride of lions trailing a caravan of "wild spear-bearing Borani, people like Somalis," herding hundreds of camels and horses to a market in Nairobi.

Roosevelt doesn't say whether the lions attacked the herd or whether the Borani asked the hunters to eliminate the threat. Regardless, the predators joined his collection of specimens. The Roosevelts were accompanied by Leslie Tarlton, a small, wiry red-haired Australian, a "white hunter," who organized the safari and whose presence ensured that neither Roosevelt sacrificed his life for a museum exhibit. Apparently, Tarlton was unimpressed with Roosevelt. A grandnephew who presumably heard it from his great-uncle wrote that Tarlton "had to ensure that a slow, overweight man with poor eyesight, riding a dumpy little pony, could grab his share of trophies without enduring too much hardship or risk."[17]

No doubt following Tarlton's instruction, the men maneuvered their horses to cut off a male lion, then dismounted, raised their Winchesters, and fired. Kermit's shot wounded the lion, who began to charge before a second shot sent him skittering away. Tarlton "stopped it with a third shot." The two remounted, found the lionesses, killed one, wounded another, and confronted the third, which charged from two hundred yards. "She at once came in at full speed, making a most determined charge. Kermit and Tarlton were standing near their horses. The lioness came on with great bounds so that Kermit missed her twice, but broke her shoulder high up when she was but thirty yards off." The lioness fell, then rose. "Tarlton stopped her with a bullet in the nick of time."

Two days later they came upon the remaining cubs and the wounded lioness. Kermit shot the latter but let the cubs go, "feeling it was unsportsmanlike to kill them," his father wrote, "a feeling which I am by no means certain I share, for lions are scourges not only to both wild and untamed animals, but to man himself. . . . In a Nairobi church-yard I was shown the graves of seven men who had been killed by lions, and of one who been killed by a rhino."

Killing a lion was risky business, particularly when hunting with Tarlton, who specialized in chasing a lion on horseback until the animal turned to charge, then quickly dismounting to fire. Dismounting was key, as one couldn't make a shot from horseback. When Roosevelt tracked two lions into a patch of thick brush "We were off our horses in an instant," Roosevelt wrote.

One burst out of the brush thirty yards off, "the tawny, galloping form of a big, maneless lion. Crack! The Winchester spoke; and as the soft nosed bullet plowed forward through his flank the lion swerved so that I missed him with a second shot."

At the third shot the lion was sixty yards off, "his hind quarters dragging, his head up, his ears back, his jaws open and lips drawn up in a prodigious snarl, as he endeavored to turn to face us. His back was broken; but of this we could not at the moment be sure; if it had merely been grazed, he might have recovered, and then, even though dying, his charge might have done mischief.

So Kermit, Sir Alfred, and I fired, all together, into his chest. His head sank and he died."

Not everyone admired the former president's "specimen" gathering. "The worst feature in the whole bloody business is not the killing of a few hundred wild animals in Africa," nature writer and former minister William J. Long told the *New York Times*, "but the brutalizing influence which these reports have upon thousands of American boys. Only last week I met half a dozen little fellows in the woods. The biggest boy had a gun and a squirrel's tail in his hat, and he called himself Bwana. . . .They were shooting everything in sight.

"How could I convince them that their work was inhuman?" Dr. Long continued. "Is not the great American hero occupied at this time with the same detestable business?"

Browning wasn't insensible to the possibility that the animals he hunted in the Utah plains and mountains possessed their own wild consciousness, and Jack describes an incident related by his father about a hunting trip with Split—the man with a split nose who offered a gold coin for Browning's first rifle. Both were armed with the famed single-shot rifle. After Browning shot one deer their packhorse skittered and stepped on his rifle, breaking the stock in two.

Browning wanted to take two deer before returning to town. "By the time a deer was whacked up among the boys in the shop and some steaks . . . for one or two others, there isn't much left." So he and Split agreed that Split would lead the horse back to camp while Browning continued the hunt with Split's poorly maintained rifle. It was so badly pitted from rust and black-powder corrosion that after every shot the spent cartridge had to be hammered out of the barrel. "He said the sticking didn't bother him much because he always got his game with one shot."

Browning worked his way along a ridge, finding no deer. As the afternoon waned, he circled back along the opposite side. "When I got to that edge I stopped suddenly and probably gasped. The ridge dropped sharply down a steep drawer and on into Ogden Canyon, and out there, filling the whole world, was a sunset that must've stopped the heavenly harps for a while." This language is almost certainly Jack's lavish paraphrasing of his father, as the account was written three decades after Browning's death.

"I sat on a rock and forgot all about deer and Split. . . . I seemed to be in the edge of the conflagration. The rocks and trees all around me had colors running over them and I tried to take it all in."

Then he saw a bear, "hunkered" on a rock outcropping. The bear, Browning realized, was staring at the sunset. It was a grizzly, already rare in the Utah mountains.

"I've never seen one before, but I knew him. I knew him the way I'd know Goliath. The outcrop was like an altar, and a priest in robes never looked more worshipful. There was no reason for his climbing up on that outcrop except to get a clearer view of the stupendous picture. I watched the colors begin to fade," his rifle in hand, "and then tiptoed away. . . . I looked back and brother grizzly was still on his altar. I thought that the Great Spirit of the mountain should be well pleased with his worshipper. I was about half ready to believe in the Great Spirit myself."

Browning never told Split. "I've never told anybody. The incident was too complicated. There was the bear, not over a hundred yards away, sitting straight up, his left side toward me, offering me the choice of any part of his anatomy to shoot at. I sat with a rifle on my knees just staring, wondering what he was seeing in the West, feeling that I had no right to interrupt his devotion with a shot. I'm a gunmaker and as much of a hunter as I've had time to be, and I had a most unusual chance at what is considered the prime big-game trophy of the Rocky Mountains, and yet I quietly withdrew."

Browning conceded a practical consideration may have influenced his decision. "That bear was a hunk for one man with the best rifle in the land, and I, limited to one shot, had no business making him mad. . . . But while I watched him he looked solemn and sad and that's the way I felt. I hope he enjoyed the full hundred years they say a grizzly sometimes lives. I never went bear hunting again."

It's a great story, even if the exact truth is not likely found in Jack's poetic rendering.

CHAPTER SEVEN

THE MUSTACHIOED MAN

The second part of John Browning's life—the part that changed history—began in the winter of 1893 when he arrived at the Colt factory in Hartford, a sprawling four-story brick building along the Connecticut River, famously topped by a dark blue onion-shaped dome festooned with gold stars.

Accompanied by Matt, John carried a much-improved version of the ungainly gas machine gun first demonstrated two years earlier. It was now sleek and slim, with a modernist look foreshadowing the next century's minimalist design movement. At forty-one inches long and a relatively modest thirty-five pounds, it had to be mounted on a tripod but remained far more portable than a hand-cranked Gatling gun, and it gave Colt a chance to compete in a market dominated by the Maxim gun.

On February 15 Browning signed the patent over to Colt in return for a royalty payment on each gun sold.[1] Potentially, it was a much more lucrative agreement than his contracts with Winchester, which set a fixed price no matter how popular or profitable the firearm. As it turned out, this was one of Browning's least successful military designs. In the hands of poorly trained troops, too often the case, it was prone to jamming and was difficult to clear. It did acquire a unique nickname, the potato digger, because if the tripod was set too low to the ground the flapper mechanism, now located on the bottom of the barrel, dug a hole in the earth with each shot.

The greater significance of Browning's trip was his introduction to Colt engineer Hart O. Berg, a short, stout man with whom Browning soon became "well acquainted," as the inventor later said.[2] They were very different in background and personality, let alone height, yet their friendship became a seminal event in the history of modern firearms. It expanded Browning's reach to a second continent, generating real wealth for the Browning brothers and giving Browning far more control over which of his guns was manufactured.

Browning was still a youthful thirty-eight, almost totally bald, and sported a mustache that before long was joined by a goatee. He was more than a head taller than Berg—Browning was six feet two inches, or six foot three: sources differ. Browning often described himself as a "mountain man" from the West, which was indeed the geographic location of his roots but belied the fact that his life was increasingly oriented toward the East. His periodic trips to New Haven—and now Hartford—became twice-annual events that consumed months. Browning must have felt a sublime sense of achievement watching the products of his imagination turned into steel, and he enjoyed the company of factory machinists. He was closely observed on the factory floor, and his habits were noted. Browning munched peanuts, and when stymied by a problem he rhythmically shelled and munched as he stood and thought amid the lathes, planes, drills, and shapers. The faster he ate, the bigger the problem. And while there is no report of Browning raising his voice, an unhappy Browning would deliver a cold stare. "Men who worked with Browning tell me he was a stern man, with eyes that looked right through you, and a face that never changed expression," according to one account.[3]

Browning was never a social animal like his brother Matt, who served a two-year term as Ogden's mayor and more than a decade as head of the city school board. He and his wife, Mary, hosted celebratory dinners and social events recorded in the social sections of the Ogden newspapers. The brothers remained close—they spoke almost every day when both were in Ogden. Together they had methodically shaved the edges off their frontier upbringing: Matt to fit in with Utah's financiers and businessmen, and John to better mesh with college-trained engineers with their city-bred manners. Growing up, they'd learned the southern Appalachian accent and grammar of their Tennessee-bred father, which didn't pass muster in bank boardrooms and factory offices. So, on their six-day train rides east, the brothers carried an English grammar book and quizzed each other on the rules and pronunciation of proper English.[4] They purchased a multivolume world history and traded the volumes back and forth.[5]

Despite their Mormon upbringing, neither brother was a teetotaler. Browning's favorite hotel in Hartford was the five-story Heublein on Mulberry Street whose owners, Gilbert and Lewis Heublein, had just introduced pre-mixed cocktails made with either gin or bourbon. The hotel, with a round conical tower topped by an American flag, became Browning's home away from home for thirty years.

The short, bushy-haired Berg was twenty-eight years old, tended toward stoutness, and sported a thick mustache. He was five feet seven and one-half inches tall, as he carefully noted in his passport application.[6] A Philadelphia native whose family emigrated from Germany earlier in the nineteenth century, Berg was trilingual, fluent in English, French, and German. He may have heard the latter language at home, but the French he learned in Liège, Belgium, where between 1884 and 1891 he studied engineering and arms manufacturing. Equidistant from Germany and Holland, Liège was a center of coal mining and steel smelting and had a history of arms production dating back to the fourteenth century.

Outgoing and genial, Berg possessed a natural charm and, as his later career proved, a keen eye for character.[7] He did not back down from a challenge. In 1900, while driving an experimental electric car on the posh Avenue Montaigne in Paris, he collided with a vehicle driven by another American, Lewis Sandford, son of an influential New York attorney. The improbable smash-up was instantly newsworthy and, in wire-service reports, Berg was described as "the popular ladies' man" and Sandford as "another prominent member of the American colony." Each blamed the other for the accident and concluded the solution was to make one or the other dead. "The two men exchanged severe words, and this was followed yesterday by a pistol duel." Their shooting was as bad as their driving. "Four shots were fired, but neither duelist was hurt," said one news report.[8] A headline was more direct: "Berg and Sandford Fought with Pistols, and Both Were Such Poor Shots That Neither Scored a Hit." They were said to be the first Americans to fight a duel in Paris.

Both Browning and Berg belonged to religions on the social fringes in old Yankee Hartford—Browning a Mormon and Berg a Jew. While Browning may have never previously known a Jew and Berg perhaps had never met a Mormon, the Jewish faith loomed large in Mormon theology. Mormon patriarch Joseph Smith taught that Mormons were linked to the ancient Israelites, and church members compared their flight from persecution, across the desert to Utah, to the biblical escape from Egypt. In 1841 an influential Mormon missionary climbed the Mount of Olives in Jerusalem to "dedicate" the Holy Land to the Jews. The Mormon faith was condemned as heresy by most Christian churches, while the Jews carried the weight of historical prejudice.

Berg and Browning worked together at Colt between 1893 and early 1896, and their friendship continued through a regular exchange of letters when Berg returned to Europe. He later was invited to the Browning household in Ogden, where the inventor's children marveled at the size of his muttonchop sideburns.

Berg also had an insider's knowledge of the European arms industry, which was racing to invent the next big thing in guns. Maxim's successful machine gun spurred widespread efforts to develop a handheld version. The era's great firearms puzzle was how to shrink a heavy, tripod-mounted machine gun into a weapon that could be held and fired with a single hand. Designs appeared and just as quickly disappeared as inventors in Germany, Austria, France, and Belgium competed to create a weapon that had never previously existed. Even its name was in flux. Initially the handguns were called automatic pistols, but that name suggested a sort of machine gun, which, engineering challenges aside, was quickly discovered to be impractical as a pistol design. Early inventors found a fully automatic pistol recoiled uncontrollably and spewed bullets up, down, and sideways. What Europe's gun manufacturers wanted was a weapon that fired one bullet with a pull of the trigger and then instantly reloaded a fresh cartridge but didn't fire again until the trigger was pulled a second time.

The concept was called a semiautomatic pistol, which did nothing to solve the engineering conundrums. Inventors strove to decide exactly what a handgun should be. How big? What caliber? Where to put the cartridges? In the grip? In front of the trigger? What kind of action? Gas? Recoil?

The difficulty was unsurprising. As Browning said, "It's not so hard figuring out the essentials of a gun mechanism. The trouble is getting the essentials in the right place."[9]

It's usually agreed that the first semiautomatic pistol to prove reliable, effective, accurate, and commercially successful—sort of—was invented by Hugo Borchardt,[10] a thin-skinned, irascible German engineer who immigrated to America in 1860, became a naturalized citizen, worked for four different firearms makers and the Singer sewing machine company before returning to Europe. Borchardt realized that the time-tested toggle link that Maxim used to move the bolt back and forth in his machine gun—also used in the original Winchester lever-action rifles—could be applied to a handgun. He came up with an odd-looking and unwieldy fourteen-inch-long gun that appeared on the market in 1893. Borchardt placed the bullets inside the handgrip, a good idea, and then ignored basic ergonomics. Rather than a grip raked at an angle so holding the gun was like shaking an outstretched hand, his grip was installed straight up and down at a ninety-degree angle, making the gun awkward to grasp and hard to aim. Worse, his design required a long, bulbous fitting for the recoil spring that added nearly five inches to the overall length.

As a German executive trying to sell the gun conceded, "It

is a well-known fact that especially the long form and abnormal shape of this pistol is a serious practical drawback."[11]

But the gun did work and, for an early autoloader it was reliable and accurate. So when Borchardt refused to shrink the size, manufacturer Deutsche Waffen- und Munitionsfabriken, DWM, called in another inventor to redesign Borchardt's gun and—to Borchardt's later unhappiness—make it synonymous with his own name: Georg Luger.[12] His work, along with turning Borchardt's pistol into an iconic handgun, launched a patent dispute with John Browning that lasted for nearly a decade as they fought over who deserved credit for a crucial element in Luger's redesign.

But that was only after Browning invented the modern handgun.

Browning joined the pistol fray in 1894. By then the breadth of his inventions had surpassed any other firearms inventor on either side of the Atlantic. Between 1890 and 1894 Browning made the world's first gas-operated machine gun for Colt, invented two best-selling lever-action rifles for Winchester, and designed what became the most popular pump-action shotgun sold in America for the next half century. He also designed that Teddy Roosevelt favorite, the 1895 box-magazine lever action, and with his brother Ed on the metalworking machines produced a dozen other rifle and shotgun prototypes that Winchester purchased merely to foil competitors. Browning guns had made Winchester the nation's leading manufacturer of civilian arms, and despite the cost of Browning's "raids" on the company treasury, Winchester's investment in Browning patents was paying off handsomely.

Now, between late 1894 and early 1896, Browning invented what the world now knows as the slide-operated semiautomatic handgun.

A division of labor between John, Matt, and Ed was now in place as they worked in the Browning store and machine shop in downtown Ogden. John did most of the creating, Ed did the metalwork, and Matt ran the business, as Matt, Ed, and John ex-

plained in a never-before-published transcript of a 1901 legal deposition.

"Formerly, we worked together in the shop on any invention
he was getting out, and some of my ideas were usually embod-
ied in the inventions, and in those days patents were taken out
jointly by us," Matt said about the brothers' early collaboration.
"But later on as our other business increased it has occupied my
time and other channels, and he has kept on with the inventions practically alone, only I was always cognizant of what he
was doing and frequently helped him in the construction of his
models, as I am a practical mechanic myself."[13]

Ed was the chief mechanic and under John's direction made
three handgun prototypes. "I have done the biggest part of the
work, that is, the manual labor on all of them, and construct the
models and guns," he said describing his work in the 1890s when
John was engaged in the most creative period of his life. With
Ed's expertise John was able to spend less and less time working metal and more time simply thinking and sketching out his
ideas.

Once the concept took shape, it required four or five months
to design and produce the individual parts, fit each together,
and produce a full-fledged prototype for testing, followed by its
presentation to Winchester or Colt, Ed said in a 1907 deposition,
also previously unpublished.

"In the first place, there are a great many special cutters, and
drills, and taps, and reamers and fixtures, and other things, to
be made" before a new firearm could take shape. Only once that
work was done could the brothers begin making the parts that
John conceived in his head and, with a rough sketch or verbal
description, communicated to Ed. There was much discussion
back and forth. As parts were developed, Browning carried them
around town, slipping them out of his pocket to manipulate
them back and forth, feeling how they interacted and imprint-
ing the movement into his brain.

"Every cut that we make we discussed whether that is right

or not, and every part is looked at and talked over a great deal to make it and make it over again may be as high as three times, probably—possibly more than that—before we leave it," Ed said.

"The parts are all thought over carefully, to determine whether they are strong enough, whether they are heavy enough, or too heavy, and possibly a part won't do, and we have to throw it away, and once in a while my brother John M. would get stuck, and would have to take some time to get it straightened out, and all this took time."[14]

Their first attempt at a handgun was a mechanical dead end, but a triumph of fundamental design and conception. There is only one example, now on display in the John M. Browning Firearms Museum in Ogden, Utah, where the gun's design innovation can be grasped at a glance.

Completed in early 1895, it looks, on first glance, almost exactly like a modern pistol.

In fact, it was a revised, simplified, and downsized version of his gas-powered machine gun, with the "potato digger" flapper— an improved version of that original paddle—swinging back and forth above rather than below the barrel. The movement likely jerked the gun up and down, degrading accuracy, though the brothers did have fun shooting the only version ever made. As described by Matt in the same deposition, "My brother John M. Browning and I took it down to the river after it was finished. We also took a .38 Smith & Wesson (revolver) and were shooting the two in some mud to see which displaced the most."[15]

The upper part of the gun, containing barrel, flapper, and recoil spring, was smoothly integrated into the bottom section, containing the grip, hammer, trigger, and magazine. Unlike many competitors in Europe, Browning's gun looked like a unified whole rather than a jumble of parts.

Browning combined form and function with such skill that the gun he designed in 1895 could all but pass for a semiautomatic pistol manufactured in the twenty-first century.

The gun's mechanism, on the other hand, was almost certainly awkward and likely of dubious reliability, so Browning tossed the gas operation and imagined a totally new mechanism.[16] This wasn't an improvement or adaption of an existing action, as so often happened with firearms design. What he created was so new it didn't have a name, and Browning struggled with how to describe it and what to call it even when he filed the patent on October 31, 1896.

The application was nine pages long, with 510 lines of text and sixteen drawings labeling each part with letters and numbers. On the second page, Browning summarized his invention this way:

> The three main parts of the pistol which I have represented in the drawings are the frame . . . the barrel . . . and the breech block or bolt carrier . . . which slides to and fro under the influence of the recoil and reaction-spring.

"Slides" is the operative word. Browning's patent described his invention of the pistol slide and its associated internal action—the slide being the steel cover surrounding the barrel and incorporating the breechblock, firing pin, and recoil spring. The upper "slides" back and forth on rails cut into the frame, which includes the grip, trigger, hammer, mainspring, and magazine.

Browning's design outlasted all its competitors to become the fundamental mechanism of virtually all modern handguns. Whenever a character in a World War II film, twentieth-century cop show, or twenty-first-century first-person shooter game grabs the top of a handgun, slides it backward, and lets it snap forward with a thick, metallic click-click, he or she is cocking what is commonly called a slide-action pistol. (Technically, it's a "short-recoil semiautomatic pistol.")[17]

It's a versatile design, as Browning demonstrated that day in October when he filed patents for three different slide mechanisms, two of which remain in use to this day. One was a "locked breech" system for high-pressure, large-caliber weapons, like the 9mm or .45-caliber guns used by police, the military, and sport shooters. In recent decades it's also become the favored design for personal self-defense weapons and the favored gun of the criminal class.

His second patent was a "blowback system" originally meant for small-caliber guns easy to carry or slip into a pocket; Browning's version was for a low-power .32-caliber round he designed himself. In mid-1896 he and Matt carried the prototypes to Hartford and opened negotiations with Richard Jarvis, the brother-in-law of founder Samuel Colt, though talks were likely handled by Hall, who'd overseen the machine-gun tests.

Not present in Hartford was Berg. He was back in Europe working as "general sales agent and international representative" for the Belgian arms maker Fabrique Nationale d'Armes de Guerre, which literally translates to "national factory of weapons of war," better known as FN. Berg was dispatched to negotiate arms deals with the governments of Serbia and Spain, which he apparently did effectively. Within a year he was promoted to director of external affairs. It may have been a job no one else wanted, because FN was in the midst of a financial crisis.

Based in Herstal, a village immediately adjacent to the larger city of Liège, FN was created in 1889 by a consortium of smaller arms manufacturers to fulfill a Belgian Army contract for 150,000 bolt-action rifles designed by famed German inventor Paul Mauser. Financing was obtained for a multistory brick factory that opened in 1892, followed by a second factory capable of producing twenty-five thousand brass cartridge cases and lead bullets a day.

With a large pool of skilled labor at hand, FN's guns were renowned for their quality. The Belgian military contract was completed in December 1894, and FN obtained orders from Brazil, China, Norway, and Costa Rica. That was the good news. The bad news began when Chile announced its intention to purchase sixty thousand rifles. Alarmed at the large incursion into its foreign market, Mauser threatened Chile with legal action and revoked FN's manufacturing license. That sent FN spinning into an existential and financial crisis, only solved in 1896 when the giant

German machine tool maker Ludwig Loewe & Co. purchased a controlling interest. While the company had a lifeline, it still had a nearly new arms factory with little to make. But it did have Berg, and he and Browning regularly exchanged letters while Browning and Colt negotiated the rights to Browning's pistol designs. Unfortunately for Colt, though fortunately for FN, the American gunmaker decided to produce only one of Browning's designs.

Colt was oriented toward military contracts and wanted to develop the stronger but technically complex "locked-breech" system. In that design the barrel and slide recoiled together for a fraction of a second until the bullet exited the barrel and the internal gas pressure dropped to zero.

The two parts traveled for about one-quarter of an inch. Then the barrel separated or "unlocked" from the slide, which continued moving backward to eject the spent cartridge. At the end of its travel, the slide cocked the hammer and the recoil spring threw the slide back forward, automatically reloading the gun from the grip magazine.[18] The entire action moved faster than the eye could see.

In Browning's "blowback" patent, the barrel was stationary while the slide moved to and fro.[19]

The small blowback design was Browning's personal favorite and he often carried it in his pocket. "When he found time, he would slip a couple of boxes of ammunition in his coat and walk up into the hills to fire it. He also practiced quick-drawing it, waiting until he had the trick perfected before he showed it to a surprised Matt," Jack wrote.

In that gun, Browning had created a semiautomatic pistol that met all but one of his design themes. The gun was effective, simple, reliable, compact, and inexpensive to produce. While it couldn't fire a powerful military round, it easily handled .32-caliber ammunition. It was simple to maintain and fit easily into a coat pocket. It fired a small bullet at a modest velocity, but for personal self-defense the cartridge was powerful enough and became the standard round in some police departments.

What it didn't have was the visual élan of Browning's first, or his future, pistols. The gun appeared to have two barrels, one atop the other. The top tube contained the recoil spring, the bottom tube the barrel. Keeping the barrel closer to the hand did reduce muzzle flip, the tendency of a gun to jerk upward after firing.

Despite Browning's enthusiasm for that pistol, Colt remained uninterested and concentrated on developing the larger .38 handgun. It provided Colt with a technologically advanced offering available for the U.S. Army when—as was inevitable—it upgraded from revolvers. A large semiautomatic pistol held more rounds, was easier to reload, balanced better than a revolver with its heavy cylinder—or at least Browning's pistols balanced better— and was proving more accurate, early experiments showed. As for the civilian market, Colt believed Americans had a limited interest in a small low-powered handgun that was inherently more "point and shoot" than a handgun intended for careful "aim and fire." Any citizen dreaming of surviving a gunfight on the western plains wouldn't buy a .32 blowback pistol. Cost was also a factor. Setting up a production line for a totally new gun—few major parts in a revolver could be repurposed for a pistol—was an expensive endeavor. Colt chose the gun it felt would succeed in the civilian and military marketplace, so it chose the .38.

Colt's decision, however, opened a door for Berg and FN, and Browning eagerly walked through.

In 1896 and 1897, Browning recalled, "Mr. Berg wrote me a number of times, asking me to come over and show some of my inventions, if I had any, to the firm that they might have an opportunity to arrange for the manufacture of anything I might have that suited them," Browning said, "and thinking that perhaps they would like to manufacture an automatic pistol, I took my pistols over to Belgium."[20]

Browning's decision to throw in with FN is an event often described in books, articles, and videos about Browning firearms, but those accounts are at best incomplete and usually incorrect.

The popular version is that Berg and Browning first met in 1897 when Berg was in Hartford scouting for bicycle designs to produce in FN's unused factory. The two men hit it off; Berg told Browning of FN's available arms factory; Berg carried a prototype of a Browning pistol back to Europe and returned with a contract. That version is neat and clean, though it assumes Browning would have surrendered an example of his groundbreaking work to an unknown man who intended to jump aboard the next ship to Europe. That version says Browning didn't travel to Belgium until 1902.[21]

Browning's own account—which was provided during the patent dispute with Luger—is very different.

It begins, as already seen, in 1893 with Berg and Browning's friendship, followed by their regular letters and Browning leaving America's shores on March 31, 1897, for the first of at least sixty-four transatlantic voyages over the course of his life. He traveled aboard a steamer, which took six or seven days to reach Le Havre, the large French port facing the English Channel. From there, he traveled to Paris and then northeast to Brussels and east to Liège.

There is, unfortunately, no clear record of Browning's reaction to his first encounter with Europe. Browning had arrived on a continent at peace for nearly three decades and, while technical marvels were speeding social and political change, Europe was still ruled by monarchs controlling foreign colonies and Belgium's King Leopold still owned what is now the Congo, overseeing a brutal regime of slave labor and torture.

While Jack Browning's book incorrectly states that his father's first European voyage was in 1902, the description may well be of the actual first voyage in 1897. It has the ring of truth, even if the date is wrong. After boarding his ship, Jack writes, his father suddenly realized that a "mountain man from Ogden" had a lot to learn about the Continent and so spent most of the voyage reading European history and travel guides found in the ship's library. Browning spent a week in Paris, hired an English-speaking guide, and visited a tailor to order a bespoke suit for his meeting in Liège. He visited the city's museums and attended a performance of the famous French opera *Faust*.

In complete anonymity, he arrived in Liège on a cold, rainy evening. Browning was little known outside firearms circles and no one in Liège would have thought that the tall American was carrying the invention that would save the FN arms factory. Browning's little blowback pistol entranced FN's managers, who were unconcerned with America's horizonless plains or hitting a target at twenty-five yards. The Europeans thought in shorter distances and, like Browning, considered the gun a weapon for self-defense, sort of a long-distance knife, a point-and-shoot weapon to be used over a distance of five or ten meters.

In Liège, Browning's prototype fired five hundred shots in a row without a single jam or failure, an achievement unheard of for any semiautomatic pistol at the time. Browning and FN's managers reached a tentative agreement, with a written contract to be signed in July when Berg was on a scheduled trip to America. FN did ask, and Browning agreed, "that when they got ready to commence to manufacture my pistol I would go over and give them the benefit of my knowledge of the invention in getting them started."

The only potential complication was that FN's chief shareholder, now DWM in Germany, had to approve the contract. DWM also manufactured Borchardt's ungainly pistol, and it turned out that the company engineer who had to affirm that Browning's device worked as claimed was Borchardt himself. "So in company with Mr. Berg I went to Berlin to try and make suitable arrangements," Browning said.[22]

One can only imagine Browning's private reaction. He was now in the unenviable position of having to depend on a competitor—essentially a failed competitor—to sign off on his deal with FN. At their meeting, Browning presented Borchardt with both his locked-breech and blowback designs. "They were first fired, and afterwards taken apart, and inspected in all the details, by Mr. Borchardt and myself." It must have been a bitter moment for Borchardt, to see Browning's advanced work just as DWM was giving his pistol over to another of its engineers, Luger, for a redesign.

Browning spent three more weeks in Liège and returned to the United States in April, visited Ogden briefly before returning with Matt to Hartford on July 7, 1897, to meet with Berg—who was indeed also looking for bicycle designs—and sign the first contract with FN. The company was licensed to sell Brownings in France, Belgium, Germany, Austria-Hungary, and Spain. The Browning brothers would handle sales in Britain. And, for the first time, Browning's name would appear on a firearm. FN didn't consider the Browning name a slight to their corporate ego and likely saw it as a positive marketing ploy; it could only help sales to identify their new gun as one designed by a tall, lean American from the Wild West. For the Brownings it was good business to develop their own identity independent of any manufacturer. The contract John and Matt signed said "Browning's Patent" would be stamped on every pistol slide. The agreement called for an immediate $2,000 payment and then a royalty of "two francs in gold" for each pistol sold. If FN sold fewer than five thousand pistols, the license would revert back to the Brownings.

The pistol FN built had only thirty-two parts and weighed only twenty-two ounces. The seven-round magazine was removable, making for quick reloads, which was unlike most other contemporary semiautomatic pistols with fixed magazines. The safety on the left side of the frame was easily reached by a thumb. With FN's experienced workforce, the "Pistolet Browning" was beautifully made. Production ramped up slowly and significant numbers of the weapon began circulating in 1902. By August 1904, 100,000 were sold. By 1909 the total reached 500,000. Sales topped out at 724,550 in 1914. A great many of the purchases were by civilians—Europe was two wars away from tough handgun controls, though the Belgian Army did order 20,000, and the gun also equipped a variety of police departments. It quickly acquired a nickname, and soon any pistol was being called *le browning* in French and/or simply a "browning" in England and Germany. Its success quickly spawned other "pocket pistols" by major manufacturers who attempted to copy Browning's design without running afoul of his patent.

The U.S. Army considered the FN pistol underpowered for a military weapon but otherwise found much to praise. "It is especially distinguished by its extremely compact construction," a report said. "The pistol is very flat and has no projecting parts, it can be fit into the breast pocket like a cigar case," and so concluded "it is very well suited for the use of the general public, as for instance, bicyclists and tourists." With the FN sales figures in hand, Colt saw the error of its decision to forgo the small pistol and began production of its own small Browning pistol. It turned out American customers would purchase a low-powered .32 caliber if the design was right.

The first "Pistolet Browning," later renamed FN 1900, would retain its popularity for decades. Throughout the twentieth century, China and Korea were "especially avid copiers" and, as of the 1980s there were still workshops in Pakistan constructing knockoffs. Even North Korea produced a sort of clone called the Type 64, which made an appearance in Tom Clancy's 1995 novel *Op-Center.*[23]

The compact pistol was among the transformative inventions of the early twentieth century. It wasn't the only small handgun sold in Europe, which had already witnessed a boom in small pocket revolvers available at cut-rate mail-order prices, but Browning's new pistol was a spectacular mechanical innovation for its time, and it became that era's emblematic handgun at a time when purchases were subject to few legal constraints. It was a high-quality, smoothly operating machine that the user could hold in one hand and in seconds fire seven shots with the little slide flashing back and forth as the brass cartridges were ejected out the side. It was, in effect, a light and sound show, only with chunks of lead that could explode glass bottles, clang off steel plates, poke sudden holes in paper targets, and, inevitably and unfortunately, put holes in people.

Records compiled before World War I by Germany's Imperial Chancellor describe the change in habit sweeping that nation, as elsewhere on the Continent, after 1900. The "culture of the knife" became the culture of the gun. Young apprentices who once saved up money to buy "some kind of exceptional knife" now went looking for a firearm, preferably "a Browning pistol, which was considered to be one of the most outstanding modern weapons," wrote one early-twentieth-century German official. "Almost nobody was immune to the fascination of the new technology," according to one study of historic records. While Germans were fond of Luger's homemade Parabellum, as his gun was called, it was Browning's gun that was "especially coveted."[24] The Luger, in comparison, was larger, complicated, and more expensive.

All those new guns and new gun owners produced the predictable. Local governments in Hamburg, Bavaria, Saxony, the Rhineland, and Prussia reported "remarkable" rates of firearms injuries, much of it accidental. While reports collected in 1911 describe husbands killing wives and wives killing husbands, many reports describe injuries and deaths of "birds, dogs and cats" shot for target practice. For young men, "shooting on trains has become an increasingly popular entertainment," and incidents were reported such as that of a woodsman who "showed his Browning pistol to young girl and shot a child dead" or "the young waiter jokingly pointed a gun at a colleague and accidentally shot him in the chest." The new technology was deadly in the hands of the many people who had no experience and no training and, indeed, may never have previously even seen a pistol. A person gripping a handgun instinctively places their index finger on the trigger, and any involuntary movement of the hand can exert the four or five pounds of pressure necessary to trip the hammer and fire the gun.

Ordinary Germans weren't the only ones charmed by the technological advance. In the decade before World War I, Europe was rife with political turmoil and Brownings became the firearm of choice among anarchists and revolutionaries.[25] The ubiquity of Browning's guns led the *London Daily Mail* to declare in 1907 that it was evidence of an international conspiracy among Europe's radicals. "It will be noticed that wherever the weapon is described as a shooting outrage it has been invariably a Browning pistol—a peculiar weapon. . . . It all points to a central organization, to one brain control that is pulling the strings of anarchism the world over; that in addition to finding funds for the work is arming the anarchists throughout the world with a weapon of uniform patent."

It was far more probable that the anarchists, like anyone else, simply wanted the best tool for the job.

In 1907 the *Salt Lake Tribune* ran an article and included a brief interview with Matthew under the four-deck headlines then commonly used: "OGDENITE INVENTS DEADLY WEAPON." "Browning Automatic Gun Utilized to Close Career of Russian General" followed by "MACHINE IS POPULAR WITH RUSSIAN REDS" and finally "Ogden Men Interested Have Other Inventions to Depopulate Court of Europe."

The Russian general slain referred to was Alexander Pavloff, the chief military public prosecutor and only the latest of a series of European officials gunned down during the height of anarchist agitation. Paraphrasing an interview with Matt, the paper reported he "stated today that the gun used by the assassin was his brother's patent of thirty-two caliber and explained that the gun is being manufactured in great quantities in Liege, Belgium, and that it is a great favorite with the Terrorists and anarchists of Russia and Poland." Matt said one hundred thousand were ordered by Czarist Russia to arm the police and military.

"Great numbers, he asserts, have been sent to other European countries where disorder reigns, and it was with one of these the attempted assassin of King Alphonso of Spain killed the policeman" guarding the monarch.

Lethality struck Utah on November 27, 1908, when Weber County deputy sheriff Seymore L. Clark was shot and killed a few miles outside of Ogden after he surprised thieves looting a railroad car. Clark was transporting a man to the hospital via horse and buggy when he stopped, tied up the horse, walked over to investigate, and was shot "multiple times in the chest." The weapon was a Colt version of a Browning gun; by then Colt had produced six Browning pistol designs for the civilian and military markets, varying them in size, caliber, and action.

A local gun expert, perhaps one of the Browning brothers, was quoted as to what made the Colt pistol so deadly: "A novice can shoot quite accurately with it, as the gun, when held in the hand, points almost in line with the index finger and furthermore there is no perceptible recoil to force the weapon out of line of aim."[26] The recoil observation was a bit off, but it was correct to say the magazine can be emptied "with the blink of an eye." Despite a lengthy investigation, no one was ever arrested for the murder.

By then Colt and Browning discovered Americans still favored the revolver and were less enthused with semiautomatic pistols than the Europeans. Browning's designs were the only domestically made pistols and faced little competition outside a few European imports, but none overtook revolvers in popularity until the last decades of the twentieth century. Between 1900 and 1911 Colt introduced seven models, but none had sales success like Browning's FN guns in Europe. The first civilian Colt pistol was the medium-sized Colt 1903, which fired the Browning-designed .32 cartridge and eventually found 572,000 customers, but it took four decades to reach sales that FN achieved in a matter of years.

Indeed, in 1906 FN introduced Browning's tiny "pocket pistol," only 4.25 inches long, little more than palm sized, with all the features and precision manufacture of a larger gun. The gun was Browning's idea, the clever inventor having figured out exactly what the public would purchase. Browning also realized that the public knew nothing about his guns, and he designed two safeties—one operated by the thumb, the other by a lever on the grip. For Browning, inventing a tiny, precise machine constituted a challenge and a fun mental exercise. In Europe it became a virtual fashion accessory, offered in engraved versions embossed with precious metals, as was also the larger Model 1900. The smaller gun was easily tucked in a pocket or purse, even if its puny .25-caliber bullet prompted a joke that "a .25 caliber is a great thing to have around when you can't carry a gun."

It was gripped with only three fingers—the index finger, middle finger, and thumb—produced almost no recoil, and yet was accurate at ten or fifteen yards. Some called it a toy, but Browning noted it could nonetheless put a hole in a person. Within a few years FN had sold nearly a half-million copies. Colt's version of Browning's tiny pocket pistol reached the market in 1908 and it sold 409,000 copies, but that sales success took thirty-three years.

America did not suffer the wave of political violence that swept Europe before World War I, but nevertheless gun crime increased as the same modern machinery and technology that produced Browning's pistols also made revolvers cheaper and more accessible. Local controls on handguns and rifles date to the eighteenth century and were usually limited to carrying weapons in public spaces. There was little discussion of licensing or regulating their sale, outside of the South, where extensive efforts were made to keep arms out of the hands of African-Americans. Then in 1908 Chicago passed an ordinance requiring a permit from the mayor's office for any handgun purchase. In 1911 New York State enacted the first major statewide gun control legislation, the Sullivan law, which required a permit to purchase or carry a handgun.

The Sullivan behind the Sullivan law was a corrupt and influential New York City legislator nicknamed Big Tim, who made gun control a campaign platform and pushed it through the state legislature with near-unanimous support. Some accounts say the impetus was the attempted assassination of New York City's mayor in 1910 or the killing of novelist and investigative journalist David Graham Phillips in 1911. One of Phillips's major exposés was a series of stories alleging corruption in the U.S. Senate, which prompted then-president Theodore Roosevelt to decry him as "the man with the muck rake," introducing into the American lexicon a new synonym for journalists

Phillips, however, wasn't killed for his journalism, but because of a novel. A paranoid schizophrenic Harvard-educated musician, Fitzhugh Coyle Goldsborough, believed Phillips used his sister as the model for the less-than-virtuous heroine in Graham's best-selling *The Fashionable Adventures of Joshua Craig*. Graham's murder was the lead story in the *New York Times*. He was shot six times before the killer turned the gun on himself. The weapon was described as a "32 caliber automatic revolver," which was a Colt designed by Browning, as in that era "revolver" and "pistol" were sometimes used interchangeably.

Less palatable explanations for the law, which remains on the books in modified form, include prejudice against eastern Europe and Italian immigrants. There is also an intriguing reason offered by historian and writer George J. Lankevich, who, in *New York City: A Short History*, said the Sullivan law "was enacted so that Big Tim's police cohorts might easily dispose of his opponents by planting guns on them and then hauling them off to jail."[27]

CHAPTER EIGHT

GEORG'S LUGER
AND JOHN'S SHOTGUN

The satisfaction Browning found at his workbench was almost equaled by the gratification he found on the shooting range. An expert marksman with rifle and shotgun, he was a "B" on Ogden's famed "Four B's" trapshooting team, so-named because its members were John Browning, Matt Browning, brewery owner Gustav Becker, and banker Archie Bigelow. They dominated trap contests in Utah and surrounding states, and Browning's score was invariably at or near the top—though not so much on November 24, 1898, at the Ogden Gun Club's Thanksgiving holiday trapshooting contest.

Reduced to its essence, trapshooting is a simple sport. Contestants armed with shotguns fire shells loaded with birdshot at clay "pigeons" catapulted into the air. That's how the sport is practiced now, but in the nineteenth century it offered a more difficult test of shooting skill, as the target was a live bird. Pigeons held in a small box—the trap—sprang into the air with the pull of a lanyard and might fly in any direction. Nevertheless, Browning rarely missed, irrespective of whether his target was a fast-flapping live bird or brittle clay.[1] Except on this Thanksgiving, which Browning must have found particularly dismaying, for it was the public unveiling of his latest invention, an autoloading shotgun that Browning expected to be as revolutionary as his semiautomatic pistols. Outside of the failed efforts of a few unheralded inventors, no commercially successful autoloading shotgun existed.[2]

Shotgun design had evolved slowly, beginning in the six-teenth century with single-barreled smoothbore guns, followed by the debut of double-barreled guns in the eighteenth century, and finally pump-action guns in the nineteenth century, most prominently Browning's Winchester 1897 model, which so domi-nated the market that the history of pump-action shotguns can be divided into two eras, before and after Browning. Now Brown-ing hoped for another leap. The prototype in his hands held five shells and, like his semiautomatic pistols, it fired a round with each pull of the trigger—no more pumping back and forth.

Browning sketched out the mechanism in late 1894 or early 1895, showed the concept to his brothers, and then put it aside to work on his pistols.[3] He returned to the shotgun idea in late 1897 and with Ed made a crude prototype before leaving for Liège in the spring of 1898. This first Browning autoloader used a toggle-link action, a venerable mechanism found in the old Winchester lever-action rifles and, in more sophisticated form, the Maxim machine gun and the too-large Borchardt pistol. What made Browning's mechanism unique was that he figured out how to reduce the length of the toggle mechanism, making the action a practical size for his semiautomatic shotgun.

The same concept, as it turned out, would shrink the ungainly Borchardt.

The shotgun design lay fallow while Browning was in Belgium, and Ed occupied himself working on the daily flow of repairs. "I never do work on a model when John M. is away," Ed said.[4] When Browning returned in the fall of 1898, he and Ed refined the prototype and tested it with hundreds of shotgun shells until on November 9 Browning was sufficiently pleased to take it "into the field." For assistance, Browning recruited James H. Emmett, manager at a soda pop bottling company for whom that day was also his thirty-second birthday. "Browning was shooting it and I was throwing objects for him to shoot at, and I was shooting it and he threw up for me while I shot it." Together they put seventy-five shells through the gun as they traded places back and forth. Emmett was fascinated. "One of the most forcible things about it, I know when I got through shooting it the last shot, these here things," and he pointed to the toggle links, "would stick up in front of your eyes."[5]

When Browning's shotgun fired, the toggle moved so quickly the links didn't interfere with aiming the gun, yet as Emmett observed after the last shot the toggle froze in the open position like a bent leg.

"A good thing to tell when it is empty," Emmett said. Over the next days Browning continued with his tests, including a hunting trip with his friend Becker, and then carried it to the Thanksgiving trap shoot.

Trapshooting spread across the nation in the 1880s and 1890s—encouraged by Browning's pump-action shotguns—and eclipsed long-range target shooting in popularity. Some shooters used glass balls or clay discs, but there was a seemingly unlimited number of passenger pigeons, a game bird, not too large nor too small, that was also a delicacy once plucked and cooked.

Hardwood forests were their natural habitat, so the billions—yes, with a *b*—in North America lived mostly between the Great Plains and the Atlantic. Into the early 1890s, passenger pigeon flocks stretched for hundreds of miles and took hours to pass overhead. In her book *Flight Maps*, author Jennifer Price said the birds were so numerous that "a typical wild pigeon roost blanketed hundreds of square miles of forest. The underbrush died, the trees were entirely denuded of their leaves, dung piled up inches deep, and century-old trees keeled over under the cumulative weight of the nine-ounce birds."[6]

By the turn of the century billions of the birds were vanishing. Farmland replaced oak forests, and a cyclical decrease in acorn production reduced that basic passenger pigeon food just as pressure on the bird population increased. But the major factor in their gradual extinction was an irresistible combination—the birds were both easy to catch and good eating, even appearing on the menus of big-city restaurants. Trapshooting contributed to the decline around the edges, but one didn't even need a gun to catch the birds. Huge numbers were taken by hunters who descended on roosted flocks armed with nothing deadlier than pitchforks and nets. Once caught, the birds were killed by snapping their necks.

As the conservation movement grew, live bird shoots were denounced as cruel and bloody. When the Four B's gathered for their holiday shoot the use of pigeons-as-targets was increasingly rare. That day was also an unfortunate public introduction for the new gun, as it apparently either jammed or misfired. "Browning shot it," Becker later said, "and didn't kill many pigeons."[7]

That setback was brief. Whatever was wrong was fixed, and, working with Ed, John produced two additional prototypes. A few months later, in March of 1899, Hans Tauscher, the American sales manager for both FN and DWM, visited Ogden and the three Browning brothers demonstrated the guns, and then John and Matt took Tauscher to dinner. That spring, the Brownings arrived in New Haven with John's new shotgun and a new demand. Thanks to John Moses Browning's inventions, Winchester was now the leading domestic manufacturer of civilian longarms, and the brothers wanted a fairer share of the profits. The repeating shotgun, Browning believed, would be an enormous commercial success. He and Matt told Bennett they wanted not just a flat fee but royalties on each gun sold. That was the agreement the brothers had with FN and Colt, and they insisted on the same with Winchester.

Winchester was trying to break free of its reliance on Browning designs, yet it was Browning guns that allowed the company to thrive when other arms makers went defunct, and it was Browning guns that cemented Winchester's hold on the lever-action and shotgun markets. Yet the Brownings received no more than a flat fee for any design.

It must have been a heated negotiation, with Matt playing the tough guy, but in any case Bennett acquiesced, as there was nothing to stop Browning from taking his gun and going elsewhere.

So for the first time in the company's history Bennett agreed to pay royalties.

"In April, July, October and January of each year thereafter, during the life of the patents, Winchester will pay to the Brownings a royalty of one dollar for each gun manufactured," reads page 2, paragraph 2, of the three-page contract bearing the signatures of Bennett, both Browning brothers, two witnesses, and the date, May 20, 1899.[8]

The contract had one other unique element—it acknowledged that Browning's toggle-link action was "somewhat similar" to the system Borchardt used for his pistol, and Winchester had to be shown there was no conflict. While no inventor could patent the toggle-link concept per se—it would be akin to patenting the wheel—Borchardt might contend Browning's shotgun idea infringed on some aspect of his gun.

It wasn't Borchardt that John Browning had to worry about, however, but Georg Luger, whose redesign of the Borchardt pistol between 1898 and 1900 turned the gun into the firearm equivalent of a celebrity. While it is Browning's pistol engineering that has stood the test of time, Luger's "Parabellum" remains the single most recognizable twentieth-century handgun. With its twin knobs on a toggle mechanism that opened and closed like a bending leg—same as in Browning's shotgun prototype—Lugers were the favorite souvenir of World War I American doughboys and World War II GIs. In the twenty-first century there remains a large base of collectors and fans with an appetite for every detail about the unique weapon, and outside Philadelphia a small shop, LugerMan, makes exquisite reproductions.[9]

To shrink Borchardt's long toggle-link mechanism to a more marketable size, Luger chose a mechanical concept previously applied by Browning to his shotgun. Whether Luger knew it or not, the idea he used was first sketched out by Browning in 1894, followed in 1897 by a working prototype. It would be at least another year before Luger's own design surfaced. Worse—for Luger—was that Browning had already filed a patent for his shotgun, proof that Browning used the idea first. It meant Browning could frustrate Luger's plans to sell his pistol in America.

So Luger went to court. The result was an eight-year-long patent battle with each inventor accusing the other of theft. It changed the history of Browning's shotgun designs and thereby Winchester's own corporate trajectory.

At issue were two small metal shapes on each gun, to a casual observer seemingly inconsequential. On the Luger they were the curved, raised edges on either side of Luger's frame. Far more than mere visual embellishments, they acted like a ramp to force open the shortened toggle link, making them integral to Luger's design. At least a year earlier Browning used the very same idea for his shotgun, though the steel shapes, approximately triangular, were hidden inside the frame when the toggles were closed.[10]

The two men had applied the same concept in different ways. But Browning did it first.[11]

Luger launched the patent dispute in the winter of 1900 with a letter to Browning's attorney, George Seymour, that claimed Browning deliberately misappropriated Luger's idea after it was inadvertently passed to him by a third party. Ignoring or unaware of evidence to the contrary, Luger claimed he, not Browning, was the original inventor of the new toggle-link device. He insisted that Browning employed the idea knowing Luger had already used it for his pistol. Luger threatened to prevent Browning from selling his new shotgun in Europe unless Browning conceded "priority of invention" to Luger. As Seymour explained in a letter to his client, that meant Browning had to acknowledge, in writing, that the toggle opening mechanism was Luger's invention. "His idea is that you shall concede that Luger was the prior inventor. . . . And you have to sign a paper to that effect."[12]

Luger had never met Browning and so can be forgiven for threatening the wrong man. Modest and unassuming in his personal interactions, Browning was immensely proud of his mechanical achievements, and it was inconceivable that he would not only say that he stole the design but also sign over the rights to the foreign accuser.

Luger's case seemed thin to nonexistent. Browning had made a prototype in 1897, and his toggle-link patent application was filed on May 6, 1899—before Luger had filed any drawings or patent or made any announcement. Seymour said his conversations with Luger's attorney led him to believe that the German inventor's threat was, in effect, a preemptive strike. Luger feared that Browning's toggle-link shotgun patent would prevent him from selling his toggle-link pistol in America, so Luger hoped the mere threat of European legal action against future sales of Browning's shotgun would convince Browning to give way.

Luger's calculation ignored an inconvenient fact—if his pistol was sold in America it would be in direct competition with Browning's Colt-manufactured handguns.

"The purpose of the agreement is to leave you free to sell your guns in Europe and to leave him free to sell his guns in the United States," Seymour wrote. "The desirability of this exchange is one which you must decide, although I suppose that you were very desirous of controlling the United States market yourself."

It was a terribly arcane dispute over slivers of steel, but unsurprising when it involved two men whose identities, not to mention livelihoods, were tied to their craft. Losing patent rights could mean paying royalties to a competitor or, in the worst case, abandoning the firearm entirely.[13]

Browning rejected Luger's threat, and in May 1900 the German moved ahead and filed an infringement case with the U.S. Patent Office.

"I, Georg Luger of Charlottenburg, Kingdom of Prussia, German Empire, being duly affirmed, doth depose and say," it began, and went on to claim that Hans Tauscher, the German who represented both FN and DWM, had seen Luger's new invention and subsequently described it to Browning during a steamship voyage from Europe to America in September 1898.

Luger claimed Browning took that idea and in two months built a shotgun around it and then tried to hide the theft.

Luger's accusation was made in legalese but was unmistakable. "Thus, Browning has been enabled to use my improvement for his firearm . . . (and) embody it into his application, not as a first claim, but as a subsequent one, for rendering it less conspicuous." Browning's shotgun patent application was eighteen pages long, seven pages of drawings and eleven of text, and Luger was accusing him of deliberately burying the contested element at the very end.

Luger's tough language couldn't erase the fact that Browning's patent was filed before any word of Luger's design appeared in any public document on either side of the Atlantic. On August 13, 1900, the U.S. Patent Office ruled that was "prima facie" evidence in Browning's favor. It added that ordinarily Luger's claim would be tossed—except that Luger had also alleged Browning stole the idea. The patent office ordered a hearing for Luger "to establish by proof, if he can, the allegation in his statement that Browning is not an original inventor."

A full-fledged legal battle was set to begin.

Then Luger did a complete about-face. Two weeks later, on August 28, 1900, he asked for the patent case to be "dissolved" and declared that neither his nor Browning's design was original and that both derived their ideas from previous inventions. Luger was suddenly contending that a key element turning the ungainly Borchardt into the svelte Luger—and that only weeks earlier he'd proudly insisted was *his* idea—was now not worthy of patent protection. That astonishing reversal isn't explained in the existing record. Perhaps Luger was pressured by his bosses at DWM, which still held a large stake in FN and wouldn't have wanted to wage a court battle against the man who had made FN a success.

Whatever the reason behind Luger's surprise filing, Browning and Seymour were having none of it.

In a sarcastic rejoinder the lawyer wrote that "if Luger had been fortunate enough in his preliminary statement to have overcome Browning's prima facie case, it is inconceivable that he would have made his motion to dissolve." The U.S. Patent Office disagreed, too, as it ruled that both designs were "so similar as to necessitate a decision on the question of priority of invention."

So the case proceeded, based entirely on the testimony of a single witness who was neither indifferent nor impartial. That was Tauscher, the German salesman who worked in America for FN—which made Browning's designs—as well as DWM, which made the Borchardt and Luger pistols. Tauscher had to choose sides, and he chose Luger. He and Browning laid out accounts of the 1898 sea voyage so starkly dissimilar that one or the other was telling a detailed string of lies.

Tauscher gave this version:

They coincidentally booked passage from Europe to the United States aboard the *Trave*, leaving from Southampton on September 7. During the six-day voyage, the two had daily discussions about firearm design, including conversations about the Borchardt pistol, the Luger, and Browning's plans for a semi-automatic shotgun. "He asked me my opinion as to what system would be good for an automatic rifle or shotgun," and Tauscher said he suggested the link system, as on the Borchardt. When Browning objected to its size, "I told him that Mr. Luger, one of our engineers in Berlin, had just found out . . . how to shorten the rear link," and he went on to describe Luger's system, "letting the central point of the rear link slide up to the curved surface." Tauscher claimed Browning replied, "Well, that would change the matter entirely," and said he would "go to work right away on the (shot)gun." Once the firearm was completed, he would sell the patent to Tauscher.

Tauscher said he interjected and told Browning that Luger had already patented the idea, but offered an easy workaround. Browning should sell the shotgun to DWM. "If you give it to us, to me . . . that would not matter."

When Tauscher returned to Berlin and described that conversation to Luger the German inventor erupted in fury. Contrary to Tauscher's belief, Luger's toggle-link design was not yet filed with any patent office. Tauscher had given away Luger's work, the German inventor exclaimed, and now Browning could do with it as he pleased.

"'I think Mr. Browning got the best out of you.' Those were his words," Tauscher testified, then added that Luger actually used a German colloquialism: "He took the worms out of your nose."

In his deposition, Browning said only one fact in Tauscher's testimony was true: They were both on the same ship.

Browning flatly denied Tauscher's entire account of their supposed shipboard conversations. Never discussed Luger, Borchardt, or firearms design, or his new shotgun, he said.

"Mr. Tauscher was not a technical man, and moreover did not pretend to be, and we both well knew it. I consider him a very clever salesman of firearms after they were made, but entirely unqualified to discuss the question of what would be good or what would be bad for an automatic gun," Browning said.

He didn't discuss his design work. "I never explained that I had done any work on the gun, fearing that it would lead to a discussion of details, and at that time I was not desirous of discussing details with anyone in relation to the automatic shotgun." In any case, "such a conversation with Mr. Tauscher would've been without interest to either of us as Mr. Tauscher only claims to be a salesman."

Nothing Tauscher knew about Luger's designs would interest him, Browning added. "In fact, Mr. Luger has not made many inventions, to my knowledge; the changes which he has made in the Borchardt pistol is [*sic*] all that I know of Mr. Luger ever having done in the way of inventions and firearms."

Browning did agree that in Liège in 1899 he told FN he was "thinking of bringing out an automatic shotgun" and Tauscher was present at that conversation. Browning's plan was to have FN make the gun in Europe and Winchester produce for the American market. "It is more than likely that such arrangements would have been consummated if it had not been for this interference."

As for the argument that Browning stole the idea, rushed back to Utah, and turned out a functioning firearm for the Thanksgiving turkey shoot, well, that was "ridiculous," said Ed. No one could build a finished gun from scratch that quickly.

Ed and Matt said they saw the original sketches in 1894, and Ed said he began the metalwork in 1897. He pushed hard to get it ready for testing. "We were very much interested in seeing whether that gun would operate or not, in fact we worked two or three Sundays on it to get it out so as to be able to test it before my brother John left for Belgium. . . . A week before he left we shot it several times; I shot it, and he shot it, Matthew S. Browning shot it, by the aid of the temporary parts that we put in it." For the months his older brother was overseas, Ed left the crude prototype untouched. "There was nothing done until he returned."

In total it took about five months to turn Browning's idea into a full-fledged working prototype, finally completed in the fall of 1898. "All things considered we done a remarkably quick job with the first gun," Ed said.

Then Browning's attorney, Seymour, made a claim that, if true, would be a remarkable revision to the history of the iconic Luger.

Seymour contended that Luger probably stole the idea from Browning.

"It is far more likely that Luger derived the invention from Browning through Tauscher," Seymour claimed. He argued that Tauscher saw a demonstration of the Browning toggle-link system when he visited Ogden in March 1899. The following month, April 1899, Luger filed a pistol patent in America, which showed the original Borchardt link system. If Luger had invented a new link system in 1898, as claimed, why did Luger file a patent for a gun design he'd already abandoned?

Seymour argued what really happened was that Tauscher returned to Berlin in the summer of 1899 and passed the idea to Luger. In his deposition, Tauscher admitted he and Luger had "frequent conversations" at that time.

"All this," Seymour wrote, "points very strongly to Browning's claim that Luger got the invention from the description furnished him by Tauscher after Tauscher had seen Browning's guns." There is no reply to that remarkable assertion in the patent office files.

Did Luger get the idea from Browning via Tauscher? It's possible but unlikely, though Luger aficionados have long noted that the history of the pistol's development is clouded by unknowns. Luger claimed to have invented his system in 1898, even though the filing with the U.S. Patent Office on April 29, 1899, does indeed show a Luger using the Borchardt toggle system. Experts on Luger's work say it was his practice to deliberately file incomplete patents to mislead competitors, and other evidence does point to an earlier prototype in Germany that used the new toggle system.

Perhaps the likeliest explanation is that both men came upon the same idea, Browning first, then Luger, who panicked when he learned of Browning's patent filing.

What is a fact is that over the course of the patent dispute Luger's attorney ceased contending that Luger was the original inventor. Instead, he argued Browning's decision to delay development during the years of his pistol work meant the invention fell into the category of an "abandoned" idea and so wasn't eligible for patent protection.

It didn't work. The patent office examiner, one Charles F. Chisholm, said that even if Tauscher's testimony about the transatlantic voyage and Luger's account of his own work were accepted as fact, Luger would still lose. "Luger cannot prevail," he declared on October 5, 1901, "as Browning already had a clear conception of the construction in issue and had nearly completed the gun" before he could have learned of Luger's work.

"There is no doubt that Browning had this invention prior to the time when Luger's embodiment of it, which was invented abroad, was introduced into this country." The final Luger appeal was to the U.S. District Court in Washington, which ruled against him, too.

Browning won, though his victory quickly fell into a memory hole. Despite the many books on Luger and his gun, and Browning's inventions, the patent case and its outcome have gone all but unmentioned for over one hundred years.

Then Browning and Colt went a step too far. In 1905 they sought an injunction to bar the sale of Luger's Parabellum in the United States. Three more years of litigation followed before they lost. The U.S. District Court in New York reheard the earlier evidence, considered new filings on behalf of Luger, and ruled Browning's toggle-link patent was "invalid for want of invention." In other words, the toggle-link design Browning said he invented—and by inference Luger's device, too—was too similar to earlier mechanisms by other inventors to warrant patent protection. Adding insult to injury, Browning and Colt were ordered to pay the defendants their court costs, amounting to $1,034, plus interest.[14]

By that time, however, the entire patent case was moot. The long court fight gave Browning time to invent a totally different, and far better, self-loading automatic shotgun that eventually sold in the millions.

That was all for the good, as throughout the early years of the Luger dispute Winchester tested Browning's toggle-link prototype with unhappy results. On July 23, 1900, Bennett returned it to Browning with a litany of complaints, including this alarming observation: "I find that other people here have become afraid of the gun and nothing that they do with it seems to fix it up."

Particularly worrisome was that the gun fired without a finger on the trigger. During reloading, as the toggle slid the block forward to chamber a new shell, the sear failed or the hammer slipped, "causing the gun to fire before the trigger is pulled. The signer has had this happen to the gun, the gun running three shots in succession on three different occasions. This will be very alarming to the outsider, and somewhat shakes up the signer. This seems to us to be the most serious fault with the gun."[15]

He also complained that some shells failed to eject, the hammer sometimes failed to ignite a shell, and "another fault, which seems to be a very considerable one with the gun, is that it must be lubricated [but] if lubrication is put upon it, this flies in the face with a spitefulness which is alarming to a party who does not know what is happening." He closed with an expression of faith: "Please do the best you can with the gun. We have no doubt you can put it in good order at short notice and let it come back to us."[16]

Browning replied on August 14 with a letter on the company's new and even more elaborately embossed letterhead bearing the name "Browning Brothers Co. Arms, sporting goods, etc.," and illustrations of a woman fishing, a man hunting, a camera, assorted sporting goods—tennis racquet, boxing glove, baseball, golf club, fencing foil, bicycles—and in a prominent spot the FN Browning pistol. In small type it listed John as president; Matt as vice president; brother George E. Browning, who ran the company store in Salt Lake City, as secretary and treasurer; followed by two names without titles, brothers T. S. Browning and J. E. Browning, better known as Ed.

"We are sorry to hear that you are afraid of the gun," Browning wrote. "I consider it one of the safest guns I have made. We are firing upwards of 3000 times without hurting anybody or anything." He explained he'd just reworked the hammer mechanism and said: "I think it is safer than the '97 repeater. . . . Let us know how it behaves this time and by all means don't get afraid of it. If your workmen get afraid of it and down on it, it stands a poor show."[17]

Fortunately for Winchester's engineers, already in hand was another Browning autoloading shotgun design using a totally different mechanism. As with his pistol development, the flexibility of Browning's inventive mind again showed itself. At the same time he was completing work on the toggle-link gun he was conceiving a shotgun that eliminated the toggle link entirely. The first prototype of that gun was produced in late 1899 and underwent two revisions in the following two years, each with a patent prepared by Winchester.

This time Browning didn't adapt a previously existing mechanism. The new gun used a unique "long-recoil" system wherein

John Moses Browning circa 1890, as he neared the height of his creative powers. *Weber State University, Stewart Library, Special Collections*

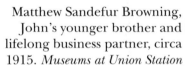

Matthew Sandefur Browning, John's younger brother and lifelong business partner, circa 1915. *Museums at Union Station*

Rachel Browning, John's wife, who raised their eight children while John worked with Winchester, Colt, and Fabrique Nationale in Belgium. Her first trip to Belgium, in 1926, was John's last. *Weber State University, Stewart Library, Special Collections*

Jonathan Browning, an early convert to the Church of Jesus Christ of Latter-day Saints, was a gunsmith, businessman, and father of the famous inventor. *Museums at Union Station*

The first Browning storefront, circa 1879. John and Matt stand in the doorway, flanked by their brothers. Frank Rushton is on the far right. All are holding the first Browning rifle, the famous single shot. It is still in production. *Utah State Archives*

The Dalton gang after a failed attempt to rob two banks at once. The rifle is Browning's Winchester 1886, believed to have been the one used by Grat (or Grot) Dalton, second from right. *kansasmemory.org, Kansas State Historical Society*

The posse of western lawmen and detectives hired to hunt down Butch Cassidy and his Wild Bunch gang. They are holding Browning's last Winchester lever-action rifle, the Model 1895, also a favorite of Teddy Roosevelt's. *Union Pacific Railroad Museum*

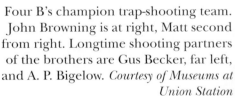

Four B's champion trap-shooting team. John Browning is at right, Matt second from right. Longtime shooting partners of the brothers are Gus Becker, far left, and A. P. Bigelow. *Courtesy of Museums at Union Station*

Browning's first pistol was widely admired for its technological prowess and purchasers considered it a mechanical work of art. Manufacturer Fabrique Nationale offered a variety of inlay options for the "Pistolet Browning," this one in gold. *Fondation Ars Mechanica*

Georg Luger is famous for his Luger pistol. Little known is that the U.S. Patent Office declared Browning the first inventor of a key mechanical element in the German gun. Browning and Luger traded accusations of theft. *G.L. Sturgess Collection*

Militarist / Alamy Stock Photo

Fabrique National employees, which always included a large proportion of women, manufacture parts for Browning's immensely successful Automatic-5 shotgun, circa 1910. *Fondation Ars Mechanica*

Belgian manufacturer Fabrique National's banquet in January 1914 to celebrate the sale of one million Browning semiautomatic pistols. Most were his first .32-caliber, seven-shot FN 1900, or his 1905 vest pocket–sized .25 caliber. *Fondation Ars Mechanica*

Browning's newest handgun, the sleek Model 1910, was chosen by the "Black Hand" terrorists to assassinate Archduke Franz Ferdinand and his wife, Sophie. The assassination precipitated World War I. *Everett Collection Historical / Alamy Stock Photo*

The first public appearance of the Browning Automatic Rifle was in February 1918, at a demonstration for Congress, the media, and foreign military attachés. *Library of Congress, Prints & Photographs Division, photograph by Harris & Ewing*

Browning's BAR was a star attraction. A soldier holds a BAR outside the New York Public Library at an event hosted by the Mayor's Committee of Women on National Defense. *Library of Congress, Prints & Photographs Division*

Browning began developing the .50-caliber machine gun when he was 63 years old. This is an early water-cooled version. His air-cooled model armed every American aircraft in World War II, and remains in use today worldwide. *Museums at Union Station*

U.S. Marines on Okinawa in combat with a BAR and a Browning .30-caliber machine gun. They were indispensable firearms used by every American infantry unit in Europe and the Pacific. *Courtesy U.S. Marine Corps*

Browning's .50-caliber machine gun armed every American bomber and fighter aircraft in World War II. Twin guns were mounted inside ball turrets underneath B-17 and B-24 bombers.

The Browning .50-caliber machine gun is still used by American fighting forces, and dozens of nations in South America, Europe, and Africa. Pictured here in 2004, an Italian paratrooper prepares a Browning .50 caliber (with night vision scope) for a nighttime patrol in Iraq. *Dino Fracchia / Alamy Stock Photo*

the entire barrel moved backward about three inches to eject the nearly three-inch-long shell. The lengthy barrel travel provided time for the gas pressure to drop before the fragile cardboard shell was ejected. Visually, its most obvious feature was a tubelike extension to accommodate the recoiling barrel, which ended with an abrupt cutoff, a feature soon nicknamed the hump.

The shotgun action required intricate, complicated machining, and, as firearms writer John Henwood has concluded, the design was ultimately "an evolutionary dead-end."[18] Only a handful of commercial firearms were ever made using the long-recoil system and four of the five most successful were designed by Browning or adapted from his guns. In Browning's hands, however, the recoiling barrel shotgun was a great success.

Browning knew he'd accomplished what no other inventor achieved—a marketable, affordable, reliable, autoloading shotgun. His recoil action solved the problem posed by a shotgun's non-metallic shells. The action worked smoothly and softly to load, fire, and eject the shells, which couldn't withstand the hard usage of brass cartridges in pistols, rifles, and machine guns. The shotgun recoil system was also adjustable and allowed the shooter to use high- or low-powered shotgun shells in either smokeless powder or old-fashioned black powder. Browning considered it his best work. By late 1901, Winchester was finished with the laborious, expensive task of preparing a patent application. But to Browning's increasing ire, Bennett left the design hanging—he never rejected it but also never ordered it into production. And he had yet to pay for it. What later became known as the A5 shotgun sat ignored on Winchester's shelf.

The reasons why can be surmised. Winchester had incurred a large expense redesigning the Model 1893 shotgun into the Model 1897 shotgun, with little or no help from Browning; now that the pump-action shotgun was selling extraordinarily well, Bennett saw no reason to spend even more money to compete against Winchester's own product with a new gun. There was a bad taste left over from the wasted time on the toggle-link design, and he couldn't be certain the new gun would succeed in the marketplace. Not only had there never been a successful repeating shotgun, but also Browning's long-recoil concept hadn't been used in any commercially successful firearm. Bennett may have feared it was too risky a project for Winchester's finances and reputation.

While Bennett mulled over what to do, Browning was busy with other work, including a new machine gun to replace the "potato digger." That gas-powered firearm saw very limited use in the Spanish-American War, and in 1900 it was used by Marines defending the U.S. legation in Peking during the Boxer Rebellion. Colt did have some success selling the gun to Czarist Russia and various South American governments, but overall the "potato-digger" gas design was barely a modest success.

It had also embroiled Colt, and indirectly Browning, in a nasty public dispute with Maxim. He published a brochure contending that Colt, and therefore Browning, stole the idea of a gas-operated gun from an early Maxim patent filing.[19] In 1893 Maxim had indeed filed a patent claiming ownership of ten different potential machine-gun designs. But while Maxim could patent a specific device, he couldn't claim the entire machine-gun concept. And he didn't build a gas gun until after Browning's invention was in production. Maxim, who never lacked for ego, must have realized his claim was on thin ice because he never filed a patent infringement case against Colt or Browning.

Browning's return to machine-gun design culminated in 1900 with a recoil system that was simpler and more reliable than Maxim's. It was patented in 1901 but received little attention. In the first years of the twentieth century the U.S. Army had no money to spend on new weapons. The brothers, meanwhile, were earning handsome profits from royalties on their civilian arms. After the filing Browning put the machine-gun design aside to work on handguns for FN and Colt.

The delay over the future of the automatic shotgun gave time for relations between Bennett and the Brownings to completely sour. Bennett's hesitation to produce the shotgun didn't sit well in Ogden, and then a new dispute arose. A letter from Bennett dated January 13, 1902, shows that Bennett and Browning both claimed credit for a new breech mechanism—though for what type of gun is unclear.[20]

"If we allow you to take out your patent, you will prevent us using the breech block in question for which we have plans in another matter," Bennett wrote. "We suggest that our patent go on."

Bennett rejected a suggestion that Winchester got the idea from a Browning gun. "There is no unfairness in the matter. We are both working on guns. You showed us yours because you want to sell it, which happened to have in it the device which is ours." Notably, Bennett denied any underhandedness. "We have never seen the inside of your gun except in your presence." He offered to license "the device" to Browning, provided Browning would do the same in the event the patent office ruled in his favor:

> It seems to me that the Winchester company is entitled to the use of this breech block and I should like to have things arranged so that you will not get in the way by using it in subsequent combinations. Would not this be fair?

A week later, on January 20, 1902, Browning forwarded Bennett's letter to Matt with a lengthy handwritten commentary. It hinted that the breechblock at issue was part of a larger disagreement. Illegible words are noted as "xxx" and punctuation is from the original:

> Thought would send you this letter of Bennetts [*sic*] You see he does not mention the main thing I wrote him about and that was that he promised to get or make claims that would not dominate us and we were to not try to dominate him. Seymour told him that would be xxx easy and in this letter you see he would like to make it a swap. We xxx have their patent killed as I write you am just sending this so you can just size the people up if anybody ever made a fair and square agreement thoroughly understood

153

by both parties we did and by the way this letter is a pretty fair lesson in diplomacy? John.

Browning may have retained that letter because it likely was the last letter he ever received from Bennett. Browning's inventions made Winchester the nation's dominant maker of rifles and shotguns—even if most of the millions of customers had no idea their guns were designed not in Connecticut but by a fellow in Utah. Bennett had relied on Browning for almost every new design since 1885, and he must have worried that his company was overreliant on one man. Indeed, he had recently hired another talented engineer, T. C. Johnson, to develop firearms in-house. And Bennett certainly knew Browning was by no means reliant on Winchester. Colt and FN were producing his new handguns and paying handsome royalties.

If Bennett didn't want the new shotgun, Browning knew that FN did.

So the highly successful nineteen-year business relationship moved toward a bitter ending. Like other stories involving Browning, however, previous accounts of the breakup are incomplete or incorrect.

The usual version says that Browning met with Bennett in early January 1902 to demand he start production of the new autoloading gun and pay royalties on each shotgun sold. Bennett refused, declared that Winchester never paid royalties and wasn't going to start with Browning's gun. So Browning walked out. That day, or the next, he arrived for an appointment with Remington Arms Company's chief Marcellus Hartley to offer that company his gun, but Hartley died of a heart attack while Browning was waiting in an outside office. Undeterred by that tragedy, Browning bought a steamship ticket, traveled to Europe for the first time in his life, and showed up in Liège with his shotgun under his arm. A surprised FN put it into production.

That's the oft-repeated story told in Jack Browning's published book. A major source is Edwin Pugsley, a former Winchester chief executive who knew Bennett and met John in 1917. It's also the account repeated in the magisterial 1952 history of Winchester by Northwestern University's Harold Francis Williamson:

> It seems clear that the break came over a request by Browning that Winchester enter into a royalty agreement with him covering the new gun. This point has been confirmed by Edwin Pugsley on the basis of subsequent conversations with both John M. Browning and T.G. Bennett.

Williamson wrote that Winchester "had always followed the policy of acquiring exclusive rights to patents and it never entered into a royalty agreement with a patent holder."

That may have been what Pugsley and Williamson were told, but it wasn't what happened. As explained previously, Bennett in 1899 agreed to pay royalties for the ill-fated toggle-link shotgun. And Browning, who had made at least four previous trips to Liège, had already advised FN that he was working on an autoloading shotgun that they would build.[21]

What actually happened, according to the unpublished, unabridged version of Jack Browning's manuscript, was that John Browning, angry at the delay, deliberately forced a break with Winchester.

"Those fellows down there are stalling and we are letting the best thing I ever made die in its sleep. I've had a scheme for having FN make it," Browning said, according to Jack's manuscript, who likely based this account on Matt's written notes or his own conversations with his father. In January 1902 John and Matt traveled east to New Haven for a meeting that lasted five minutes. "I named a down-payment and royalty so high there wasn't a chance he'd accept, but if he had it would've left me feeling satisfied," Browning said.

"When I told him my terms, his reply certainly was not diplomatic. We were both hot, for that matter." Once Bennett made his refusal clear, Browning merely said, "I suppose the guns were in the drafting room." Bennett nodded and the two brothers walked out, took their prototypes, and left.

The outcome was perhaps inevitable when a hardheaded, financially conservative Yankee gunmaker butted up against a proud inventor who knew that no matter what Winchester paid him in the past, the company had earned back that and far more. Jack's account continues with this additional anecdote, told in Browning's voice:

> As the door closed and we started along the corridor to get the guns, Matt said in a hoarse whisper, "Hell I didn't get to say a word." I laughed and asked him if he wanted to go back and make a few remarks. At that he burst into his loud ha-ha which Bennett must've heard back in the office. He probably thought of us as those uncouth mountain men and wondered how we could break with the great Winchester company, and go away laughing.

News of the split alarmed Winchester's many dealers, accustomed as they were to having new Browning designs arrive with regularity. Bennett had to explain himself. In August 21, 1903, a letter was distributed to the company sales force that was a remarkable display of anger, resentment, and defensiveness, even ingratitude, from a company executive smarting from accusations that he'd made a very bad decision by letting Browning escape to FN, after already neglecting the pistol market:

> For a number of years it seemed best to us to employ the Messrs. Browning brothers. We bought everything which they invented which had merit, whether we used it or not. It seemed to us at the end that they had become rather high-priced, and we let them go to Colt's. They had got to feel that they were the only people who could invent guns, that our suggestions as to what

was needed by the public were of no value, and that they were really the "whole thing."

Clearly, the bad blood between Bennett and the Brownings was about more than royalties.

"Mr. John Browning was a very nice man, and we were sorry to part because he was in many respects a genius," Bennett wrote. "His younger brother, Mr. Matthew Browning, was a more difficult proposition."

Then Bennett took a whack at the genius.

"None of the things invented by them were made by us exactly as presented. They were all worked over by the people in our employ to get them into such shape that they can be manufactured successfully." The example Bennett offered went all the way back to Browning's first lever-action gun. "The model 1886 gun is more largely the invention of Mr. Mason than it is of the Browning brothers. The Browning brothers having supplied us with the locking features only," Bennett wrote, exaggerating Mason's contribution and ignoring the fact that the "locking" design was the heart of the rifle.

"We shall be perfectly able to get along without the Brownings and shall probably be better off without them than with them," Bennett concluded. "On the other hand we do not believe they will get along as well without us as they did with us."

Neither of Bennett's predictions proved true.

FN began production of the "Automatic 5" shotgun in 1903. In 1905 the design was licensed to Remington for manufacture in America, where it sold for $35 or $40, though prices ranged higher depending on options; many shotguns boasted ornately engraved steel receivers. Over the years the A5 would be made in four different gauges, or barrel dimensions. FN's factories churned out over 1.5 million of the guns, while Remington produced more than a million and another two hundred thousand were made by Stevens Arms and an unknown number by the Savage Arms Corporation. Other versions were made by European firms and knock-offs appeared once the patents expired. It is, in fact, impossible to accurately estimate sales for shotguns using Browning's action, other than to say it was one of the most popular shotguns in history.

The success must have been a bitter reality for Bennett, particularly as Winchester found it impossible to break Browning's patent—written by Winchester's own attorneys—and its engineers were unable to produce a successful alternative for fifty years.

Then, in 1908, Remington introduced the world's first autoloading hunting rifle, another Browning long-recoil design. Winchester leapt to meet the competition, but none of its attempts were particularly successful, while Browning's rifle remained in production until the 1950s.

One version or another of the A5 remained in production until at least 1998.

Browning didn't set foot in the Winchester factory again until his talents were called upon when America went to war in 1917.

In the meantime, Browning designed the most famous handgun in American history.

CHAPTER NINE

A MECHANISM FOR THE AGES

Lake Lanao sits on the northern edge of the island of Mindanao in the Philippines, its 137 square miles a bright splash of blue amid green-covered hills. On September 12, 1903, Maj. Robert Lee Bullard, Alabama native and West Point graduate, watched the shoreline creep by as his troops rowed their barge to a meeting with the Sultan of Toros, leader of a small inland town. Under a new American strategy called pacification Bullard and his troops intended to talk, not fight.

Bullard could not be certain of their reception. America occupied the Philippines after the Spanish-American War in 1898, only to discover the Filipinos were uninterested in replacing one Western overlord with another. Two years of warfare followed before a settlement was reached with Catholics in the north, while on the southern islands, starting at Mindanao and stretching westward toward Indonesia, the Americans became ensnared in a guerrilla war with Moro tribesmen. The warrior society had a zest for battle amplified by Islamic religious zeal and personified by suicide swordsmen called *juramentados*, who carried the kris, a two-foot-long sword sharpened on both sides and forged with S curves near the hilt. The juramentados, an American general told Congress, had "taken an oath to die killing Christians."[1]

The Americans didn't want to convert the Moros to Christianity, as did their Spanish predecessors, but did insist the Moros cease enslaving their neighbors and submit to the central government in Manila. The two sides talked, fought, and talked.

After four years of inconclusive combat, American commanders hit on a plan to combine aggressive military patrols with civic improvements. Bullard's battalion had recently constructed a road linking villages along Lake Lanao to a seaport on the island's north shore. Nevertheless, the strategy proved problematic, as Bullard was to discover.

The barge was rowed ashore and an apparently peaceable Moro stepped aboard as Bullard sat in the stern.[2] "I suddenly heard a death groan and a fearful struggle," he later wrote, and looked up to find that the Moro was a juramentado who had already "half severed the head from the body of my soldier steersman."[3] The warrior worked his way along the deck, striking down a second soldier and heading toward Bullard, who grabbed his .38-caliber Colt revolver and fired four rounds at near point-blank range. All four shots struck home, "but to my consternation they seemed wholly, wholly without effect." The warrior kept coming and Bullard, trapped by the confines of the boat, prepared to meet him. Americans had discovered they invariably lost one-on-one fights with Moros, who were trained from childhood in hand-to-hand combat. But this Moro was on a boat with oars and benches and had to clear an obstruction before raising his sword arm. "In that hundred part of an instant . . . I thrust my muzzle against his close cropped head and fired," Bullard said.

With that shot the Moro died. He had killed one of Bullard's men and gravely wounded another and had kept coming after taking four revolver rounds. Bullard had survived by pure luck—the Moro was tripped up by the unfamiliar terrain of a boat deck. That wouldn't happen in the jungle, as Bullard wrote in an essay calling upon the Army to replace the .38-caliber revolver—which he derided as a "toy gun"—with a weapon purpose-built for stopping a charging enemy. He wanted a handgun with "stopping power," and that meant a .45-caliber gun, "and nothing else." As Bullard noted, the handgun is a short-range weapon for "close quarters [when] you must kill your enemy, and kill him quick, or he will do as much for you."

"Give us, I say, a gun that will kill, not a pepper-box which, when we use it, only so irritates an enemy that he comes and chops us up with a knife," Bullard wrote.

Bullard was not the first trooper to dismiss the .38 Colt as inadequate, even as the Army prioritized switching to a semiautomatic pistol rather than upgrading its standard handgun ammunition. Borchardt's original pistol was examined and rejected, and in 1898 tests compared an early version of Browning's semiautomatic design to four autoloading guns from Germany. All were chambered in .38-caliber or equivalent rounds, and none were found to be as reliable as a revolver. By 1900 an improved version of Browning's pistol persuaded the Army to purchase five hundred for testing by troops in the Philippines, Cuba, and Puerto Rico. The Army was also considering Luger's pistols (which helps explain the vigor of Luger and Browning's patent dispute). Troops considered the Luger a refined example of German engineering but found the toggle links prone to jamming in the dirt and dust of field conditions. There were complaints about the Browning, too, and even as that first version was being distributed Colt and Browning produced a revised gun called the Model 1902. It proved that the semiautomatic pistol was indeed the future when it fired six thousand rounds in a row with no failure, a record matched by no other autoloading handgun.[4]

But that was a test on a shooting range. Army officers who used the Colt-made Brownings in training and combat churned out written reports that chronicled a long list of complaints. One officer called the Browning unreliable and "completely unsuitable," while another said it showed "potential"—provided various defects were resolved: The grip was short, leaving the little finger waving in the air; the six-inch-long barrel made the gun muzzle heavy; the slide was too sensitive to dirt and grime and tended to jam after a dozen shots. Most important, virtually every soldier complained that it took too long to fire the first round.

"When a pistol is needed it is needed in a hurry, and delay in firing the first shot is fatal," wrote Lt. James Hanson from the Philippines. "Therefore, if the pistol is to be of any practical value I have to have it made so it can be fired on the first shot as quickly as the Colt's double-action revolver, by pointing and pulling the trigger."[5] Pressing a revolver trigger turns the cylinder while cocking and then dropping the hammer. In a pistol, loading and firing the first round takes two hands. One to hold the grip and the other to cycle the slide back and forth to put a bullet in the chamber. Only then can a pistol be fired.[6]

Critics did like the pistol's accuracy. "This is a point greatly in its favor," Hanson wrote, and closed his report on a positive note: "If the suggestions for its improvement be adopted, I think it is an improvement in the present revolver." Then the stopping-power question intervened, and work on the gun was halted. The Army was finally dropping the .38-caliber round, so there was no reason to perfect a .38-caliber pistol if the Army was going to adopt a larger, more powerful cartridge. Exactly what size ammunition was debated. To settle that question the Ordnance Department began a series of macabre experiments on human cadavers, live cows, and dead horses.

Browning was in the meantime preoccupied with other work. With each trip to Liège his overseas sojourns lengthened. The inventor found himself embraced by managers and workers alike, not only as *le maître*, the master gunsmith, but as the savior of the company itself. At Winchester and Colt, Browning had navigated long-established hierarchies and company cultures; no matter his technological contributions—or sometimes perhaps because of them—he would have encountered jealousies, backbiting, and second-guessing, all elements of human nature. At FN there were disagreements over money—the Belgians discovered the Brownings kept close watch on their royalties—but on matters of gunsmithing and inventions John Browning was given wide latitude. What he proposed, FN was likely to build. So as the company geared up for production of the A5 shotgun, while also preparing to manufacture a second Browning handgun, the Liège factory became the inventor's priority. When work on the Colt gun was halted while the Army tested new ammunition,

Browning's reaction was likely indifference. He was immersed in Belgium.

The first decade of the twentieth century was a delightful moment to live in French-speaking Belgium, flush with wealth from mining and manufacturing. The years before World War I were Europe's Belle Epoque, the "beautiful age," when the standard of living increased, the middle class expanded, and there were daring innovations in art and architecture. Liège was part of the Belgian state of Wallonia, a region immersed in French culture. Daily life in the city on the banks of the Meuse River was in sharp contrast to still-small Ogden, three days from Chicago and two from the West Coast. Ogden hadn't existed until 1844, while Wallonia's recorded history began with Caesar's conquest of Gaul in 57 BC and Liège is mentioned in records dating to the sixth century AD.

In Liège Browning found the food, architecture, culture, the very manner of daily life, that would later entrance decades of American tourists. A visitor like Browning, whose arrival by rail required a stop in Paris, found that Liège was infused with Gallic charm and resembled the French capital in miniature. Laid out along the Meuse, Liège's streets were lined with five- and six-story-tall houses with small shops on the first floors, the homes ending in peaked roofs and a skyline of chimneys. The heart of the city still contained blocks of medieval-era half-timbered buildings. The massive redbrick and gray stone Hôtel de Ville, the city hall built in 1714, overlooked a plaza with a stone fountain that was surrounded by café tables served by bustling waiters. Along the river was the grand seventeenth-century mansion of Jean Curtius, a merchant who made his fortune supplying arms and gunpowder to the Spanish, which was being converted to a public museum. Within a day's travel were the famous hot springs and spa of Chaudfontaine, and a short train ride north was the ancient university town of Maastricht in the Netherlands. East was the industrial center of Aachen in Germany. To the south were the hunting preserves of the dense Ardennes Forest.

Browning cemented his relationship with the Belgians by

teaching himself French, at first to forgo the awkwardness of using a translator to communicate with workers on the shop floor. Browning didn't hire a tutor or take a French-as-a-second-language course. "He does it by reading," explained granddaughter Judith Browning Jones, whose father, Val, would become the Browning representative in Liège. "My father told me how he did it. He had a French dictionary. Not a French-English dictionary, a French dictionary. And he would read a [French-language] book. . . . He comes to a word he doesn't understand. And he looks it up in the French dictionary. He obviously doesn't understand the definition, either. So he looks up each and every one of those words."

Browning looks up French word after French word "until he comes to one he understands."

Then he would start on the next unknown word. And the next. Then he repeated that process, slowly compiling a vocabulary that began with gun parts and eventually was sufficient to read books and newspapers.

"He spoke a very bookish French, my father said, and he was medium-ly fluent." He read French literature, including Honoré de Balzac, best known for *The Human Comedy*, a novel set in post-Napoleonic France, and Jean-Jacques Rousseau, the eighteenth-century writer and philosopher, whose *The Social Contract* was famously an inspiration to the French Revolution of 1789. Its first lines proclaim: "Man is born free, and everywhere he is in chains. Those who think themselves the masters of others are indeed greater slaves than they."

Records indicate that between 1897 and 1902 Browning spent some two years in Liège, including six months in 1898, four months in 1900, and six months in 1902. There was certainly another trip in 1899, as FN and Browning made final revisions to his first pistol. His eldest son, Jack, then twenty years old, and brother Matt accompanied him in 1900 for a tour that included a stop at an International Exhibit in Paris, where FN's pistol was awarded a "Grand Prix."[7] That trip coincided with Matt's term as mayor of Ogden. Upon his return to Utah, he fulfilled his political responsibilities by telling the local paper that while the trip was very enjoyable, "I didn't strike anything in my travels that suited me quite as well as Ogden."[8]

During that time the brothers completed construction of new homes, each similar in exterior design and material, except that Matt's home had the front porch on the left and John's had the porch on the right. The first floors were built of red sandstone, the second two stories of brick and stone trim. Despite Browning's well-known reticence toward any publicity, the Ogden newspaper in 1901 printed a photo of the exterior and included a detailed description of the sixty-seven-hundred-square-foot interior. Either the writer was allowed in or visitors provided this account:

> The arrangements of the interior are very fine . . . on the right of the hall are the large double parlors separated by a handsome arch finished in solid oak. On the left of the hall is the fine library filled with valuable books, and the dining room, the two being connected by solid oak folding doors . . . the works of art and ornate furnishings render it one of the most beautiful homes in the state.

There were five bedrooms on the second floor and three rooms on the third floor, with a laundry and children's play room in the basement. When the children became teenagers it became a sort-of ballroom where Rachel hosted dances for the Browning teenagers and their friends.

Now on the National Register of Historic Places, the home had an exterior porch that is long gone, but the interior of the house is largely intact and still boasts the striking polished oak staircase—stretching up to the third floor, a very masculine design with square, closely spaced balusters and thick handrails and stringers. Massive sliding oak doors, built of solid wood more than an inch thick, separate the main first-floor rooms, and large windows provide a bright interior.

● ● ●

When FN began production of the A5 shotgun in 1903, Browning arrived for an eight-month stay, as there was much to be done to manufacture a type of gun never before built anywhere in the world. Upon his return to the United States in January 1904—after the Christmas and New Year's holidays—he was met in New York City by his wife, Rachel, and one of their daughters. Together they journeyed back to Ogden, where he didn't stay long before heading east once again.

What Rachel thought of her husband's long absences is unfortunately unknown, though much later an elderly aunt told Browning granddaughter Judith Jones that the inventor's treatment of his wife was "not fair," though never explaining exactly why. The reason may have been found in Belgium, as will be explained.

Throughout their marriage, Rachel served as the family caregiver, a responsibility for which Browning had little inclination, but he intervened as he thought necessary. He refused to allow their children to be vaccinated against smallpox, which resulted in Val contracting the disease as a teenager. The Browning home was declared under quarantine,[9] though not before John made plans to depart his household for Europe. As Val later told the story, John was planning to leave without saying good-bye until an angry Rachel forced him to stand within view of Val's bedroom and wave from the street.

Few relatives found fault with Rachel. For starters, she was a "fabulous cook . . . everyone said she was," said Jones. She was of even temperament. "Everyone describes her as being a saint," Jones observed, adding it was a greater praise than ordinary. "They say she was a good person," Browning's granddaughter observes. "She was a saint, I don't know why, but she was. That's how they describe her.

"She was a caregiver, and my theory is that he became so worked up in the inventing that he kind of, and this is very, very natural, he also kind of got worked up about himself." His singlemindedness increased as the years passed. "I think he had to keep producing to prove himself to himself," Jones said.

• • •

By 1906 Browning's first pistol was famous throughout Europe, with more than 250,000 sold to military, police, and civilians alike. For the Browning brothers, sales earned them 500,000 gold Belgian francs, a sum difficult to convert into modern dollars, but well into the millions.

For many customers his pistol represented more than a weapon—it was a mechanical work of art, and they demanded it be decorated at such. Ordinarily, firearms were shipped from the factory in gunmetal rust-blue—literally a protective rust coating polished to a gleaming brightness—but, for an additional cost, pistols could be engraved with one of six intricate floral and scroll designs. FN established a famed engraving department staffed with graduates of an arduous training regimen, as mistakes made carving steel couldn't be erased and redone.

John found a favorite residence in Liège, the Hotel D'Angleterre, which, along with an emphasis on serving English-speaking guests, was ideally located adjacent to the city's Royal Opera House. The person associated with the hotel in guidebooks was one Pierre Quaden, who may have taken refuge in Liège during the Franco-Prussian War of 1870 and who ran a well-known restaurant, La Becasse, on the ground floor. Tourist guidebooks list the hotel as among the city's preferred accommodations, and in 1904 it underwent a renovation to install an elevator and extend electrical service to each room. A few-minute stroll away was a shopping district with cafés and department stores. A favorite restaurant of Browning's was a ten-minute walk toward the Meuse. It occupied a sixteenth-century building of wood, brick, and slate that still stands on the riverbank. Browning's prominence and patronage inspired the restaurant to reserve him a special dining room, a perk no doubt encouraged by FN's financial success, by now washing across the region.[10]

The Belgians celebrated Browning even as they found this tall American from the "Wild West" to be unique, if not indeed odd. A photograph of Browning flanked by twenty FN executives shows him nearly a head taller than most anyone else. And it was a head "whose smallness contrasted with the length of his neck, and was extraordinarily smooth," wrote FN manager Henri Chevalier. Browning had a penetrating gaze, but Chevalier found his ordinary countenance affectless and his expression typically a poker face, prompting a comparison to the static image on a coin. Then there was his clothing. "He liked to wrap himself in a cape and wear a wide-brimmed hat, which only added to his strangeness." In America his headgear was called the Panama hat, a common enough accoutrement in the United States that nevertheless stood out in Liège.[11]

Despite his visual peculiarity, Browning's character was praised. He was declared to be kind and quiet, with modesty verging on shyness. He was never boastful and listened courteously to comments and advice from customers and FN engineers, even when he knew them to be wrongheaded. Browning believed that human flaws were to be tolerated, wrote Chevalier, who was struck by Browning's willingness to suffer difficult personalities. "This was one of the secrets of his success," Chevalier wrote. "In fact, it was a character trait of his. One day, I was speaking to him about one of his collaborators, whose lack of subtlety was well-known, and he responded to me: 'I have known X for a number of years and I know that he has this defect, but apart from that, he has some rare qualities. I use these and close my eyes to the rest.'"

Chevalier gushed: "With such principles, coupled with great modesty and perfect simplicity, Browning could only have friends—and this despite the jealousy that could have been aroused due to his amazing success."

"For everyone he had a pleasant word," but he was not much of a conversationalist in either French or English, even with close acquaintances. "This great man was also a shy one," Chevalier said, which explains the relative dearth of Browning stories from Belgium. "Those who knew him best can hardly recall any anecdotes that would shine a light on his character, or any 'words' that one could quote regarding him," Chevalier wrote.

Browning could take a joke at his own expense, however, as

when a handgun he was demonstrating to visiting army officers failed to operate. Taking the gun apart, Browning discovered that he had earlier removed and then forgotten to reinstall the firing pin. "That incident became legendary among the ordnance officers," with Browning smiling along with every humorous recounting of the incident.

While Browning worked in Liège, in America the Army Ordnance office continued its search for a handgun round that—theoretically—could stop an attacker with a single shot. There were many elements to consider. What caliber? What weight? A round nose, a flat nose, or some other shape? Was a small, fast bullet better than a slow, big bullet, or vice versa? Lacking computer algorithms or plastic gel facsimiles of human flesh the Army, perhaps not unreasonably, decided to measure the "shock effect" by using real flesh and bone.

Two officers were tasked with that unpleasant but not unimportant duty. In charge was Maj. Lewis A. La Garde, an army surgeon since 1874 who was descended from a French colonial family in Louisiana. Working with him was Capt. John T. Thompson, with a reputation for efficiency gained during the Spanish-American War, and who later invented the Thompson submachine gun. For testing they selected nine pistol bullets, ranging in size from a .30-caliber round suitable for a small pistol to an experimental, and massive, .476-caliber cartridge. They obtained two Lugers, two Colt pistols, and four Colt revolvers and set out for the Philadelphia Polyclinic at Eighteenth and Lombard streets in that city, which billed itself as "the finest hospital in the world devoted strictly to post-graduate teaching." From there they moved to the New York University Medical Department at the corner of Twenty-Sixth Street and First Avenue. Between the two hospitals they experimented on eleven cadavers, followed in Chicago by thirteen head of cattle.[12]

Each cadaver was suspended by the head so it was free to swing with the impact of rounds fired into a specific body part—hand, leg, arm, or torso. Thompson and La Garde decided to give each

round a numerical score of 1 to 100 determined by simple observation. The greater the motion of a body part after it was struck
by a bullet, the higher the score. No instruments were used.

Leaving aside any ethical concerns, the test was on its face
unscientific. The results varied according to the test subject; a
muscular 250-pound corpse would have larger bones and therefore greater mass and a very different reaction than the limbs
of a 135-pound woman, though neither sex nor body size was
identified in the report. Also, the transfer of energy from the
bullet to the body depended on the body part hit. As the report noted, a bullet striking a leg bone "was noticed to throw the
limb back in the direction of the flight of the bullet" and then
"was apt to sway back and forth several times." The same-caliber
bullet fired through soft tissue offered little resistance and provided no movement to measure. A bullet in the soft tissue of the
heart, a wound invariably fatal to a real life, produced little or no
"shock effect" in a cadaver compared to a bullet striking a femur,
a serious but not necessarily fatal wound. There was no attempt,
of course, to measure the "shock effect" of a bullet on a living
human being.

After compiling comparisons from each of the cadavers,
Thompson and La Garde scored the .38-caliber bullet fired
through the regulation service revolver at between 50 and 65. A
.45-caliber round fired from a Colt revolver scored 80 or higher.

The shots fired into live cattle showed the larger the caliber
the greater the damage, and the report suggests the officers
found those tests, which amounted to the slow execution of each
animal, particularly disturbing. In one instance, six .45-caliber
rounds were fired into a thirteen-hundred-pound bull over a period of three minutes. The noise from the first shot, fired through
the chest cavity from left to right, startled the animal but otherwise had no discernible effect. A second shot followed, and one
minute and twenty-five seconds later the animal began bleeding
from the mouth. Two more shots were fired over the next forty-
five seconds, dropping the animal to the ground, where it was
shot twice through the abdomen. "After the second shot to the

abdomen the animal got up, walked about and fell again. One minute and 10 seconds after the last shot the animal was struggling to get up on his feet. Finally orders were issued to kill him in accordance with the method pursued at the slaughterhouse."

The horses were shot in the head—the cavalry needed a handgun capable of putting down injured animals—and then rounds were fired into soft tissue, which was examined to determine the damage done by each bullet. All in all, it was terribly gruesome, though done with the purpose of finding a cartridge that would allow American soldiers to kill an enemy before the enemy killed them. In the end, Thompson and La Garde concluded that while any handgun round had sufficient "shock effect" if the bullet hit the brain or heart, they judged the size of the bullet, rather than the velocity at which it was shot, as the more important factor. A .38-caliber bullet passing quickly through a human body was less injurious than the larger .45-caliber round traveling at a slower speed. In short, bigger was better.

The validity and usefulness of the Thompson and La Garde report has been widely debated ever since, often without noting that the officers included a major qualification—they emphasized that the only truly effective handgun bullet was the one that hit a vital spot. A smokeless powder rifle bullet, larger and traveling at a high velocity, might ordinarily incapacitate with a single round, but no pistol-caliber cartridge could do the same. Unless there was a shot to the brain or heart, "there was no hope of stopping an adversary by shock or other immediate results when hit" no matter which round was used. In other words, the most important factor was accuracy, and what the Army really needed to do was drill soldiers "unremittingly."

As has often been reported by police forces and armies and as the troops observed in the Philippines, a human being hit in soft tissue can absorb multiple shots and remain upright and in motion for a surprisingly long period of time. At the infamous 1892 Dalton raid described earlier, the town marshal was shot in the head and died instantly, while Emmett Dalton received twenty-three wounds—some from shotgun pellets rather than pistol

171

or rifle bullets—including shots through the right arm, below a shoulder, the left hip and groin, surviving to move to Hollywood, where he died years later, in 1937.

So the Army chose a .45-caliber round. The final design and dimensions were the product of a joint effort by Browning, Colt, ammunition maker Union Metallic Cartridge, and the Army's Frankford Arsenal in Philadelphia, which manufactured the first ammunition commonly referred to as ".45 ACP" for the "automatic Colt pistol." Its lead bullet was almost twice the weight of the .38-caliber round and the powder behind it generated twice as much energy. Its effective range in a handgun—the distance it could be accurately aimed—was an optimistic 50 yards, though it would travel 1,650 yards before gravity and air resistance brought it to the ground. Various manufacturers designed pistols around the ammunition and in 1907 the Army began comparison tests with eight guns, including revised models from Colt and Luger and a new entry from Savage Arms in Utica, New York. Yet again, ordnance officers rejected all and declared no firearm had "reached such a stage of perfection as to justify its adoption."[13]

Throughout the duration of the Army's quest, Colt was usually considered the favorite. It supplied the Army's revolvers, was a domestic maker, and was offering a gun by John Browning, his reputation proved by the success of Browning's FN pistols and shotgun as well as Winchester's rifles. Among arms makers Browning's reputation for inventiveness was by then well known. "He developed his ideas in a different manner than any other inventor I have worked with" was the observation of Samuel M. Stone, who joined Colt in 1905 and rose to become president; "When he conceived an invention in his mind he conceived it in its entirety instead of getting a thought and then gradually working it out as is usual in inventions. When the picture was complete in his mind he then went to the laboratory and used mechanical means to put his idea in steel or iron."

Georg Luger's more expensive gun was praised for its mechanical elegance, but American troops said it was too fragile for combat. "The mechanism, while comparatively simple for a complicated machine, will not stand the wear-and-tear of service. Exposure to rain, water, dust and field service will render the pistol unserviceable," wrote Capt. M. W. Roel of the Eleventh U.S. Cavalry. Eventually Luger withdrew from consideration, declining to produce the two hundred guns sought for field testing as European orders for the 9mm pistol already exceeded manufacturing capacity.

That left Colt and Savage, and the domestic competitor prompted Colt and Browning to finally address the long list of army complaints. The barrel was shortened to five inches, making the gun balance better in the hand. The grip was revised from near vertical to rake backward at eighteen degrees to make aiming easier and more accurate. The springs operating the hammer, sear, and trigger were combined into a single part. Colt and Browning may also have realized that allowing more play between the slide and frame reduced costs with only a marginal effect on accuracy and, more important, increased the gun's ability to operate in dirty, rusty combat conditions.

Browning's renewed focus also resulted in a major change in the internal barrel mechanism. In his prior guns the barrel was supported by two swinging joints, called links, at the muzzle and breech, which allowed the barrel to move backward and retract downward at each shot. That small movement separated or "unlocked" the barrel from the slide and allowed the slide to continue its rearward travel to eject the spent cartridge and load a fresh round. That brief delay was crucial. It wasn't safe to open the breech to eject the brass case until the bullet left the barrel and the gas pressure dropped to a safe level.

In his redesign, Browning replaced the link at the muzzle with a circular solid steel bushing. When the barrel recoiled, it still moved backward but now was pulled down only at the rear. That created an unusual, counterintuitive tilting action. Each time the slide recoiled and the barrel unlocked, the muzzle tilted up until the returning slide pushed it back onto a horizontal plane. It seemed the antithesis of accuracy, but it worked. It's the mechanism used by most semiautomatic pistols today.

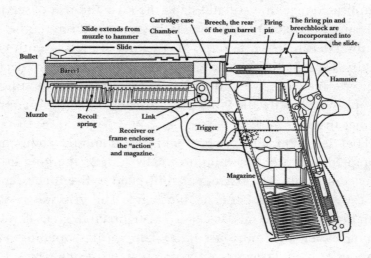

Browning's revisions also simplified manufacture, or would once Colt improved its quality control. In February 1910 at Fort Myer in Virginia the metal cap retaining the recoil spring cracked, halting tests while Browning fixed the part at a nearby blacksmith shop. A second failure required a second repair job, and "Mr. Browning stated that it was made too light and to a lower grade of steel."[14]

Nevertheless, two hundred test guns were ordered and favorable reports started flooding in, with one artillery unit declaring "the Colt automatic pistol is attested to for convenience, serviceability and reliability, the best automatic pistol known." Horse troops were still unenthusiastic about cocking it with two hands. Carrying the gun with a round in the chamber would allow it to be drawn and fired with one hand, but the Army considered that unsafe. "It would require no great effort of the imagination to picture a nervous soldier with his horse out of control, puncturing the atmosphere in all directions and making the life of bystanders an uncertain proposition," wrote one officer. That brought a biting response from the Ordnance Department, which believed it finally had, or would soon get, the version of a

Colt pistol it wanted. "It looks as if the cavalry were afraid of the automatic. It seems strange to me that anyone can prefer the old gas leaking and fire-spitting Colt revolver to the present perfect automatic."

Not quite perfect.

In late 1910, the Army conducted a head-to-head test of the Colt and Savage pistols. Each gun was put through the six-thousand-round reliability test, with cleaning and oiling allowed between every thousand shots. The once-reliable Colt suffered failure after failure. Fifteen times it either didn't fire, didn't eject, or didn't load a cartridge. The receiver cracked in six places, the slide was bent, and there was even a crack in the barrel. The ordnance officers blamed that on the new bushing and link interface between barrel, slide, and receiver, which required metal to be cut away at "the point of greatest pressure." Even the magazines failed, and the screws attaching the pistol grips worked loose. Colt was saved because the Savage was even worse. Both companies went back to try again.

What turned out to be the final test was in early 1911. By now Browning had addressed the cavalry's two-hand versus one-hand issue by adding a second safety. The gun already had a grip safety, a lever-like protrusion on the back of the grip that froze the action unless it was firmly pressed—gripped—by the palm of the hand holding the gun. Without a tight grip, the gun wouldn't fire. The additional "thumb safety" was a small lever on the upper left rear that held the slide in place once the hammer was cocked. It immobilized the slide even if the trigger was pulled and the grip safety compressed. The combination made Browning's pistol safe to carry with a round in the chamber. Grip the gun, pull it out of a holster while thumbing down the safety, and the gun was ready to fire. No two hands needed.

On the morning of March 15, 1911, Browning, company executives and engineers from Colt and Savage, and a bevy of Army officers gathered at the Springfield Armory. The John Browning described by the Belgians—phlegmatic, preternaturally emotionless—made an appearance, as Jack wrote that his father "strolled about, or stood with his hands in his pockets, sat on the bench, never appearing to be the least bit nervous." The first day was taken up by the usual tests for accuracy and dust resistance. Day two was the six-thousand-round competition, a slow process, as each magazine held only seven rounds. A routine was established; one man fired the gun while other soldiers reloaded magazine after magazine, pressing seven rounds into a spring-loaded magazine with sheet-metal edges 857 times in a row, a task that no doubt produced very sore thumbs.

The gun was periodically splashed with water for cooling, and it was cleaned after every one thousand rounds. If Browning appeared phlegmatic on the outside, on the inside he was counting each round, "from 1 to 7 as each fresh magazine went into action, and did not have time to breathe even a little sigh of relief before he was back at it again," Jack wrote.

The test reached two thousand rounds without incident. Then four thousand rounds without a failure . . . and five thousand cartridges without a malfunction. As he had years earlier with his gas-powered machine gun, Browning lost count of the number of rounds. When the firing stopped, he was momentarily uncertain whether the pistol had broken or had fired all six thousand rounds. It was the latter. The gun was disassembled and each part examined under a microscope for cracks or deformities. This time Colt metallurgy and machining met the challenge. No problems were found. The Savage suffered thirty-one malfunctions; plus, shooting it produced a sharp, distinctly uncomfortable recoil. The new Colt 1911 remained the standard-issue military side arm until 1985.

The initial government order was for 31,344 pistols, a significant number for an army that numbered ninety-five thousand troops in 1914, the year World War I began. Another 515,000 Colt 1911 pistols were made before that conflict ended, a large number but a small percentage of all the 1911s made since, and a minuscule percentage of all pistols made using Browning's slide and tilting-barrel design, as it is the world's dominant handgun mechanism. (The once-competitive Borchardt-Luger toggle-link design eventually dropped out of use and most production ceased at the end of World War II.) The current best-known example of Browning's mechanism is the ubiquitous Glock pistol, designed in 1982 by an Austrian curtain-rod manufacturer, Gaston Glock, and used by two-thirds of America's police departments. Glock, like most other major manufacturers, did away with the swinging link and uses a steel cam to tilt the barrel as it retracts with the slide.[15]

In its final form Browning's 1911, with input from Colt, is a distinctly American weapon. It's not elegant like his European guns—the 1911 has a boxy, aggressive look. It's a serious tool. Its trigger mechanism is considered the best ever designed. It can be set up so it requires a heavy, deliberate press of the finger, the sort of trigger weight used by police officers and soldiers to prevent accidental discharge, or adjusted to be crisp and delicate for competition so that pressing the trigger turns the mechanism into a virtual single piece of steel and the shot "breaks" like a pane of glass.

The 1911's continuing cachet is also rooted in its military history. A pistol is an intrinsically more intimate and personal weapon than a rifle and, obviously, a machine gun, and beginning in 1917 and continuing through Vietnam millions of American soldiers, sailors, and Marines were taught to use the 1911. Yet as a combat weapon Browning's pistol, or any pistol, is a firearm of last resort. It's a very short-range weapon, when the enemy is not much more than one or two arm's length away, and its "terminal ballistics," the technical term for what a bullet does to flesh, verges on inadequate compared to a rifle round.

To win wars the Army turned to three other Browning inventions.

CHAPTER TEN

ARMING THE ARMY

An unexpected bonus from the success of the "Pistolet Browning" was that in 1914 FN easily found space to host a celebratory sit-down dinner for five hundred guests. The FN factory that had occupied 7.5 acres of land prior to Browning's arrival had expanded to four times that size, and its brick buildings now sprawled over 30 acres.

The company had undergone a rapid expansion thanks to Browning's invention and was now a major European arms maker aiming to become a major industrial power. Four thousand machine tools filled its factory floors, operated by a workforce of five thousand people, an increase of 550 percent. FN was also producing a successful line of bicycles and firearm profits helped it venture into motorcycle and automobile manufacture, but its prime product was Browning's guns, and when sales crossed the 1 million mark in 1912 the company began planning, albeit very slowly, for a grand celebration. More than a year passed, and on January 31, 1914, guests entered a factory hall cleaned up and decorated with carnations, roses, and the national flags of Belgium and America. By then the total number of Browning pistols sold was 1.3 million, or about one FN handgun for every 265 Europeans.[1]

A tuxedo-clad Browning sat at the head table, flanked by government ministers and FN's top executives. Rising behind them was a tall, curiously shaped object draped with an American flag. Each guest received a celebratory menu printed on thick paper, and once the meal was served—turtle soup, foie gras, venison, chicken, and veal, followed by ice cream and fruit—FN managing director Alfred Andri took to the podium and detailed what Browning's "creative genius" had wrought. FN had produced 740,000 of the original Browning pistol, followed in 1906 by a gem of industrial manufacture, his tiny pocket pistol, which sold an astonishing 550,000 copies in a mere seven years. In 1912 the larger, graceful Model 1910 entered the market and found customers in the military and law enforcement in Germany, Brazil, Russia, and France. Andri took advantage of the moment to announce the latest sales contract, "the very recent victory, after a fierce competition and against the most serious of competitors, with the Serbian government."

Andri praised the company's skilled workers and described FN's offer of long-term, employment, "where merit and professional skills are not only appreciated but justly remunerated," he said. Andri said "workmen," though a year earlier Browning noted that a third of the employees were "women and girls" who were "as efficient as men in the operation of machines."[2] The entire region had profited from FN's expansion, particularly the small village next to Liège where FN had its plant. "Herstal owes to you, Mr. Browning, I would say, almost its life."

The evening culminated with a royal honor authorized by Belgian king Albert I, the "Knights Cross of the Order of Leopold." The king's representative, Minister of Industry and Finance Armand Hubert, held up the medal, a Maltese cross wrought in silver with white enamel, topped by a crown, and pinned it on Browning's coat. He praised FN, Browning, the workers, and noted a profound fact of Browning's inventions: "It is either a terrible or reassuring weapon Mr. Browning, that you created there! Terrible if one finds oneself on the side of the muzzle, reassuring if one finds oneself on the side of the trigger."[3]

Hart O. Berg was in the audience, now famous thanks to his escorting Wilbur Wright and his airplane through Europe in 1907. Also present was Browning's eighteen-year-old son, Val. In a letter to his mother, Rachel, Val reported "wine and champagne flowing like water."[4] He described Andri's "fine speech talking about daddy's life and work and finished by presenting daddy a large statue which had been covered by an American flag." The presentation then turned a bit slapstick, for as everyone craned their neck for a view Browning sat stock-still facing the diners. He'd just turned fifty-nine and had spent the previous decades firing tens of thousands of pistol, shotgun, rifle, and machine-gun rounds. As Val wrote, "Daddy did not hear what the director was saying, so when they unveiled the statue," the goddess Victory cast in bronze, "which is right in back of daddy, everybody looked at it but him."[5] Andri ordered the statue quickly moved in front of the head table, where Browning could see its arms uplifted, both hands holding laurel wreaths to symbolize "the victory to which you have led Fabrique Nationale," Andri declared.

Browning arose. His remarks were brief: "During fourteen years of collaboration, not the slightest cloud has troubled our excellent relations," he said in French. "Everywhere, and in whatever place I find myself, a friendly greeting is addressed to me, and this I esteem much more than gold or honors. I have confidence that the future will not be any less good than the past. I thank all of you. My wish is that Belgium and Fabrique Nationale will continue prospering and progressing so that we can soon celebrate the second millionth Browning." He raised his glass in a toast.

Not all reaction was as celebratory as the Belgian newspaper *La Meuse*'s front-page account. The competing *Le Soir* did not cover the dinner but offered the editorial observation that FN and Browning's 1 million-plus handguns "will make a large number of good people excellent shooters, and a few low and high underworld *chevaliers* all over the globe, shiver with delight." The newspaper noted that the noun "browning" had "become part of the everyday vocabulary of sportsmen, honest citizens who have no other care but to defend both their skin and their property, as well as for less distinguished characters."

With sarcastic understatement, the unnamed author added: "We owe to the inventor, that one celebrated in Herstal on Saturday, a few misfortunes, a few crimes that it would be unbecoming to reproach him for."[6]

In Ogden, Matt issued a statement to the newspaper incorporating the text of a cable from Andri extending his thanks to the Browning family, "especially to M.S. Browning, the clever collaborator," and summarized Browning's Belgian achievements—a total of five handgun models, the semiautomatic shotgun, a new autoloading hunting rifle, and a planned .22-caliber rifle. For good measure, the newspaper added that major arms makers in the United States produced Browning designs—including Winchester, Colt, and Remington.

Then the article veered from pedestrian press release to philosophical treatise—or as philosophical as the publicly taciturn Browning brothers ever offered on the printed page.

"I, at one time, had a man infer that he expected to find a set of desperados when he met the Browning brothers," Matt wrote. "He found them different. He had the idea that we invented something for the slaying of man. I told him that we did not consider it so, that the perfection of firearms meant the ending of war rather than its continuance.

"People will take a chance of being killed, but when guns are perfected so that death is certain, they will not stand up simply to be killed. It is not human nature. Perfection of guns means the ending of wars and of deaths from the use of such arms."

It was unvarnished idealism, and while it was a commonly held belief in that era it was run over by history. Five months later, on June 28, 1914, a FN Model 1910, exported to Serbia by a private arms dealer,[7] was used by Princip, the young, radical nationalist, to kill Archduke Franz Ferdinand. Princip would die in prison of tuberculosis in April 1918, watching from behind bars as the Continent exploded. He told a prison psychiatrist that he felt no responsibility and "could not believe that such a World War could break out as a result of an act like his." Nevertheless, Germany declared war on France on August 3 and the very next day invaded Belgium and advanced on Liège, only twenty-six miles west of its border and astride the ancient invasion corridor between France and Germany. It was not unexpected, as the Belgians long believed their neutrality would be violated in case of war. "Now the German Army has invaded the little country," Browning told an Ogden reporter, "the very thing that they have always feared has come about."[8]

Browning had left Belgium in June and, after likely stopping in Connecticut, reached Ogden on July 31. By August 5 there was street fighting in Herstal, and on August 6 Liège became the first European city attacked from the air when a German zeppelin, floating slowly through the sky, dropped a load of bombs, killing nine civilians.

Browning expressed surprise at the speed of the German advance and news reports that German troops were already in Liège, as the city was defended by a ring of twelve fortresses built specifically to deter an invasion. "I can scarcely understand how this is true . . . these forts are not more than five miles apart and some are as close as two miles," he told a reporter.[9]

He conceded some small German units might penetrate the defensive ring, as in fact occurred, but larger German formations were indeed delayed by the forts' thirteen-foot-thick poured-concrete walls, and heavy artillery mounted in 171 steel gun turrets. However, the concrete was unreinforced and the guns had been installed forty years earlier, before smokeless powder and twentieth-century metallurgy.[10] One by one the forts fell, the last on August 16, more than a week later than the Germans planned, which gave the British and French extra time—exactly how many days remains debated—to prepare for the coming onslaught. The Belgian government fled Brussels on August 17 and Hubert, the minister of industry and finance who'd presented Browning with the king's medal, fled to Paris with the government in exile. From occupied Liège, FN workers and managers were deported to factories in Germany. Andri, the general manager, was jailed for refusing to cooperate with the invaders. Arms manufacturing ceased, and the complex was used as a hospital for the wounded and a repair facility for German military trucks.

A firsthand description of the war's start reached Browning in

October with the return of a nephew, Jonathan Browning, who had spent twenty-nine months in Belgium as a Mormon missionary. The young Browning witnessed the invasion and was shocked as wounded troops flooded into Brussels. "They cannot be taken care of, and many died before being moved from the railway station," he said. A German plane flying overhead was struck by machine-gun fire, and he watched it explode when it hit the ground, making him one of the first people to witness a plane shot down by ground-based antiaircraft guns. Traveling with a pair of American war correspondents, he saw Belgium troops blow up strategic bridges over the Meuse River as long lines of refugees fled what became known as "the rape of Belgium." There were lurid accounts of atrocities: nuns forced to strip naked to prove they were not male spies in disguise, uncountable rapes, civilians killed in retaliation for a smattering of guerrilla attacks. In the city of Leuven, German troops burned a university library with three hundred thousand volumes of medieval books and manuscripts, killed 248 residents, and expelled 10,000 civilians. Another 674 civilians were massacred after a bitter battle in the city of Dinant. Some atrocities were exaggerated to whip up Allied support for the war effort, but more often than not the war crimes were real.

This was no mere abstraction for Browning, to be clucked over in the morning and forgotten by lunchtime. Since 1897 he'd spent nearly half his life walking the streets of Liège and the FN factory floors where workers' nickname for him, *le maître*, the master, was a tribute to his genius and an honor for his unassuming modesty. Those workers were now deported, and Browning must have known soldiers and civilians who were made casualties by the invader. In addition to those horrors and in addition to eviscerating the Browning brothers' royalty income,[11] the German invasion may have been an attack on family, too.

On his prewar visits to Liège, Val Browning discovered that his frugal, forthright father bundled him off to live not only in a different room but in a different hotel altogether. Val described the arrangement to his children years later, leaving unstated why Browning sought to avoid inadvertent morning meetings in the

Hotel Angleterre. It didn't take much figuring to assume Browning was in a relationship with a local woman that he wanted to conceal from his son. Such stories travel, however. Browning may have told his brother Matt or perhaps Val eventually heard it from Liège gossips, for family members believed that the rumored relationship also resulted in a child. The truth is unknown, though the story is plausible. Browning by then had spent as much or more time in Liège, Hartford, New Haven, and traveling in between than he did in Ogden living with Rachel, whom he once asked to join him in a plural marriage.

In Utah, Browning returned to his workbench at the brothers' newest Ogden location, on what is now Kessler Avenue, in the downtown.[12] Browning settled in among milling machines, lathes, and drills housed in a spacious wood-floored and brick-walled second-floor workshop, brightly lit by windows on three sides. His workbench, as always, was covered with tools and gun parts seemingly spread about at random. There, between the fall of 1914 and spring of 1917, Browning completed two of three machines that went on to arm the American Army in the greatest war of the century. That was World War II. During World War I, despite an enormous effort by the inventor, his brothers, and American industry, the much-anticipated and then well-reviewed weapons that made Browning a figure of national reputation had to be manufactured as well as invented, and manufacturing took time.

The first firearm completed was a tripod-mounted machine gun based on the design he patented in 1901 and revised in 1910. Colt received a working prototype in mid-1915 and set up demonstrations for ordnance officers in Hartford and Washington. The Army was replacing a machine gun selected in 1909, the "Benet-Mercie," whose principal designer, Lawrence V. Benet, was a son of a previous ordnance chief. It was called a machine rifle and was supposed to do double-duty as a stationary tripod-mounted gun and a portable weapon for troops maneuvering in the field. Armies had been slow to realize that soldiers needed two very different automatic weapons: a heavy machine gun, mounted on a stationary tripod, fed by belts loaded with hundreds of cartridges and worked by a two- or four-man crew; and a light weapon carried by a single solider to support advancing troops with short bursts of automatic fire.

The Benet-Mercie did neither job well. Its ammunition was loaded via awkward metal strips that carried only thirty rounds, it was air-cooled and quickly overheated, and it was complicated and expensive to manufacture. Its reputation plunged further at 4:15 a.m. on March 9, 1916, when Pancho Villa raided Columbus, New Mexico. The American troops defending the town were said to have found the guns too complicated to load in the dark, prompting controversial complaints about "daylight" weapons, which added to the clamor for an American gun comparable to the Maxim. The Benet-Mercie's failings, however, were in fact irrelevant, because the U.S. Army was too small and ill equipped to wage any war larger than a police action.

In Europe tens of thousands of machine guns were deployed in trenches stretching from the English Channel to the Swiss border, while in America the Army could field only 670 of the problematic Benet-Mercier, 282 versions of an aging Maxim design, and 158 of Browning's gas guns. With pressure mounting, the secretary of war named a board of seven officers and two civilians to select a new American machine gun. The board conducted preliminary tests and in October ordered up four thousand of the British Maxim-based Vickers gun as a stopgap measure and scheduled a competitive test for all contenders in May 1917. The decision was fortuitous, if a bit late, as war was declared on April 6, 1917. The Army with only one hundred thousand troops in 1914 and two hundred thousand in 1916 now had to recruit, train, and equip a force of 4 million who would need fifty thousand machine guns.

There were only five serious contenders when trials started at the Springfield Armory: an initial model of Browning's new water-cooled gun, which Colt and Browning struggled mightily to prepare; the British Vickers gun, now made in America, also by Colt; two versions of Browning's earlier air-cooled gas gun, which were revised and upgraded by rifle manufacturer Marlin; and the French heavy machine gun, called the Hotchkiss.

To say the results were one-sided is an understatement. Browning's gun fired 20,000 rounds in fifty-three minutes and seventeen seconds, not counting the time it took to reload the gun eighty times in a row with 250-round ammunition belts. The Vickers fired the same number of cartridges in ninety-eight minutes and seventeen seconds, as forty-one minutes and forty-six seconds were absorbed clearing jams and replacing broken parts.

Browning's new Colt was out of action for forty-six seconds.

The gun seemed perfect.

The result was so surprising a second test was ordered up, and both guns fired another 20,000 rounds pausing after each 1,000 shots. This time they were better matched. The Vickers spent eleven minutes and forty-three seconds down for repairs compared to the Browning's six minutes. The Browning jammed five times, mostly due to faulty ammunition. The Vickers suffered fifty-six "other malfunctions."[13]

The tests also measured how long it took to load the 250-round cartridge belts, a not-insignificant fact, as troops at the front were supplied with crates of loose ammunition. Thanks to a simpler belt of Browning design—it was canvas and used no metal parts—plus a reloading tool also of Browning's own design, it took two men ten minutes to load 1,000 rounds in four belts. It took four men twenty-three minutes to load the Vickers's belts.

Perhaps even more important to an army in dire need of thousands of weapons quickly was that the simpler Browning was cheaper and easier to produce. A Browning gun cost $283 while a Vickers ran to $490, though the final price of either gun at least doubled or tripled once tripods, mule carts, and spare parts were included. A glowing report reached the secretary of war: "Lightness, simplicity, reliability of function, and endurance and action as such to make it superior to any other of the so-called heavy water cooled type known." The excited machine-gun board rushed two members down to Washington, D.C., to meet with the secretary of war on May 9, where the results were received with skepticism. A third test was ordered up, and to make sure the first gun wasn't a ringer, Colt was instructed to provide another from its still-small stock. On May 24 that gun fired 20,000 rounds and quieted the Ordnance Department cynics. Brig. Gen. F. H. French, who oversaw the tests, produced a report a day later declaring Browning "the master machine gun mechanic of the world."

What Browning did was what he always did—he figured out a simple, elegant way to accomplish a complex task.

To visualize how his machine gun worked, consider an assembly line churning out new iPhones. Each smartphone is carried along on a conveyor until it reaches a mechanical arm that picks it up, swings it around, and drops it into an empty box moving on a parallel conveyor. There another arm lifts it up and drops it onto a shipping pallet. Now imagine the objects are cartridges rather than iPhones, and imagine the first conveyor is a canvas belt with 250 rounds of ammunition, the second conveyor is the machine gun's bolt, and the shipping pallet is the barrel.

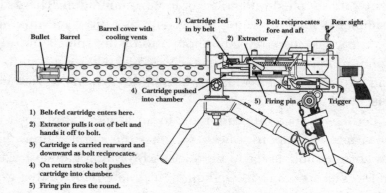

.30-Caliber Browning M1919A4

The ammunition belt is fed into the side of the gun above the barrel, where a mechanical "arm"—the extractor—pulls a cartridge free and hands it off to the bolt as the round is lined up with the barrel. The bolt moves forward, inserting the cartridge into the barrel. The cartridge is fired, and the recoil throws the bolt backward, extracting the spent cartridge. The recoil simultaneously causes a fresh round to be extracted from the belt, which is handed off to the bolt for insertion into the chamber as the spent case drops to the ground. Then repeat.

To perform that function some 500 times a minute, the maximum rate of fire, the Maxim-derived Vickers used a twenty-two-part mechanism of clockwork intricacy. The Browning machine gun used six parts, including a small coil spring and two short steel pins. Only two parts required intricate machining.

As Browning completed his .30-caliber machine gun, he was finishing a second automatic weapon with a totally different action. The government wanted a portable machine gun for troops maneuvering in the field, hoping it could help break the muddy, deadly stalemate on the Western Front, where trenches defended by barbed wire and machine guns ran from the English Channel to the Alps. These never-before-seen industrial-era defensive lines withstood successive frontal assaults that only served to keep the gravediggers busy. The Battle of the Somme, a series of Allied attacks and German counterattacks from July to December in 1916, resulted in 325,000 dead and no change in the strategic stalemate.

A new tactic initially believed to have merit was "walking fire," where troops carrying light automatic guns would advance firing from the hip, knocking out entrenched enemy machine guns with concentrated bursts as they worked their way through the crater-filled no-man's-land. In practice, walking upright toward the German lines was a recipe for getting killed. But the idea of a portable automatic weapon was a good one. The British used the Lewis gun, a heavy, sometimes problematic automatic weapon encased in a large aluminum tube that acted as a radiator to cool the barrel. The French developed the Chauchat, its design heavily influenced by the long-recoil system Browning invented for his 1908 semiautomatic hunting rifle,[14] though what worked in a hunting rifle that fired a few shots a day wasn't the best system for a battlefield. Chauchats were cheap to produce—they used metal stampings rather than expensive forgings—and more than 250,000 were made, but they were ergonomic monsters, heavy, hard to balance, hard to aim, and equipped with poorly designed magazines prone to jam in the ever-present mud. In 1917, when the gun was hurriedly converted to handle American ammunition, a design error resulted in constant stoppages.

By comparison, the Browning Automatic Rifle was an ergonomic and mechanical work of art. It weighed not quite sixteen pounds, carried a 20-round detachable magazine, and was fired from any position—the shoulder, prone, or from the hip. A selector on the left side converted it from semi-automatic to full-automatic.[15]

Recognizing the automatic rifle's potential, the Army tested it in secret and began production under wraps, and Browning was forbidden from applying for a patent, which would require disclosing the design, until after the war. The government was meanwhile beginning to adopt the Lewis gun—it had a genuine combat record, no matter any issues—and some wondered if this rumored weapon really existed. Doubters included Theodore Roosevelt Jr., who reportedly called it a "gun on paper," which he no doubt regretted following the highly choreographed and highly successful unveiling of both the Browning guns on February 27, 1918.

On that cold winter morning, three hundred members of Congress, military attachés, diplomats, and reporters gathered at a shooting range, outside Washington, D.C., for a demonstration unlike any in their experience. Standing in a line were ten soldiers carrying what resembled an ordinary rifle, if a bit larger. On command each man fired twenty shots in a row just by pulling the trigger twenty times. Then each pressed a button and the rectangular metal magazine dropped to the ground. Another was instantly inserted, followed by short bursts of automatic fire. The soldiers reloaded and began "rapid automatic fire from the hip, emptying the magazines," the *New York Times* reported.

"Quicker than it takes to tell it, each of the ten riflemen had fired twenty cartridges." Then two Browning .30-caliber machine guns fired more than 1,000 rounds each. The crowd buzzed in astonishment, more so at the automatic rifle than the machine gun. They'd seen or read about the Maxim and Vickers, and to an idle observer the Browning machine gun didn't look much different, but this automatic rifle was something new. Its appearance was familiar to anyone who handled a hunting rifle, but it was quite unlike the Lewis gun, which looked like a drainpipe, or the Chauchat, which looked like a badly designed fire hose.

Senators and congressmen lined up to take turns firing the machine rifle, remarking on its mild recoil. It was chambered for the same .30-06 cartridge used in the standard infantry rifle, but in single-shot mode the new rifle's heavier weight dampened the recoil. The onlookers raved, as did the newspapers the following day. In fact, the ten demonstration guns were early production models and suffered a variety of faults, though none obvious to the excited onlookers.

The Army gave Browning full credit for conceiving and building the arms. "The Browning machine rifle and the Browning machine gun came from the hands of the inventor, coincidentally with the imperative war needs," the Army said, admitting in government-speak that the weapons were neither sought nor conceived by the government bureaucracy or a military contractor but imagined and built by one man, and his brothers, in a second-floor workshop in a small city in Utah. Because most Americans had never heard of Browning, including the parents and wives of the men who would use his weapons, the Army pointedly noted he was a "distinguished firearm designer, inventor of several Winchester rifles, automatic pistols, repeating rifles, . . . and numerous other arms."

While the many press accounts made much of the "Browning" guns, there was all but no mention of John Moses Browning, the inventor, and some believe he did not attend. In recent years a photo from the event has surfaced, apparently lacking identifying data, that shows a tall, gray-haired man with a small belly—as described to the author by a grandchild—comfortably demonstrating the heavy automatic rifle. Though his face is partially obscured, what can be seen resembles other photos of Browning. Photos of the event are on glass negatives, according to the Library of Congress, which meant the photographer chose his subjects carefully. And it is all but impossible to believe Colt would have demonstrated potentially balky, early production models without the inventor on hand for a quick fix.[16]

The sudden appearance of what was soon named the BAR, or Browning Automatic Rifle, has been an unexplained mystery, as it was not commissioned by any military power, American or European. Author James L. Ballou wrote in his detailed history of the gun, *Rock in a Hard Place*,[17] that the BAR made its first stop in the historical record on February 27, 1917, at Colt's plant in Hartford, where a handmade prototype was demonstrated to military officers. The extensive work necessary to turn the prototype into a mass-produced weapon began almost immediately. By May, Colt had test models that fired 480 rounds with no faults. The first contract, for twelve thousand, was awarded July 16, 1917, an exceeding short time frame.

So where did the BAR come from? Pretty much from off a shelf in Ogden. Browning, with his brother Ed, began working on the automatic rifle five years earlier, driven not by a government order but Browning's own inventive curiosity. That's according to a never-before-published letter, written in 1939 by Ed Browning to Edwin Pugsley, then the Winchester vice president. By then Ed had resumed friendly relations with Winchester, and Pugsley was working on the new M-1 carbine, a lightweight rifle that became a widely used World War II small arm. It originated with a prototype developed by Ed in the 1930s that used a replaceable box magazine like the BAR. As Pugsley oversaw the redesign he resisted pressure to use an alternate system to feed ammunition, and Ed wrote a letter thanking Pugsley for "how you stood up for the box magazine principle." Ed's remarks are worth quoting in full:

It reminds me of the experience my brother, John, had at the time the government asked for the machine rifle. Five years previous, he and I had started on one using the box magazine, and he received no encouragement from the government so we stopped our work. At that time I had made the box magazine and it was laid aside with the unfinished gun. Five years later, when the government, facing war, asked for such a gun, we started work again.

As usual the experts were recommending a belt magazine or a French Hotchkiss long fixed clip [*Ed. Note*: an unwieldly device that sticks out the side], I distinctly remember John thrashing over these for about a week, and in disgust he threw them away and picked up and used the original box magazine we had made years previously. The crisis ordnance faced and the manner in which the model performed forever silenced any in Washington from mentioning their temperamental theories as to gun feeds.[18]

Exactly how far advanced work on the machine rifle progressed circa 1912 is unknown, but if Ed was making box magazines the gun was certainly operable before Browning stashed it away for a future war.

To explain how the new machine rifle worked, the government used as an example another new, though more familiar, technology, the internal combustion engine. "This gun is gas operated on the same principle that is used to operate a gasoline engine." As the bullet exited the muzzle a small vent in the side of the barrel extracted a pulse of high-pressure gas from the burning gun powder and directed it into a tube where a piston was installed. The impact of the gas on the piston moved a rod that actuated the mechanism that ejected the spent round and loaded and fired a fresh round. The back-and-forth movement of the gun's piston was similar to a cylinder in an auto engine. This new machine rifle was named the Browning Automatic Rifle, making it the first Browning firearm in America to carry his name.

Accounts of the Washington test were followed by profiles of the inventor, illustrated with photographs that put Browning's aged and lined face on full display. The inventor America saw was a phlegmatic man. In no photograph did he smile or offer a twinkle in his eye. He didn't look into the camera. The self-aware, confident gaze on display in a studio photograph from the 1890s is absent. Browning didn't look avuncular and accessible like Thomas Edison or display the sharp intelligence seen in photographs of another great inventor, Henry Ford. Browning's photos show a man expressionless. Also absent from each article was the standard ingredient of celebrity profile—words from the celebrity. Even in the seventh decade of his life and on the receiving end of nationwide accolades, Browning continued his policy of never giving an interview. No matter that he became known as the "Edison of guns." As one profile put it, just as Thomas Edison was the "wizard" who invented all things electrical, Browning was the "wizard of firearms" who invented all types of guns—lever-action rifles, semiautomatic rifles, pump-action shotguns, autoloading shotguns, pistols of all shapes and sizes, and now two different sorts of machine guns.[19]

He was declared "the world's greatest inventor of sporting firearms" by the popular West Coast magazine *Sunset*, which added: "In foreign countries he has been honored by royalty; in his own country he is practically unknown outside the circle of close friends in his home community." Browning was said to be "indifferent" to the honors bestowed on him, the magazine noted: "He enjoys the noise of firearms but not public clamor and dislikes publicity." And the magazine tried to answer the question always asked when people discovered the breadth of Browning's inventions: "Mr. Browning's patents bring the princely income from royalties on the sale of guns, but he is unostentatious in his manner of living and is quiet and retiring." It cited no number to define "princely." However, in the years immediately prior to World War I the Browning brothers received about $40,000 a year in royalties from FN, about $1 million a year in current dollars.[20] They also earned additional royalty income from Colt and Remington.

The *New York World*, a popular mass-circulation newspaper, echoed *Sunset*, writing that "throughout his own state he is hailed as the firearm wizard, but the great majority of newspaper readers probably have never heard of him."[21] As in other articles popping up across the country, the *World* included a summary of Browning's life—his father's history of gun making, early adventures in the trade, Winchester's purchase of his first gun. Readers were assured Browning was a peace-loving man who deplored war, indeed had spent most of his career making sporting arms, but was compelled to answer his nation's call. The *World* article did include a quote from the inventor, who admitted to playing the banjo "tolerably well for an old 'un," and said that "The Blue Bells of Scotland" and "The Beautiful Blue Danube" were his favorite tunes.

The many profiles are stuffed full of similar details. Technical explanations are alike and sometimes articles display an uncannily similar structure, all suggesting that Matt, the successful businessman and former mayor, the outgoing and sociable brother, was distributing press kits to inquiring reporters. Interestingly, Matt himself is virtually absent from the articles, as is Ed. John's decades-long status as head of the Browning clan, not to mention the siblings' recognition of his genuine genius, led them to put him forward while they stepped back from public acclaim.

Browning's automatic rifle was a particular crowd pleaser, and was dispatched to war bond rallies, including one outside the New York City Public Library hosted by the Mayor's Committee of Women on National Defense. Society ladies posed with the rifle, among them a veiled Anne Louisa Ide Cockran, the well-known wife of a congressman, photographed holding the heavy BAR in white-gloved hands. Ms. Cockran was famous thanks to author Robert Louis Stevenson (*Treasure Island, Strange Case of Dr. Jekyll and Mr. Hyde*). Cockran's birthday was December 25, meaning she suffered the misfortune of receiving a single present on what was for her a double holiday. So in 1891 when she was age fourteen, Stevenson "formally deeded his own birthday, Nov. 13, to the young girl." So said the *New York Times*.

Only once did Browning address, obliquely, the deadly nature of his inventions and explain the time and effort he spent inventing machines with the primary purpose of killing. His automatic weapons weren't for hunting or self-defense, unless one considered the self-defense of the nation, as Browning did. On March 1, 1917, the *Ogden Daily Standard* ran a lengthy article on the hometown inventor, which paraphrased Browning's response when asked "Why he didn't turn his attention to perfecting the automobile":

> He replied to the effect that the world's need of guns still was greatest; that the field of arms invention was infinitely larger yet than that of the motor-car. He is, however, an ardent peace advocate, but recognizes the need of preparedness and the fact that generations probably must pass, through an era of evolution and the use of force, before the nations will be ready, by reason of scientific advancement and intellectual culture, to beat their guns into plow-shares and their swords into pruning-hooks.
>
> Since the world must have guns it was the great inventor's business to supply the best guns ever made by man . . .

For the Army, selecting guns turned out to be the easy part. Figuring how to make them fast enough and in large enough quantities was a daunting challenge. Colt held the rights to both guns, but its factory was already missing production deadlines, so Remington and New England Westinghouse were contracted to make the .30-caliber guns and Winchester became the lead producer of the BAR. To compensate it for its lost revenue, Colt received a $1 million payment from the government, which it believed "was very much less" than it deserved.

There was also the matter of the Browning brothers' royalties. By October 1917 existing government orders entitled the Brownings to at least $5 million, and with combat expected to continue into 1919 that sum would double as plans called for a total of one hundred thousand machine guns and an even larger number of automatic rifles, not to mention tens of thousands of 1911 pistols. Hoping to cut costs, the Ordnance Department opened negotiations and at a meeting on October 31, 1917, asked the brothers to accept a maximum royalty of $1.5 million for both automatic guns. Pistol royalties would presumably continue as contracted. As recorded by Matt, "I supposed that John would ask for a little time to think things over and get my opinion," but instead, "Without hesitating a second he said . . . 'If that suits Uncle Sam, it's all right with me.'" Browning noted that if he and Matt were younger they'd be in uniform across the Atlantic and covered in French mud. The cut-rate agreement was a significant concession by Browning, who always paid close attention to contractual details, fought Luger for years, and was described by Colt and FN as a fair but hard bargainer. It was the act of a genuine patriot—and a wealthy man—but what Browning never considered was the steep federal income tax hike passed to pay for the cost of war, which reduced the $1.5 million in royalties to some $600,000.

"For their famous machine gun they had an enormous disappointment," wrote an FN executive following a postwar meeting with Colt managers. "The government dealt with them for a set sum, payable once. Yet, having paid, they reclaimed 60 percent in taxes on said sum. John Browning almost died from it."[22]

Winchester's BAR contract led to Browning's return for the first time since 1902. The task of rebuilding a relationship with the inventor was assigned to Winchester's chief engineer, Pugsley, who met Browning in his Hartford hotel. "Mr. Browning couldn't have been more cordial and inquiring about all his friends," Pugsley wrote later. Someone at Winchester who obviously knew Browning well, not former president Bennett, who was retired, provided Pugsley with the wooden forestock to a BAR, which Pugsley used as a bit of show-and-tell to prove the company's commitment to the new firearm. Browning turned it over in his hands and told Pugsley, admiringly, "Nobody can handle wood like Winchester."

Ed, Matt, and at least one other brother, Sam, also moved to

New England nearly full-time to help Winchester, Remington, Westinghouse, and other smaller firms set up their tooling and production lines. Rachel came east and she and John resided in Hartford while he worked with Colt. "They have a nice big apartment and are very happy," Matt told his daughter Telitha in a July 7, 1918, letter. Family members took John on weekend excursions, including to a dinner in New Haven on Long Island Sound, but it was a rare break from his work. With affectionate sarcasm Matt wrote his daughter that John's youngest child, Elizabeth, fourteen years old and soon to turn fifteen, was upset by her father's single-mindedness. "Uncle John has a great time with Elizabeth 'wont go to the pitcher show, wont go to the circus, wont read a book, wont eat' etc etc. & he is looking better than I have seen him for over a year."[23]

By 1918 sufficient firearms were available to train new recruits, which posed another problem. Few soldiers, in fact, few people anywhere, knew how to maintain or operate either the automatic rifle or the machine gun, so at his father's request Val left Cornell—Browning had in fact discouraged Val's enrollment, not seeing the need for four years of classroom learning[24]—and accepted a lieutenant's commission in the Ordnance Corps. He joined a small unit training the instructors who would then train the troops, not only in how to use the weapons but also to "instill confidence in the man in the gun you're going to use and in that way to better the morale," he wrote in an August 1918 letter to a first cousin, Marriner Browning, Matt's oldest son. "This matter of not only having a better weapon but of having the men feel and know that they have a better one is very important nowadays."[25]

Val soon decided the troops, from enlisted men to officers, were unreasonably impressed with his father's weapons: "Everybody from highest to lowest of all allied nations are openly and outspokenly enthusiastic. The fact is too much so. They actually have so much confidence in the guns that they don't think it worthwhile to study them mechanically. Which is exceedingly important and we have the devil's own time trying to teach them anything beyond how to put in a belt or a magazine and then pull the trigger with the gun pointed in the direction of Berlin."

He was dismayed by military boasting: "One colonel got up and made a speech about it in which, among other things of a like nature, he said that all one had to do with this gun was to whisper the Boches' names and addresses to it and give it a kick in the—and it would go over the top and bring them in by hundreds. He said also, 'The Boches haven't a chance. John Browning isn't dead yet!'"

Marriner, twenty-six, was helping Matt handle the Brownings' investments and Val's letters touch on business and financial arrangements, and more than once Val bemoans the monetary fallout from the cut-rate royalty agreement: "It would make you sick, though, to see all the fellows getting enthusiastic over the guns and trying every way to get ahold of them by the thousands, and then to think that no matter how many they get, we are not better off—excepting in reputation, perhaps."[26]

In April, Val was dispatched to France for the first overseas demonstration of the .30-caliber machine gun. Before a mixed group of American, English, and French officers and troops, one machine gun fired 2,500 rounds and another 2,200 rounds without a problem, which surprised the French, who said they'd never seen automatic weapons that reliable. By then both guns were arriving in quantities sufficient to arm American troops. But just as Browning's BAR was deployed it was suddenly recalled, stored in depots, and the troops were given the much-disliked Chauchat. It appears Gen. John J. Pershing thought the new automatic rifles "were so greatly superior to any machine guns in use by any armies in either side" that he feared that distributing them in advance of a planned fall offensive would give the Germans an opportunity to capture the guns, reverse engineer them, and turn the German version against the Allies.

When Pershing finally ordered BARs reissued, Val was attached to the Seventy-Ninth Infantry Division, the first to be fully equipped with both Browning arms—it received 960 BARs and 260 heavy .30-caliber machine guns. They actually used *three* Browning guns, as the troops were already issued 1911 pistols.

The BAR was deployed with regular infantry units, while the tripod guns went to fourteen specially designated machine-gun companies of 173 men, who transported their guns, ammunition, tripod, cooling water, and assorted accessories in specially designed mule carts. If the gun had to be moved under fire, it was detached from the tripod and each part was carried forward by a soldier. Each machine gunner was issued an individual side arm for self-defense, sometimes a revolver but usually Browning's seven-shot .45-caliber pistol. A fourth Browning weapon made an appearance, too. The 1897 Winchester pump-action shotgun turned out to be an ideal weapon for trench warfare and in fact was so deadly in the confined spaces of a trench that the Germans—who introduced poison gas and flamethrowers—claimed its use constituted a war crime.[37]

Modern weaponry was no replacement for practice, however, and that was sorely lacking. Between May and July the Seventy-Ninth Division machine gunners expended 450,000 machine-gun rounds in training, a seemingly impressive figure diminished in that it amounted to only 1,750 rounds per gun, or enough for each crew to fire their weapon for ten or fifteen minutes. The guns were capable of firing 500 rounds a minute, but allowing for target spotting, aiming, and changing ammunition belts, machine gunners in combat typically fired 100 to 150 cartridges a minute, usually in short bursts.

The Seventy-Ninth entered the front line on September 14, 1918, taking positions west of the Verdun battlefield. A machine-gun barrage was ordered, which meant elevating the guns to fire in an arc over the enemy trenches to strike rear units. Val helped aim the guns, "and the gun I was handling quite possibly fired the first shot" ever fired in combat by a Browning machine gun.

Twelve days later on September 26, the American Expeditionary Force launched the Meuse-Argonne offensive, deploying fifteen divisions, about 220,000 troops, along a twenty-six-mile line,

part of a larger Allied assault intended to break the German line
and end the war. It was the deadliest military campaign in American
history, in which the Seventy-Ninth played a key and controversial role. American battle plans called for the division to
advance nine kilometers on the first day and seize fortifications
around the town of Montfaucon, an area Germans spent four
years fortifying and nicknamed Little Gibraltar. They believed
it was impenetrable, and the French said the Americans would
need three months, not one day, to reach that objective.

One of the American machine gunners was a New Jersey man,
Sgt. Harry L. Frieman, who went over the top at 6:00 a.m. with
the 313th Infantry regiment.[28] Their initial advance under enemy
shell fire was speedy but dangerous. "One man . . . carrying ammunition was hit by a shell and killed. All that was found of him
was an arm." At 1:00 p.m. they paused to set up their machine
guns and came under sniper fire. "I located a sniper in tree and
we shot at him. I shot at him seven times with my .45 caliber and he
fell out of tree," Frieman wrote in his daily diary. They continued
to advance, supported by artillery fire, until they were halted by
heavy machine-gun fire. "We had to back about 200 yards and lay
in shell holes overnight." By morning a cold rain was soaking the
battlefield and they moved forward under enemy machine-gun
and artillery fire. Bodies from earlier combat dotted the ground.
"This morning we cleaned out many M.G. nests—captured many
prisoners and took Montfaucon." At twelve hundred feet above
sea level the town served as an important German observation
post, where in 1916 the German Crown Prince arrived to view
the battlefield of Verdun where one hundred thousand soldiers
died, Frieman observed.

The feat of capturing Montfaucon in two days turned out to
be inadequate. The extra day slowed the overall advance, a delay
blamed for allowing the Germans time to regroup.[29] There was
also a high cost. Between September 26 and September 30, the
division of roughly 16,000 men suffered 798 killed and 2,731 injured, a steep casualty rate of 22 percent. The unit spent October in a defensive position before returning to the offensive in

early November. On November 11 they launched an attack at the village of Chaumont, Frieman wrote. "Took our guns and ammunition off the carts and started to walk. It was very foggy this morning and couldn't see over 10 yards in front of us. We were caught in a barrage and had to hide behind a slope at road. The shells were bursting all around us. We were lucky that the ground was very soft and shells stuck there and only threw a lot of mud over us." At 10:30 a.m., "we received orders to open up a M.G. barrage. Just as we set our guns up to fire an officer passed by and said, 'Boys take your time I have a message to stop firing at 11 AM. We could hardly believe it.'"

The war had ended. The unit remained locked in fog until noon, when visibility returned and Frieman realized they had walked into a trap. There were Germans on three sides. "If the war would've kept up a few hours longer there would not be many of us left to tell about it."

One 313th soldier who didn't survive was Henry Gunther, a Baltimore man who was earlier reduced in rank from sergeant to private after censors found him complaining about frontline living conditions in a letter home. Intent on proving his patriotism, at 10:59 a.m. Gunther jumped out of a foxhole and carrying his BAR attacked a German machine-gun position. Nearby Americans said the Germans waved him away, but Gunther kept coming, opened up with his rifle, and was cut down by a burst of fire. Gunther may have been the last American killed in the war.

Frieman's machine-gun company was one of the relatively few to use Browning weapons in combat. While the government ordered 150,000 heavy machine guns, only 41,806 were produced by war's end and not all of those reached the front before the Armistice. Numbers for the BAR were similar. Orders were issued for 288,174, but Winchester and other manufacturers churned out only 51,798 by war's end.

The delays in getting Browning's guns to the front were inevitable, given the months it took to set up an assembly line. At the Winchester factory, production was temporarily halted after the first 1,800 BARs failed to meet design specifications. They ran fine, but the parts were not interchangeable with the guns coming off other production lines. Most American troops ended up using the Vickers or French Hotchkiss, and the ungainly Chauchat.

That was the case with the Eightieth Infantry Division, which went into combat in September with the European guns and during bitter fighting discarded four hundred Chauchats "ceasing to function" and tossed aside fifty Vickers machine guns. The division was reequipped with Brownings for the final offensive, a battle "which was even more bitter than the former," wrote one soldier, but only one disabled Browning machine gun was left on the battlefield, and that was damaged by enemy fire. Only seventy-three BARs were lost, mostly after the troops carrying them were killed or wounded.

The Browning weapon that did see wide service in World War I was the 1911 pistol. About 510,000 were manufactured by eight different companies and most got to the front lines, beginning in 1914 when air combat was in its infancy and pilots were scrounging for weapons. The Royal Flying Corps armed observers in its open-cockpit reconnaissance aircraft with 1911s carrying twenty rounds in an extended magazine to attack their German adversaries. T. E. Lawrence, the one from Arabia, had two Colt 1911 pistols supposedly gifted to him by Gertrude Bell, the writer and British political officer who played an influential role in the empire's Middle East policy. A grainy photo of Lawrence in the desert shows him reloading what appears to be a 1911 pistol.

But it was American corporal Alvin C. York whose combat record led the gun to popular fame. A crack shot from years hunting in the hills of his native Tennessee, York was a drunken troublemaker—"hog wild" was his own description—who hung out at one drinking establishment where twenty-five people were killed in bar fights. Then he met his future wife and on New Year's Day 1915 York joined the Church of Christ in Christian

Union, which considered the Bible the direct word of God, including the command "Thou Shall Not Kill." When war came he declared himself a conscientious objector.

As York later wrote, "So you see there were two reasons why I didn't want to go to war. My own experience told me it weren't right. And the Bible were agin it too."[30]

Nevertheless, he was denied conscientious objector status and drafted at age twenty-nine. A change of heart came after a late-night meeting with his unit commander. "I remember he begun by p'inting out that Christ once said: 'He that hath no sword, let him sell his cloak and buy one.' I 'lowed that was in the Bible. But I reminded him that Christ also said: 'If a man smite you on one cheek, turn the other to him.' He admitted that, but he asked me if I believed that the Christ who drove the money changers from the temple with the whip would stand up and do nothing when the helpless Belgian people was overrun and driven from their homes."

York conceded the point and in France on October 9, 1918, he was part of a sixteen-man patrol sent to clear a row of German machine-gun nests.

Working their way behind enemy lines, the Americans surprised a German headquarters unit of seventy men eating a meal of bread, marmalade, and canned meat. With no choice but to take them prisoner—otherwise the Americans would be killed or captured themselves—the Germans were rounded up at gunpoint. Just then enemy machine gunners on higher ground realized they'd been infiltrated, yelled in German for their compatriots to get down, and opened fire. Six men in York's patrol were wounded and three were killed. York was left in command.

With no time to give orders and no way for his troops to hear him amid the machine guns, York opened fire with his bolt-action Enfield rifle. "Every time I seed a German I jes teched him off. At first I was shooting from a prone position," as in Tennessee. "But the targets here were bigger. I jes couldn't miss a German's head or body."[31] Within a few minutes York's rifle was overheating and he was almost out of ammunition. More than a dozen

Germans lay dead when suddenly six enemy soldiers emerged from a trench twenty-five-yards away and charged at him with fixed bayonets.

That was pistol range, so York dropped his Enfield, pulled out his 1911, and opened fire the same way he hunted wild turkeys, back to front. "You see we don't want the front ones to know that we're getting the back ones, and then they keep on coming until we get them all." All six Germans fell, the last only a few feet away, shot in the abdomen and screaming in pain. York had killed twenty-five Germans, and a moment later an English-speaking German officer among the captured prisoners offered to negotiate a surrender: "Good Lord! If you won't shoot anymore I will make them give up." They did, and York, with the remnants of his patrol, took 132 Germans prisoner. York received the Congressional Medal of Honor.

Recent archaeology at the battle site by American Douglas V. Mastriano has added an addendum to the role Browning's Colt 1911 pistol played in the historic encounter.[32] Mastriano recovered twenty-four .45-caliber cartridge casings from around York's position and discovered the spent cartridges marked by two different firing pins. That meant two 1911 pistols were in action, one firing fifteen recovered rounds and one firing nine. Mastriano concluded a second American soldier, Pvt. Percy Beardsley, unnoticed by York amid the noise and violence, was also firing a Colt at the charging Germans. Beardsley later signed an affidavit testifying to York's courage. He made no mention of himself.

CHAPTER ELEVEN

THE SIXTY-FOURTH
OR SIXTY-FIFTH VOYAGE

Time was running out and there was much to do, so John Browning was not going duck hunting.

That was a surprise to Charles G. Adney, a friend, farmer-and-shooting partner. He had stopped by Browning's second-floor shop on a late summer afternoon following the end of World War I, and as he departed observed they'd be meeting again soon for the start of waterfowl season.

For years Browning marked the date by meeting friends and family at a camp north of Ogden, where the Bear River flowed into the upper edge of the Great Salt Lake. Adney worked land in the river valley and usually joined Browning at the visually striking spot, ringed by distant mountains above blue water. Adney's reminder to Browning was a mere parting politeness, a simple social formality. Not so Browning's response.

"He promptly said no," Adney later wrote. "He was not going down this fall, to which I expressed not only surprise but also a strong belief in the existence of a real need for his taking a holiday, for I knew he dearly loved to shoot and over a period of years made the duck shooting a holiday."

Browning said that was not happening this season, and likely wasn't happening the following year, either. As Browning explained, "He had unfinished work well underway which could not be interrupted." Adney must have protested, because Browning laid down his tools and offered a glimpse of his inner life. "Only an ardent inventor could understand his situation," he said, for the urge driving his work lay outside the ordinary parameters of decision-making. "If he had an arch-enemy on whom he could invoke the most dire calamity, the worst that he could afflict him with would be to make of him an ardent inventor," said Browning. There were also the infirmities of age. "He had reached a point in his life where he got no enjoyment from indulgences which formerly were dear to him."[1]

By way of example Browning offered an anecdote. Rachel and his children had "put forth strenuous effort to interrupt his work sufficiently to get him out to an evening entertainment at home or at the theater." Tickets were booked for a three-act play, specifically in box seats to place him in full view of the audience and actors. So exposed, the idea was he wouldn't drift off into his mental workshop. Perhaps he'd actually have fun.

"He said that the curtain went up and he enjoyed the opening features and felt that his resolution to lay aside his shop work long enough to indulge in the play was being accomplished and realized." Or so he thought until Rachel pulled at his elbow at the end of the first act and asked, "John, why don't you applaud?" Browning looked about puzzled. The inventor had zoned out. "He didn't know just why they were applauding. He was back in the shop."

"Now you probably can understand why I will be unable to go down to the club and shoot ducks this fall," Browning told his friend.

By Browning's reckoning he'd wasted nearly a decade of his early life. Subsequent successes failed to squelch his regret at spending his late teens and early twenties muddling along in his father's workshop, doing rote repairs, when he could've been inventing. So although Browning was sixty-five in 1920, he threw himself into six distinct projects—at *least*—each with its own set of mechanical challenges.

His greatest satisfaction was found conceiving a new shotgun.

It wasn't a tool, like his pump-action guns or the A5 autoloader, but an instrument for an expert, in design and function an expression of art produced in steel and wood. He chose an "over-under" gun with two barrels stacked vertically, one above the other. Compared to the venerable side-by-side double-barreled shotgun, it would be better balanced and easier to handle and aim. Drawing on his lifetime of shooting experience, Browning told his friend Gus Becker that it would be designed around the spot on the "shooting plane"—a metal rib atop the barrel—that Browning had concluded was the intersection between gun and target where the shooter's eye naturally settled.

There was also a very practical reason for a two-round gun. Autoloading shotguns were still resented by many wildfowl hunters as unsporting tools for "game hogs," and there were periodic attempts in various states to forbid their use.[2] Browning figured his over-under gun offered a source of income if the worst ever came to pass.

For FN this highly crafted shotgun, called the Superposed, wasn't the product it needed or wanted as it tried to rebuild factories torn apart by the war. The company was extraordinarily short of cash, so much so that John and Matt for a time considered loaning FN their own money. What the company wanted was a high-volume product suited to mass production, and so they pressed Browning to design a new handgun for the French Army. Drawing on their experience in World War I, the French sought a semiautomatic pistol using a 9mm cartridge and holding twice the seven rounds of existing FN firearms, and with a slanted grip like the Luger. That would require a longer grip to hold cartridges stacked in two parallel rows. Browning didn't think much of the idea. In a 1920 letter to Val he said: "A double row in mag . . . is very difficult" and was likely to cause jams. "I am inclined to think single row is better [*sic*]." He was more emphatic in a January 26, 1921, letter sent directly to FN, where he seems to reject a 15-round magazine outright, declaring: "Fifteen cartridges in the magazine, especially such cartridges as the 9mm Luger, is almost an impossibility."[3] Browning would soon be proven wrong by an FN engineer, Dieudonne Saive, who converted the earlier Browning gun, the Colt 1903, to handle a "double-stack" 9mm magazine, though without the slanted grip. Saive sent it off to Ogden for Browning's inspection, who began work on what eventually become the best-selling handgun ever made by FN, the Browning Hi-Power. After its introduction in 1935, the final design completed by Saive, it was adopted as the standard side arm by a multitude of European armies and police departments and remained in production until 2017, with more than 1.5 million sold.

In that 1921 letter, Browning was more prescient on the future of another military firearm he had designed, a light, quick-firing automatic rifle much different from his BAR or the heavy, long-range bolt-action rifle that was the standard infantry weapon worldwide.

"I have, as you know, been working on an automatic rifle using what might be termed pistol cartridges. We are finishing one of these rifles and it works entirely satisfactorily." It emptied a magazine of thirty-three cartridges in 2.3 seconds, and Browning wrote: "This class of gun, I am satisfied, is the coming military arm." He dismissed FN's military customers who wanted a smaller, handgun-like weapon as a complementary arm to the bolt-action rifle, rather than a replacement. "I think the military authorities calling for what they term a pistol are off on the wrong foot as they generally are. . . . The advantages are so plainly in favor of a light rifle and the arming of part of the troops with this arm and nothing else that it seems too bad to be fooling with some kind of makeshift which is neither one thing nor the other."[4] A patent for that gun was filed in 1923, though the prototype is now lost. What Browning designed resembles an "assault" rifle, though it would be some forty years before the American military acted on the concept and adopted what became the M-16.

His letters included long-distance advice to Val, who was in Liège as FN struggled to resume manufacture of a Browning .22-caliber pump-action rifle. In more than two dozen letters written in 1920 and 1921 Browning filled three or four pages with his hard-to-decipher scribble, offering advice on topics ranging from firearm design to FN royalties to family investments. He pondered crop reports and rejected a plan to invest in hotels. He sometimes sketched out parts and frequently jumped from subject to subject—veering from describing a spring or ejector in the .22 rifle to problems with the magazine for a version of the BAR for the British Army—and often closed his letters with fatherly advice. He ended one very technical letter in February 1920 with the remark: "Look strictly after business son and do all the good you can while away with love Daddy."[5]

Another letter reflected on the drawbacks of fame and fortune, as he asked Val to make amends to an unhappy acquaintance in Belgium: "Smooth over my not writing as well as you can tell him I am away a lot. He wanted me to use my influence with the FN to get him something better in the way of a [unintelligible]. He like a good many others takes advantage of friendship to lay down on you." He closes by advising Val to consider business propositions "from all angles . . . and do what you can to make your life profitable. Oh well, with love Daddy."

A letter written on May 1, 1920, includes a rare mention of politics: "May Day and looks like there may be good many broken heads before the day is gone. Looks like they are going to buy the soldiers vote by levying another tax." Organized labor had promised demonstrations amid warnings that Soviet Russia was fomenting international revolution, while Congress was debating a bonus for American war veterans. Thousands of troops and police were called out across the country, and while 360 people were arrested in Chicago, the day passed relatively peacefully.

In Liège, Val was negotiating an extension of royalty payments from FN, as the Brownings sought to make up for revenue lost during the war years. It placed Val on the receiving end of letters from both his father and Uncle Matt. "You must learn to trade and don't just accept what they offer," his father wrote. "The FN should extend them or in other words should pay at least five years longer than life of patents. We made contracts expecting them to be profitable 20 years not 14 or 15. . . . Bring it right up to them and everything else that is to our interest."

In a following letter he wrote: "I realize you are in rather difficult position over there with no one to consult" but went on to say: "I'm afraid you are giving them too much . . . in order to keep goodwill."

Matt chimed in on a major sticking point, whether royalty payments would be made in the gold francs as agreed to in the original 1887 contract, or in paper money as FN sought. Matt rejected any change and warned Val: "I fancy I can see that they are working you. You must remember that while they act like children in a great many ways they are as shrewd as anyone and working for their own interests every minute."

Most of Browning's letters are written on Hartford's Heublein Hotel stationery, where he spent the spring and summer of 1920 working with Colt to complete the new .50-caliber machine gun. It was proving difficult to make combat ready but held promise as a weapon of war. Indeed, it became the most widely used machine gun in the world and is still deployed by the U.S. Army and some one hundred other nations.

The original impetus for the design dated to World War I and the British deployment of a new motorized armored vehicle shaped like a parallelogram with treads and armed with machine guns and cannon. It was called a tank, the code name used during development. Once Allied tanks were deployed, the Germans rushed out an oversized rifle that fired a cartridge approaching a small cannon shell in size. Its heavy two-ounce bullet sped down the barrel at three times the speed of sound and was capable of penetrating an inch of steel armor. A predictable arms race ensued as Pershing ordered up an American anti-armor round, but fired by a machine gun, not a single-shot rifle. The task fell to Browning, Winchester, and Colt.

In his five-volume history of the machine gun, retired U.S. Marine Corps colonel George Chinn wrote that Browning was already mulling upgrades to his .30-caliber machine gun when Pershing's specifications arrived. The general demanded a bullet five times heavier and moving at 2,700 feet per second, which meant the new cartridge and Browning's new gun had to generate—and withstand—five times more explosive energy than the existing .30-caliber rounds. Browning used the .30-caliber gun design as his starting point but needed months to produce a larger prototype, while at the same time helping Winchester design the first version of a .50-caliber cartridge and its half-inch-diameter bullet.

By the fall of 1918 Browning assembled a single gun with parts built to his design by Colt, while Winchester constructed six other prototypes. For the first test on October 15, 1918, Browning fired 870 rounds in bursts of 100 to 250 rounds, proving that the basic mechanism was sound but confirming a host of challenges remained. Recoil from the .50-caliber cartridge made it "practically impossible" to hold the barrel level. And the laughably brief 870-round test proved nothing about the gun's reliability. Nevertheless, with the war expected to continue through 1919 the Ordnance Department immediately put in an order of ten thousand, which was immediately canceled when peace was declared a month later.

Postwar development of the gun continued, though at a much-reduced pace and with a much smaller budget. Browning's surviving letters provide a glimpse of his work with Colt engineer Fred Moore, to whom Browning confided his private worries about Val's dealings with executives at FN and Colt. Those managers found Val demanding and intransigent compared to his father and uncle, while Val bridled at what he considered those same executives' condescension.

"Expect to leave next week for the East Coast to discuss the 50 cal gun," John wrote Val in March 1920. Browning and Moore were testing examples of .50-caliber ammunition produced by the government's Frankford Arsenal in Philadelphia and found that cartridge posed challenges never faced with the .30-caliber gun. "Work on the 50 caliber going along rather slow," Browning wrote on April 23. "I am not satisfied with the new cartridge and afraid it will kick the gun around so it will have no accuracy. You can about figure what a [indecipherable] gun will do with cartridge having five times the energy of the US govt. The cartridge we have jumps too much and new one will be 50% worse."

Browning discovered firing pins were prone to breakage, as was the "accelerator," which resembled a crooked finger and added extra thrust to the recoil so the gun's moving parts interacted in an exact, repeatable cadence. The barrel and the bolt reciprocated 500 times a minute, so an error could be catastrophic. "They broke two or three accelerators, they should be made stronger as shown above," Browning wrote, and at the top of the letter drew a small sketch of the redesigned part.

On May 30 a pleased Browning announced he'd solved the recoil problem by adding what he called a buffer, a small, oil-filled shock absorber that controlled the rate of fire and moderated the recoil. It turned the machine gun from a barely controllable beast into a more practical, accurate weapon. "50 Cal is coming along. I have been shooting with new buffer which reduces the speed from about 650 to 450 and easy on everything." As usual, he told Val to keep watch for business opportunities. "See if there is any 50 caliber talk over there how about the 22. Be alert son and don't let anything get by you. Nice and warm here now."

Work on the gun was slowed by the lack of government urgency and money as well as Browning's visits to Liège and trips home to Ogden. Two versions of the gun were under construction, a water-cooled weapon for ground troops and an air-cooled model for the Army Air Corps. A year later, in June 1921, Browning wrote he was ready to test a revised version of the buffer: "But they have no cartridges yet expecting 8000 shipped from Frankfort about a month ago and are lost somewhere, tough luck?" He also completed revisions to the air-cooled prototype. "Shipped the aircraft gun yesterday to Dayton and it sure works fine here I made quite a number of changes that made it better." The latest version of the .50-caliber machine gun was adopted as the government's Model 1921, but fewer than one hundred were purchased as the Army, Navy, and Air Corps struggled to adapt to the powerful and still awkward-to-use weapon. The recoil remained too great for the fragile fighter aircraft of that era, and the antitank role originally envisioned was already rendered moot by a simple countermeasure—thicker armor.

It wasn't until 1923 that the government officially adopted the first of what would be many variations of the .50-caliber round. It was 5.45 inches long and fired a steel-core bullet that weighed 1.8 ounces. It had a horizontal range of about four miles, though the effective range was less than half that.

The sluggish pace of work allowed Browning time for his other projects. The Army asked him to take over design work on a .37mm automatic cannon and he completed a preliminary prototype of the new 9mm pistol for the French Army. Colt retained the rights to his 1911 design, so Browning came up with a new version that literally eliminated a weak link. On the 1911 the barrel was tilted down on recoil by a swinging link, which could break under heavy use. His new design replaced it with a solid piece of machined steel pushed down, technically "cammed down," by a steel lug in the frame. It was nearly impervious to wear and used in the enormously successful FN Hi-Power. Nevertheless, the French reaction was so-so. Browning's gun was declared the best of all designs submitted but was rejected as too large and too heavy.

Browning's reaction is unknown, but it can be safely stated that he cared little, because on the afternoon of Monday, April 9, 1923, the Browning family's good fortune—affluence, success, respect, and no hint of scandal—came to an abrupt end.

Ten years earlier Browning's daughter Elsie, then twenty-three, married an Ogden man, Benjamin Franklin Ballantyne, a half first cousin of Browning's long ago companion in missionary work.[6] If it was ever a happy marriage it wasn't so for long, and resulted in a tragedy for both families. When Ballantyne wasn't entreating his in-laws for financial help he was reviling them for their condescension. When John Browning paid the newlyweds' past-due furniture store bill from his personal checking account

Ballantyne was infuriated. He wanted to hide his father-in-law's charity by routing it through his own bank account. Ballantyne berated Elise, declaring that she'd allowed her father to "humiliate" her husband.

In 1915 the couple moved to Florida, where Browning had purchased a half interest in a grapefruit farm—one letter suggests it was worth $2 million—and on his arrival Ballantyne allegedly attacked the co-owner's wife. Browning, often an absent or distant father when his offspring were children, now set aside his work and arrived in Florida to take his daughter home to Ogden. Some weeks later Ballantyne turned up at the family home in Utah, demanded Elise leave with him, and threatened that "if anybody interferes I'll kill them."[7]

The couple spent the next eight years moving erratically from town to town as Ballantyne moved from job to job, sometimes threatening suicide if Elsie's father didn't cover his debts. Soon he was drinking heavily. By 1923 the couple were living in Salt Lake City and Ballantyne had a job as a teller at the Utah State National Bank, employment he considered beneath him as a member of the Browning family. "I'm tired of wasting my life as a bank clerk when the Brownings could place me in a position at a good fat salary," he reportedly said. When Elise refused to ask her father for more financial help Ballantyne called her a "dirty black skunk."

The couple now had three children ranging from an infant to a nine-year-old, but Ballantyne's behavior had become so intolerable that, with her family's agreement, Elsie began divorce proceedings. Ballantyne said he wanted a cash payment "to go away," so on a Sunday afternoon in April 1923 John Browning, his wife, Rachel, son Jack, brother Matt, and a family attorney, William H. Reeder, met to develop a plan to bring Elsie home to Ogden from Salt Lake City.

The next day Jack and Marriner Browning, Matt's son, to whom Elsie was particularly close, climbed into a car with the family attorney and made the thirty-six-mile drive south. They arrived to find Ballantyne drunk and initially regretful. He conceded he was acting badly and asked the visitors to empty a bottle of liquor down the sink. He acquiesced to Elsie's departure with the children, but once she was in the car he suddenly ran out, pulled open the automobile door, and ordered her back inside the house. She obeyed. He followed her up the walk, pushed her to move faster, pushed Jack out of the way, and unsuccessfully insisted the two Browning men remain outside.

Ballantyne, Elsie, Jack, and Marriner all entered the house. Testimony was that Ballantyne rushed into the library, where a revolver lay on a bookcase. Ballantyne picked it up and Jack and Marriner yelled at him to put it down, but Ballantyne swung the barrel toward Jack. "The next instant Marriner fired a shot," according to Reeder, the attorney.

Ballantyne fell. The bullet perforated his windpipe and nicked the left jugular vein. He was rushed to a hospital, where he lingered into the evening, long enough for police to arrive with a stenographer and take down his version of events, which was that while he'd been drinking since morning, he never picked up a gun. He didn't know which of the two Brownings shot him. Among his last words were: "They tried to break up my home."

Jack and Marriner were arrested, jailed, and charged with second-degree murder. The sad, titillating story became more so when it was disclosed that Elsie wouldn't attend her husband's funeral and would testify for the defense. Both Brownings were released after their fathers put up a $25,000 bond.

"You have no doubt seen through the paper that our boy killed a man," Matt wrote to a friend in Los Angeles, "and as most of the newspaper accounts were calculated to give a wrong impression of what really happened thought I would write you so that our friends in Ocean Park would know the shooting was done entirely in self defense, it being purely a question of speed as to who got shot." To his sister Mary, Matt wrote that "the boys had to do what they did . . . it will come out all right in the end."[8]

Their plea of self-defense, however, became more problematic to the public when the Salt Lake City prosecutor filed new charges of first-degree murder, based on Ballantyne's deathbed testimony that he was unarmed when Marriner shot him. There was also the question of why both Browning men arrived at the home armed. Marriner explained his practice was to always carry his uncle's tiny pocket pistol, though for the trip to Salt Lake City his worried father, Matt, asked him to carry a larger, more powerful, and more accurate .380-caliber Colt.

The two men were scheduled for arraignment on the new charge when another tragedy intervened. At four o'clock in the afternoon of June 29 Matt Browning arrived at his attorney's office in downtown Ogden. He'd driven down from the family's vacation home in Bear Lake, Idaho, where he'd gone in an unsuccessful attempt to relax with his wife, Mary, and two daughters. Matt walked in, asked for a place to rest, sat down on a chair, and toppled to the floor. Marriner was nearby. They'd planned a game of golf that afternoon, and so he arrived in time to hear Matt speak his name before dying. An autopsy cited heart disease as the cause of death.

Mourners overflowed the hall and spilled out into the street, honoring Matt's term as mayor, his years presiding over the school board, and, as the local newspapers put it, his success as a "capitalist" investing in coal, water, ranching, and banking. Retail stores closed when his funeral cortege passed. The family's eulogy was given by Thomas Browning, a son of patriarch Jonathan Browning's third wife. Thomas pointed out that Browning Bros. was the fruit of two talents, John and Matt, and offered them up as examples to the youngest generation of Brownings. "When it came to the proposition of business, never in my life do I remember one of these boys telling me anything that was not absolutely true," Thomas Browning said. "Not that they were perfect men. No not by any means. They had just as many faults as you and I and all of us, but this is one of the things that makes my heart proud."[9]

In the months after the shooting and his brother's funeral and before the murder trial, John decamped to Hartford to work on changes to the BAR and improvements to the .50-caliber machine gun. The emotional fallout inside his family followed him there through letters from his wife. To Marriner, the older Browning offered awkward counsel as his nephew weathered his father's death and awaited his own trial.

"Just heard through your aunt Rachel that you are not well and I am very sorry," he wrote. "As our health is the main thing in life thought I would advise you to take a vacation and go away, California or southern Utah. You may think you can't but you can. Your daddy is gone and no amount of worry is any good so try to get to thinking that way. Val is here now. We are trying to get things in shape so he can go back in about two weeks. Better take my advice son and try and think of something else and get a change. With love uncle John."[10]

Browning returned to Utah for the November trial but appeared at the Salt Lake City courthouse only once, to be chased away by attention from the press and public. The spectacle peaked in the third week when Elsie testified. Over the objections of the prosecutor, the judge allowed her to tell the all-male jury about her history with Ben, so she recounted a litany of unhappy moments, including her husband's threat to commit suicide if John Browning didn't pay for the purchase of a horse and buggy when Ben and Elsie already had an automobile. A monthly subsidy of $300 to $400 didn't prevent Ballantyne from cursing the inventor and his eldest son.

By 1922 Ballantyne was drinking regularly and at Thanksgiving dinner declared, "What have I got to be thankful for," and threw his plate of food on the floor. "All the rest of the day he kept on drinking and continuously talking in a loud voice, calling me a coward and sometimes abusing my family, my father and brother. . . . He abused daddy, saying he hadn't treated him fair and never given him a chance. . . . He said a young man had never been known to get anywhere without a pull. I contended that any man with brains could get along without pull but he didn't agree with that. He said my duty as the daughter of a wealthy man was to see that he was put in a good position at a good fat salary." Once she escaped him by sleeping in the basement coal bin, and on another evening he ripped the sleeve of her dressing gown and was so drunk Ballantyne's brother, William, had to put him to bed.

When he ordered her out of the car and back into the house Elsie called on Jack to follow her inside despite Ballantyne's objection. Jack replied, "Elsie wants me to go in and I'm going," Elsie testified. "Then Ben pushed me through the door and said, 'I'll kill the whole bunch.' I saw him rush into the library and I put hands to my head and I said, 'Oh, he'll kill us all.' I must've screamed loudly, for Marriner heard and rushed past me. I remember hearing a shot and I think I said, 'He has killed Jack.'"

Jack took the stand and said he was in the hallway at the entrance to the library and saw Ballantyne raise a revolver. He grabbed at his own gun when a shot came from over his right shoulder. Marriner had fired once, and Ballantyne fell to the floor.

Marriner testified next. "Ben was whirling with a gun in his hand and as I saw him I reached for my gun and yelled, 'Drop it, Ben, drop it.' He didn't stop so I fired . . . to keep Ben from shooting Jack." Prosecutors argued that Ben's "dying declaration"—a medieval English concept that a person about to die has little incentive to lie—that he didn't pick up a gun demanded a guilty verdict. After four weeks of testimony the case went to the jurors at 5:00 p.m. on the evening of December 8. An hour later the twelve men announced they had a verdict, returned to the courtroom, and declared Jack and Matt not guilty. Later that evening, Jack Browning was tracked down at a local hotel and uttered his only public reaction: "It was a just trial and a just verdict."

The bitter events of 1923 reverberated through John Browning's life. A memo in FN's archives reports on a meeting between a Colt vice president, Frank Nichols, and the inventor the following spring. "John Browning is very transformed following the death of his brother Matthew and by the anguish he has had when his two sons [sic] were imprisoned." The FN memo is unsigned but was almost certainly written by Gustave Joassart, then

FN's managing director. Joassart adds: "The Browning family lost its commercial head with the death of Matthew Browning," and that John didn't step in to fill Matt's role. "He is too occupied with his inventions."[11]

Indeed, Browning's inventing wasn't slowed by the death of his brother or the scandal of the trial. He could do nothing about the former and little about the latter. His son was forty-four; his nephew Marriner was thirty-three; they were grown men with families. Between the shooting in April 1923 through December of that year John filed eight patents, beginning with the prototype of what became the FN Hi-Power pistol, followed in July with a thirty-page patent for the .50-caliber machine gun, followed in October with a seventeen-page patent for his over-under shotgun, ending in December with a forty-eight-page patent for a 37mm aircraft cannon developed at the government's request. Even though Colt employees and its longtime engineer and patent attorney, Carl Ehbert, prepared the machine-gun and cannon paperwork, each filing represented hours of detailed work by Browning. In 1924 another eight patents were filed, including an updated Superposed shotgun patent, a revision to the BAR, and updates to the 37mm cannon. Three more patents were filed in 1925, for a cartridge-feeding device for the 37mm, a rotary drum magazine for aircraft-mounted machine guns, and an improved machine-gun water jacket design. The final patent was for an aircraft machine-gun magazine. The idea was to package the ammunition belts in a removable magazine to be replaced after each mission. The concept was sound, but Browning's design verges on crude, looking more like a wooden shoeshine box than the component of a modern weapon.

Browning was finally old. His photographs on two separate Belgian residency permits offer a stark illustration. One dated May 15, 1922, is attached to the two-page application—the standard form that required the names of children, parents, and spouse—and shows him at sixty-seven, looking vibrant and healthy. His face is fleshy but not fat, in the black-and-white photo he appears to have a ruddy complexion, and any health problems are not apparent. The best evidence of his roots in the prior century is his old-fashioned wingtip collar.

The other photograph is dated December 28, 1925, when he filled out the same application and attached a photograph that is unlike any previous image. In this photograph Browning has an expression, and it's not a happy one. He wears a modern shirt and tie, but the thin, lined face with loose skin glares angrily at the camera. It's a photograph of an aged and unhappy man.[12]

The reasons likely extended beyond the miserable events of 1923. Val's day-to-day management of technical and business relations with FN was proving problematic. Surviving FN memos— much paperwork was lost in two wars—show that FN and Colt executives considered Val's demands to be both excessive and inconsistent. Val dashed off angry letters and from FN's perspective made ill-considered demands, and then later apologized. At one point Val threatened to "offer his [Browning's] inventions elsewhere," until FN pointed out that it had rights to the "Browning" name in Europe and that John and Matt had signed those binding contracts. Colt had similar problems, and at one point Nichols, the Colt vice president, told his counterpart at FN that thanks to Val's father "I did not have to worry about Val's attitude. He added he had often seen his father scold him for occurrences like this and that he was convinced that his father would not follow him in a similar attitude."

A June 1924 FN memo, titled "generalities on the Brownings" states that the younger members of the family, presumably Val and Marriner, were considered to lack business acumen. Nichols, the Colt vice president, told FN that John Browning "believes them to be excessively rich, but he does not judge the commercial skill to be very good.

"Colt considers as we do that Val is not of the same essence as his father. One doesn't find him sincere. Nichols remembers that John Browning said several times to Mr. Moore, with whom he is very close, that he was worried Val didn't write, didn't come back." The phrase is not explained, and the memo ends with advice to recipients in Liège: "Briefly, one must be prudent."

The memo closes with Nichols telling his FN counterparts that "contrary to what we think," Browning will make "at least one more trip to Belgium."[13]

He made two more trips. In October 1925, Browning left Ogden to resume work on the 37mm cannon in Hartford, and then departed to Belgium, arriving on December 28, where he spent the next six months living with his son Val and wife, Anne. "Daddy is out for his morning walk," Val wrote in a letter to his brother Jack in March, providing a unique glimpse of Browning in the eighth decade of his life. "Anne puts an orange or two in his pocket and he goes up to his little observation point and eats it, or them (yesterday he ate three.) He seems to feel tip top, sleeps well most of the time and eats if anything too much. He particularly likes the soup, and eats two steaming plates at the factory at noon and then two plates here at night. He generally fills his glass about half up with beer at supper and then keeps taking a little more from time to time as the meal progresses. I give him wine sometimes and he thinks it makes him sleep. One morning about two weeks ago he came up to breakfast and said he had never slept as well before in his life—slept right on through and didn't even have to get up to make water all over the bathroom floor. I pulled him in from the factory around 4 o'clock every day before his mind 'gets to wool gathering.' I think his stay here is, perhaps, doing more good than harm."[14]

Relations between Val and FN were also improving. After a blowup with FN over production of the Superposed shotgun, Val was abashed, and "he declared spontaneously to Mr. Nichols that he had acted too quickly and that he had let himself go with a moment of anger. . . . He regretted the letter that he had written us" according to an FN document likely authored by Joassart.[15]

While Browning was in Belgium, Rachel spent the winter of 1926 in Pasadena with her recently married daughter, Monida. They returned to Ogden in June and Browning arrived home the first week in August, after a stop in Hartford. In September Browning's youngest daughter, Elizabeth, visited Ogden with her

newborn son, Stuart S. MacLeod, and there was a round of dinners and family gatherings as Browning prepared for his second
trip to Liège that year. For the first time ever he was accompanied
by Rachel, his wife. It is often reported that this was Browning's
sixty-first transatlantic voyage, but that calculation does not include the three, or likely four, trips he took between 1897, when
he arrived with his pistol, and 1902, when he left Winchester with
his shotgun for what has been incorrectly called his first voyage.

In that autumn of 1926, on the day before his departure, John,
Rachel, and their children gathered on the Brownings' wide
porch. It was a warm fall day, and Browning turned to his wife
and used a pet name. "Pretty thing," he said, "when we board the
ship people in the crowd will whisper, that old chap must be rich
to have such a young wife!" Conversation turned to family history
and Browning reflected on how he lived at the best time and
place for a gunmaker, an ideal moment for the confluence of his
imagination and technology. By that day Browning's career had
encompassed nearly half a century. He'd been lucky with good
health and lucky with his wife, "Mama to straighten my tie and
make me change my shirt as often as she could" is how Jack wrote
it. "Those who listened that day remembered; they later felt that
John . . . had been saying goodbye to his mountains, to the locust
that shaded the shop of many memories, to a rich and bountiful
life, that he had been intuitively if unconsciously informed."

Once in Liège and ensconced in their son's apartment at
20 Rue Dartois, a multistory building of brick and stone near the
train station, Rachel, sixty-six, found the city difficult to navigate
as compared to Ogden. "Daddy and I went out for a walk this
morning he made me lead the way home I had to stand and look
up and down to see which way to go finally I got him home safely,"
she wrote to a daughter in Ogden. "The roads are so crooked,"
Rachel wrote, "I don't venture out alone." There was a hint of
reproach in the letter as she described Val and his wife Anne's
high-flying social life: "Val and Anne were going out to dinner
at 8 o'clock to the club and didn't get home until this morning. Anne got up and gave the baby her bath at nine o'clock

then went back to bed. They are still sleeping. Nearly 12 o'clock. Daddy and I may have to eat our dinner alone."

On Thursday, November 25, 1926, John and Rachel celebrated Thanksgiving with Val, Anne, and their two infant children, John Val and Carol. The next morning Val drove his father to the FN factory, where they walked up a few stairs and down a short hallway to Val's first-floor office. Its two windows overlooked a swath of green that led to a narrow street, with private homes on the other side. John Browning walked out toward the manufacturing floor but returned a few minutes later complaining of chest pains. Val called for the factory doctor, while his father "strode to and fro swinging his arms back and forth" attempting to alleviate the pain. He then laid himself down. The doctor arrived, "stimulants were administered"—family members say the physician gave Browning an injection—and the doctor "massaged his body." After a moment Browning looked up at Val and said, "Son, I wouldn't be surprised if I am dying," and he did so a few moments later.

The next day Browning's body lay in state in the FN boardroom, a few feet from the office where he'd died. The room's ornate woodwork was covered by dark hangings and flowers surrounded the casket as FN employees paid homage to the man whose inventions saved the company and created their jobs.

Browning's remains were returned to America via ocean liner on December 7, 1926. Rachel, Val, and Jack traveled along and all disembarked in New York City. They were met by a uniformed honor guard from the Army Ordnance Department who escorted the casket to Grand Central Station and a train bound for Ogden. Services were held on Sunday, December 12, amid a heavy snowstorm that gave the day an eerie solemnity. A funeral cortege carried Browning's body from his home and across town to the Latter-day Saints tabernacle, filled to overflowing. A string quartet played the "Largo from Hayden." Eulogies included an emotional tribute by shooting friend Gus Becker, whose remarks, intentionally or not, referenced the powerful antiwar and anti-firearm movement that swept the country after the horrendous casualties of World War I. "The greatest inventor of firearms for all the ages, he was withal as gentle and peace loving a man as the world has ever known," Becker said.

A family friend and Treasury Department official, James H. Anderson, represented the federal government and laid out a practical and philosophic rationale for the nation to celebrate Browning and his inventions. "As Americans we detest war," he said, insisting the nation was forced to arms by "the human self-ishness and ambition of others." Americans lionized the "man behind the gun," he said, but equally important was the man who invented the gun. "Unarmed we would have been held in bondage. Poorly armed we would have been brought into captivity. Well-armed with Browning devices . . . God gave us victory and we remained free."

In 1926 that sentiment was both eloquent and at that moment an exaggeration. With the exception of his 1911 pistol, Browning's inventions saw little use in World War I, but Anderson was prescient and correctly described the nation's, and the world's, future debt to the inventor.

The deaths of Matt and John added some facts to public speculation about the family's wealth. Over the years various newspapers theorized that between FN, Colt, and Remington the Brownings were earning $1 million a year in royalties, a stupendous sum in the early twentieth century. That would have been true during World War I, had the brothers not signed away their rights, but otherwise it appears an exaggeration. Details, however, remain difficult to ascertain. The documents that do exist are sometimes incomplete and show that royalty payments from FN and Colt were regularly renegotiated. Some payments also expired at the expiration of Browning's patents, while other payments continued for more than a decade. The significant earnings from Matt's business investments, typically shared by the brothers, are also largely a matter of speculation.

After World War I the Brownings filed an unsuccessful reparations claim against the German government for profits lost by the occupation. Between 1907 and 1913, that document states, their FN royalties averaged $40,744 year, or about $1 million in today's currency, a respectable but not awe-inspiring sum. They also would've earned another $47,680 during those years had Remington been able to sell FN shotguns under the company name.

Another glimpse of the family's wealth came when inheritance taxes were paid. In 1924 Matt left an estate appraised at $446,807—about $7.3 million in current dollars. The lengthy state inheritance filing showed him to be a conservative investor, as $200,197 was held in cash at his death. In his wallet was $315. There was also a claim by the IRS for $150,000 in income taxes.

Tax appraisals also required a limited listing of personal effects, which were few. John left behind a six-cylinder Overland auto valued at $600, a .22 target pistol worth $10, two versions of his autoloading shotgun, one twenty years old made by Remington valued at $100 and a FN version thirty years old valued at $25, which today would be worth a small fortune to a collector. There was also a .22 autoloading rifle worth $10. Reported as valueless were an old gold watch, one dress suit, two business suits, and an overcoat. His total estate was appraised at $369,452, or about $5.4 million in current dollars. Previous distributions by John and Matt to their children aren't reflected in those tax filings.[16]

Browning was gone, but not his inventions.

CHAPTER TWELVE

TWENTY THOUSAND FEET HIGH

Five days after his twentieth birthday Roland Beamont stood his fighter plane on its wing tip and dove toward a fleet of German planes five thousand feet below him. As his single-engine Hurricane closed on the cluster of small dots they resolved into seventy to eighty enemy bombers, flying north over the English Channel. Using a tactic that had kept him alive over the beaches of Dunkirk two months earlier, Beamont sought out a single target. He'd make a swift pass and fire his wing-mounted machine guns, followed by a steep dive away. Lingering amid a confused jumble of aircraft was a sure way to get shot down.

So on the afternoon of August 15, 1940, as the Battle of Britain entered its most deadly phase, Beamont closed in on a Dornier 17, a narrow twin-engine bomber nicknamed the "flying pencil." His Hurricane jigged up and down in the turbulent airflow as Beamont manipulated the throttle and control stick. At point-blank range he pressed the red "gun button." Eight Browning machine guns, mounted four on a wing, shuddered as they fired a combined 152 rounds a second. He kept his thumb on the button and within seconds saw the Dornier fall out of formation. Beamont pointed the Hurricane's nose toward the ground and advanced the throttle.[1]

A few thousand feet later he spotted a German ME 109 fighter. "I got onto his tail, fired a long burst," Beamont said, though "long" was a relative term, as the Hurricane carried ammunition for only sixteen seconds of continuous fire. "He slowed up and then he rolled very violently up to the right. As he came out of his roll I was back on his tail close in for another burst, when I could see that his undercarriage was coming down."

By then the two aircraft were over land and only twelve hundred feet above the Dorset countryside. The ME 109 slipped sideways and descended. "I thought either he's going to go in or he's actually aiming for a forced landing." It was a landing. The cockpit flew open and the pilot jumped out, ran a short distance, threw himself onto the ground, and lay still as a puzzled Beamont circled low overhead. Then the German rose, retrieved an item from the cockpit, and walked off to be captured by the British Home Guard.

A day or two later a soldier arrived at Beamont's air base carrying a German Luger pistol and a message. The ME 109 pilot had expected Beamont to swoop in and turn his eight Brownings on the defenseless, ground-bound Nazi, so the pistol was a gift, a thank-you to Beamont for letting his enemy live.

Beamont was nonplussed. "Wasn't a thing that would've occurred to me to do."

Between July 10 and October 31 of 1940, the Royal Air Force destroyed 1,733 German aircraft and won the Battle of Britain. The cost was 1,023 fighters and 510 pilots.[2] The Nazis' defeat was thanks to the Hurricane and Spitfire fighters, their pilots, and the British foresight to have constructed a primitive but effective early-warning radar system. Another factor was largely unremarked on by anyone but the British—the RAF used John Moses Browning's machine guns.

"During the crucial period of the war when we stood alone and were outnumbered in the air, the RAF's fighter armament was superior to the German," wrote Graham F. Wallace, who served in and authored a history of the Air Ministry's armaments work. "There is little point in a pilot, however good he or his aircraft, getting an enemy in his sights if, when he presses the firing button, the gun jams or the ammunition proves ineffective. In the last analysis a fighter is only as good as its guns."[3]

World War I fighters, built of cloth and wood, carried only two guns that were mounted on the fuselage within arm's reach of the pilot. Despite the advent of aluminum-skinned aircraft in the late 1920s and early 1930s, RAF doctrine held that two or four guns remained sufficient. But in 1934 a group of young officers successfully argued that four guns were completely inadequate, rejected a compromise of six guns, and insisted on eight machine guns. The unprecedented number of guns was needed because the RAF still used the British Army's .303 rifle cartridge, a low-velocity round, underpowered for air-to-air combat. So, a three-second burst from eight .303 Browning machine guns firing 1,100 rounds a minute compensated for that by dispatching 440 lead projectiles toward the enemy—adequate enough, as Beamont demonstrated.

With the number of guns settled, the RAF convened trials to select a weapon from among five contenders, including the Browning, adapted by the armaments works to fire the British cartridge. The Browning's main competition was a British-designed Vickers gun already in service. The Browning was chosen, largely because of its proven reliability. Wing-mounted guns made it impossible for the pilot to reach out and clear a jam, and Brownings rarely jammed. They also fired more rounds per minute than the Vickers. In 1940 those decisions gave the RAF's Hurricanes and Spitfires a short-lived edge over the Luftwaffe.

"It became increasingly apparent that the Germans were badly shaken by the firepower of our fighters,"[4] recalled RAF group captain J. A. Kent. For a very brief window, only a few months, the British fighters outgunned German fighters armed with two machine guns and an inadequate aerial cannon. The .303 Brownings also proved capable of slicing through the skin of German bombers. Then the Me 109 was rearmed with a more powerful aircraft cannon and armor plate was added to protect the German bombers. The .303 machine guns were made obsolete for air-to-air combat, but the RAF's advantage lasted long enough to end Hitler's dreams of invading the United Kingdom and so change the course of the war.

Wallace and Kent weren't neutral observers, of course, but U.S. Marine lieutenant colonel George Chinn, author of a multivolume machine-gun history, who was writing with postwar perspective, said "students of warfare are generally in agreement that the most far-reaching single military decision made in the 20th century was when a small group of British officers . . . decided to mount eight caliber .303 Brownings on their Hurricane and Spitfire fighters. The single act undoubtedly brought about the turning point of the war."[5] It can be argued that Chinn's flat declaration is a bit hyperbolic, but it's an ironic fact of Browning's life that his firearms' greatest impact on the course of history came years after his death. It is, in fact, impossible to tell most any story about American combat in World War II—on air, land, or sea—without also telling the story of Browning's firearms.

Every American fighter plane and bomber—numbering nearly three hundred thousand by war's end—was armed with Browning machine guns, in all but a few cases the heavy .50-caliber gun. On the ground, four of America's seven major infantry weapons were Browning inventions, and a fifth, the .30-caliber M-1 carbine,[6] had roots in a design—albeit extensively revised—that John's brother Ed Browning delivered to Winchester before Ed's death in 1939. Browning's firearms were so ubiquitous they became mere background noise in the great conflict, always there, always reliable, used everywhere. Every battle on or over the cities and fields of Europe, and the islands of the Pacific, was won with firearms that John Browning designed. Even battles that were lost, as by the war's end Imperial Japanese fighters took to the air armed with a 20mm cannon based on a 1921 Browning design.

The Allied dependence on Browning's weapons places him within a historical category occupied by only a select few: John Garand, the American whose work led to the M-1 rifle, the standard U.S. Army combat rifle of World War II; and R. J. Mitchell, the British aeronautical engineer lauded as the driving force behind the Spitfire. But, as noted, without weapons Mitchell's plane was no more than a high-speed ornament. American ground troops, even armed with M-1 semi-automatic rifles, still depended on Browning's two machine guns, his automatic rifle, and, in an emergency, his 1911 pistol. Unlike the American Sherman tank, the Russian T-34, or the German Panzer, Browning's firearms were the invention of one man, assisted by his brothers, working out of a small shop in Utah decades before World War II. His effective, deadly machines underwent changes and revisions over the years as metallurgy improved, planes and tanks were redesigned, and flaws in Browning's original work were made visible in the crucible of combat. But by appearance and function, each Browning gun used in World War II remained a Browning gun.

Informed by the British and German experience, the American Army sped up its adoption of Browning's heavy .50-caliber machine gun, and when war began for the United States on December 7, 1941, that gun had largely supplanted the lighter .30-caliber weapon on American aircraft. It was only a matter of good fortune, however, that the .50-caliber gun was in the American arsenal, as it survived a near-death experience after Browning's passing in 1926.

The .50-caliber weapon was heavy at around eighty pounds, and for ground combat it needed a tripod of fifty or so pounds. The cocking mechanism was difficult to manipulate, and even with Browning's recoil buffer soldiers struggled to keep it on target. There was also no single "correct" barrel length or diameter; both varied according to how the gun was used. The barrel was not a static tube but pumped back and forth five hundred to six hundred times a minute, working in concert with the action to eject spent rounds and load fresh cartridges. Barrel design and dimensions affected cooling, velocity, the rate of fire, and durability. The variety was a potential manufacturing nightmare, as a water-cooled version was needed for antiaircraft defense, a heavy-barreled air-cooled version was needed for armored vehicles, and aircraft demanded a lightweight version. Plus, proponents of his .30 caliber gun calculated that 400 rounds of .30-caliber ammunition weighed the same as only 100 rounds of .50-caliber ammunition, providing a fighter pilot with a greater volume of fire for a longer period of time, even if each individual bullet was less effective.

"The .50 caliber gun is a special weapon. It is assumed that there will never be a great demand for them," one report said. But the Navy had a different opinion. That service conducted its own review and decided whatever its flaws, the gun had potential, and in any case the water-cooled version would serve as an effective deck-mounted antiaircraft gun.

The .50-caliber gun was ultimately made ready for widescale deployment by Samuel E. Green, an engineer at the government's Springfield Armory in Massachusetts, who took over development work in 1927.[7] He revised the cocking mechanism and redesigned the recoil springs. He and his team developed a feed mechanism so that ammunition belts could be loaded from either the left or right side, important if multiple guns were mounted in the confined space of an aircraft wing or fit into a tank turret. He also figured out how to produce a version of the gun for use on land, air, or sea that could be made on a single assembly line. It was officially adopted as the "Browning, Caliber .50, M2" to differentiate it from Browning's first version. By the end of World War II, more than 2 million M2s had come off American assembly lines, and the gun acquired its still-used nickname, Ma Deuce.

Some doubts about its aerial deployment arose when European arms makers introduced rapid-fire, lightweight 20mm cannons in the 1930s. In military parlance, a machine gun becomes a cannon when the projectile is large enough to incorporate an explosive charge. A new round of studies by the Army judged the .50-caliber M2 as adequate, and, at any rate, a switch to an air cannon would have been near impossible in a reasonable time frame. Peacetime budgets were tight, existing cannon designs were of uncertain utility, and there was already a supply chain to manufacture the .50-caliber gun and ammunition. The gun also worked, and worked well enough so that Browning's heavy machine gun underpinned the creation of America's new fleet of long-range bombers.

While the British RAF debated how many machine guns to fit in a fighter, its counterpart, the American Army Air Corps, argued whether to spend its limited budget on new fighters or bombers. Ideally, there would have been simultaneous development of both, but one had to take priority and the bomber advocates won out.[8] They eagerly endorsed the new concept of strategic bombing, which held that quick and comparitively bloodless victories were possible if accurate air bombardment destroyed an enemy's industrial base. Without factories, power plants, oil refineries, and transportation centers, the theory went, a nation rendered unable to manufacture or distribute food, weapons, and ammunition would have no choice but to surrender.

To become a reality, the theory needed an airplane, which arrived in 1935 when the prototype of what became the B-17 Flying Fortress bomber took flight at the Boeing plant in Seattle. The aircraft had provision for five defensive machine guns, sufficiently impressive for a newspaper reporter to dub it a "flying fortress," a catchy name Boeing quickly adopted and which, as it happened, implicitly endorsed the bombing strategy developed at the Air Corps Tactical School at Maxwell Field in Alabama.

The captains and majors at Maxwell went on to lead the American Air Force in World War II. They believed that large fleets of fast bombers with precise bomb-aiming sights, well armed with defensive weapons—Browning's machine guns—and flying in close formation could fight their way through enemy air space, hit a target from twenty thousand feet or more, and return, all without fighter escorts and without incurring major losses. Air-to-air combat between fleets of fighters was dismissed as improbable at best.

"The spectacle of huge air forces meeting in the air is a figment of imagination of the uninitiated," wrote one officer. "Military airmen of all nations agreed that a determined air attack once launched is most difficult if not impossible to stop," another concluded. The concept was that large fleets of bombers could be assembled into formations and positioned so any attacking fighter would be vulnerable to fire from dozens of guns from multiple bombers, creating an impervious lead bubble.

It didn't work out that way. Mounting casualties showed that the B-17 in combat was less a flying fortress and more a flying gun platform, as the aircraft were eventually armed with thirteen Browning M2s.

The easiest entry into the B-17 was through a small access hatch on the right rear side of the fuselage.[9] Inside to the left on entry was the tail turret, with twin .50-caliber guns. To the right was the bomber's waist, an open twenty-nine-foot length of fuselage with a Browning machine gun mounted at cut-outs on either side. Those waist gunners were clad in heated suits worn under sheepskin jackets and overalls for protection from high-altitude cold, topped with a layer of body armor to resist shrapnel from exploding antiaircraft shells.

Set in the floor of the fuselage a few feet farther on was the ball turret, an aluminum and glass sphere forty-four inches wide supported by a steel frame. The ball gunner slid through a hatch into a seat between guns flanking either side of his head. With the barrels aimed at the horizon the gunner rested on his back; pointing down at the ground he half-stood on two stirrups. Gunners were usually small, as they had to fit in while wearing a heat suit, a flight suit, and cold-weather gear. Two handles mounted at head height swung the hydraulically powered turret through a full 360 degrees. The gunner's view was at once panoramic—he could look anywhere left or right, up or down—and restricted by the single circular bulletproof window less than two feet wide. Smaller flanking ports were of little practical use.

A step forward and up was the radio compartment with a small desk and chair for the radioman, shelves lined with vacuum tube receivers and transmitters and, in some B-17 variants, a .50-caliber gun mounted overhead facing rearward.

Another couple of steps onward was the bomb bay, surprisingly small given the B-17's size. A bomb load was five thousand to six thousand pounds, usually made up of five-hundred- or one-thousand-pound bombs mounted on either side of a narrow, shoe-width catwalk that could be crossed in four or five steps. It led to the top turret directly behind and above the pilot and co-pilot. The gunner, whose primary duty was as flight engineer, spent most of each mission leaning over the pilots' shoulders monitoring the bank of dials for each engine.

The pilot and co-pilot sat in a small, cramped space jammed with control wheels, throttles, levers, and dozens of switches and dials. Vision was forward and to the sides and only adequate. As American losses mounted, bulletproof glass and armor plating were added for protection. Beneath the cockpit a small passage led to a spacious navigator and bombardier's cabin in the nose with seats for two men and a small table for the navigator. It had a dramatic forward view through the plexiglass nose and in flight gave the sensation of being both in and separate from the sky.

Single .50-caliber guns were mounted on either side of the nose, and between them was the top-secret Norden bombsight. It had demonstrated unparalleled accuracy in the clear, peaceful air of the American southwest but proved a frequent disappointment in Europe. Above it was a set of handles and an optical sight, remote controls for twin guns in a turret beneath the bomber's nose.

The nose compartment was cocoon-like, situated as it was below the cockpit, immersed in the high-decibel soundtrack from the four unmuffled engines and with a wide vista of European sky passing by inches away. It was a cocoon easily burst by German fighters.

They are making frontal attacks and coming in 15 at a time in a staircase formation. I pick up one in my sights and fire a five-second burst. They are firing cannon shells at us. I feel them hitting our ship and I am beginning to sweat now. I pick a FW 190 up in my sight track for one second and open fire. I followed him. He was going by off our left waist. . . . Got him. He explodes in a ball of fire. . . . I see five of our Forts going down on fire and explode, throwing flames around the sky. I see seven men bail out of a Fortress. . . . I fire at the enemy ship for eight seconds. I see smoke trailing from his engine and sincerely hope that I got the rat.

This account is from Sgt. Sam N. Fain, the ball turret gunner on the B-17 *Lady Stardust II*:

A man bailed out of the ship in front of us and comes into our ship, breaking our Plexiglas nose, injuring our bombardier and navigator and throwing them into the catwalk of the ship. I looked down at the ground and see many small fires and large ones burning. They are enemy fighters and our Forts.[10]

Losses were horrendous and unsustainable. On August 17, 1943, the Eighth Air Force dispatched 363 bombers, armed with 3,900 Browning machine guns, to strike a Messerschmitt factory in Regensburg. They were met by 300 German fighters backed up by ground-based antiaircraft artillery. Sixty planes carrying 600 men were lost, and another 47 bombers were damaged beyond repair. Eighth Air Force commanders initially took solace in crew reports that 228 attacking fighters were destroyed, though those claims were sliced to 148 after a review. The real number, as discovered after the war, was 25. Fatalism overtook the bomber crews. "It has come to be an accepted fact that you will be shot down eventually," wrote one crewman after his unit lost 12 of 17 planes.[11]

The strategic bombing theory faced its most significant test of the war, so far, on October 14, 1943, when the Eighth Air Force dispatched 290 bombers to attack ball-bearing-manufacturing plants in the city of Schweinfurt. The factories were prime targets, since without ball bearings wheels don't turn and engines don't operate. The short-range Allied fighter escort was forced to turn back at the German border, leaving the bombers unprotected for two hundred miles of flight to and from the target. At the day's end, only 197 bombers returned to England, and 22 of those crashed during landing or were too damaged to fly again. The total bomber loss was 28 percent, with 594 Americans airmen declared missing in action. A few more raids like that and there would be no more Eighth Air Force.

What had happened? By World War II, fighter speed and armaments surpassed projections made a decade earlier. In the 1930s existing fighters were no faster than the new B-17. Speedier, longer-range, single-engine fighters were unknown, and none seemed on the horizon. Allied planners underestimated the difficulty of shooting down small, nimble fighters flying at 300 mph in one direction while aiming from a bomber moving in another direction at 200 mph. During the war Air Force gunner-training programs quickly expanded—eventually lasting two months—and a series of improved sights were rolled out, including early mechanical computerized sights. Still, a gunner had only a handful of seconds to aim, fire, and hit a fighter hurtling past. Confounding attempts at accuracy was that each bullet moved in three directions: forward in the direction of fire, sideways at an angle according to the direction and speed of the plane, and downward due to gravity and air resistance. The trick was in figuring out the correct "deflection" angle, where to aim from the moving plane to hit the moving fighter. To their amazement, gunners discovered they often had to aim behind an attacking fighter, as a bullet fired from a B-17 traveled both toward the target and forward at the speed of the aircraft. If a gunner led a fighter, as a trapshooter leads a clay pigeon, the .50-caliber bullets could pass harmlessly in front of the enemy plane.

There was also the physical stress of combat at high altitude. Flying at twenty thousand to thirty thousand feet over Europe, B-17 and B-24 crews—by war's end the larger, longer-range B-24 was the dominant American heavy bomber—spent up to eleven hours at temperatures reaching -12 degrees. The bomber interior had no creature comforts—it was a bare, drafty aluminum tube, always noisy and always in motion. There was predictable turbulence generated by a large group of planes flying in close formation, and hard, jerky motions when pilots jiggled the controls to throw off an enemy fighter's aim.

Powered turrets on the nose and tail and above and below the fuselage did help gunners swing their twin machine guns and their ammunition belts, smoothly and quickly horizontally or vertically, but suffered inevitable glitches in combat. Effective fire from the single, manually controlled "flexible" waist guns was particularly problematic. Swinging the .50-caliber machine gun forward and aft, up and down, was exhausting. Gunners manhandled not only the mass of the gun but also the ammunition belts, which were extracted from plywood boxes hung on the fuselage. Movement was constant, all while the bomber bounced about and spent cartridges piled up underfoot. As one historian said, flexible gunnery in an aircraft was "capable of doing little more than spraying bullets in the general direction of the target."[12]

And when they did shoot down an enemy plane, getting credit could be its own battle. "The roughest thing about combat is trying to get an enemy plane confirmed. Even if you shoot one down, even if you see him blow up in midair doesn't mean you get credit for him," wrote B-17 gunner Thomas J. Hansbury. "First at least two other men on your crew or any other crew must also see you get him. Nine times out of ten they are shooting at one the same time that you are getting yours. Even so it is hard to get them to say that you got him. But after you come back and get to the interrogation officer you must be able to convince him. This is a very hard thing to do."[13]

Yet strength, skill, luck, and witnesses could combine to produce the unexpected.

On July 5, 1943, S/Sgt. Benjamin Franklin Warmer III was a waist gunner on a B-17, one among one hundred aircraft bombing the largest German fighter base in Sicily. A wild fifteen-minute melee ensued when groups of four to sixteen enemy fighters attacked head-on. After the mission, air crews claimed forty-five enemy fighters shot down, which intelligence officers dismissed as more of the usual exaggeration. In the midst of air combat, with multiple gunners firing at the same attacking aircraft, crews always overestimated enemy losses. But Warmer's debriefing was particularly notable. The waist gunner said he'd shot down seven enemy fighters with his single-barreled Browning machine gun.[14]

How unlikely that was can be illustrated by the fact no American fighter pilot—with the advantage of six or eight guns at his command—had ever claimed seven enemy planes in one mission. It was, in fact, a virtual impossibility, for American fighters typically carried enough ammunition for twenty seconds of continuous fire. To shoot down seven planes with three-second bursts seven times in a row was unheard of. Warmer said he'd used only twelve hundred rounds, a part of his claim that was easily checked—and confirmed after inspecting the ammunition boxes onboard his B-17.

Intelligence officers launched an investigation. They called in Warmer's crewmates and interrogated pilots and gunners on the surrounding B-17s. Witnesses were interviewed repeatedly to unearth inconsistencies, and each was subjected "to the most exhaustive scrutiny possible." In the end the intelligence officers concluded Warmer had indeed done what he said.

A photo of Warmer standing next to his waist gun provides the explanation. Warmer is bent over so his head won't hit the B-17's fuselage. He was six feet six inches tall, weighed between 225 and 250 pounds—reports varied—and was a college football player. He also was a law school graduate and former guard for U.S. treasury secretary Henry Morgenthau Jr. Warmer was big, strong, athletic, and bright and had the strength, body mass, and presence of mind to control and accurately aim the gun in a 200 mph slipstream. Compare Warmer to the average World War II gunner, who was five feet eight inches tall and weighed 140 pounds.

The Air Force issued a special dispatch written by Warmer himself:

The first plane I got a shot at came in at the start—a Messerschmidt peeled off from our right and leveled straight at us with guns winking. I winked back until the German was 50 yards away and I saw him burst into flames and plough down under our Fortress. Number two and three were daisies. Two ME 109's made a run together at the Fortress. I got one on the way in. The other came on but broke his run at about 50 yards and I opened up on his belly when he exposed it in a turn.

The next victories I didn't even intend to claim, but the gunners in some other plane saw them parachuting down. I got two more fighters but didn't have time to identify them positively.

Warmer, who said he had given up a chance for an officer's commission because "he wanted to get some action," closed his dispatch with a glimpse of the anger common in post-action reports: "I knew every one of our boys who went down. We had been eating together, palling around together and living together for eight months. I only wish I could've gotten a plane for every one of them."

Warmer received the Distinguished Service Cross, second only to the Congressional Medal of Honor. But gunners with Warmer's skills were few.

After Schweinfurt, American long-range strategic raids into Germany didn't resume until January 1944, when the P-51 Mustang fighter arrived and external metal fuel tanks called drop tanks that extended flight range became readily available. (Previously the Air Force had been reduced to using coated cardboard tanks cobbled together in Britain.) Such snafus and errors were unsurprising. Prewar air planning by all sides—the Americans, British, and Germans—was inevitably a hit-or-miss venture. No one had ever fought an air war with comparable flying machines and there had never been large-scale, high-altitude air combat. William R. Emerson, a P-47 Thunderbolt pilot turned postwar military historian, wrote: "All they had to go on was hunches and guesses. In such a pioneering venture, error is unavoidable."[15] Fortunately, the mistakes made by the Americans, British, and Russians were fewer than those by the Germans and Japanese.

The failure of the Air Force's bomber-alone concept sped the deployment of long-range fighters and it was those fighters, all armed with .50-caliber Brownings, that destroyed the German Luftwaffe as an offensive fighting force. By D-Day, June 6, 1944, the Allies had complete air superiority over the Normandy invasion beachhead. The result of the American strategy was to give B-17s and B-24s an unintended and bitter role—bait for traps sprung by the American P-47 and P-51 fighters armed with .50-caliber guns. The official Air Force history concluded that control of the air "must be considered in the last analysis a by-product of the strategic bombing offensive. It is difficult . . . to escape the conclusion that air battles did more to defeat the Luftwaffe than did the destruction of aircraft factories."[16]

A four-second burst from six guns in a P-51—each firing at 800 rounds a minute—sent 300 rounds of armor-piercing projectiles with incendiary tips into what was called the convergence zone, where the bullets are concentrated into a close-packed mass. For the P-51, the zone was typically a six-by-ten-foot rectangle 250 or 300 yards distant, which meant that in four seconds twenty-six pounds of lead and phosphorus would slam into an area smaller than Ford's 2020 Mustang coupe.[17]

The American bomber losses may suggest the Germans found the B-17s an easy target. They didn't. For inexperienced pilots attacking a massed flight of close-packed bombers, the encounter was terrifying. Bomber fleets were divided into groups called boxes of thirty to thirty-five planes flying in tight formations, staggered up and down and left and right for the maximum degree of mutual protection. A German fighter attacking a single B-17 from astern faced a half-dozen twin .50-caliber tail guns. "The size of the heavy bombers and their formations and their unprecedented offensive firepower could not be described adequately to a green pilot. They had to experience it firsthand," Luftwaffe veterans told American historian Donald Caldwell. The Germans found it was hard to shoot down a B-17. The aircraft kept flying with engines shot away, fuselages bullet riddled, and wings holed by antiaircraft fire.

Luftwaffe fighter commander Adolf Galland wrote a worried report after inspecting a downed bomber in 1942. Even shattered on the ground, the B-17 had "every possible advantage in one bomber; first heavy armor; second enormous altitude, third colossal defensive armament; fourth great speed." Luftwaffe reports show some pilots never edged closer than a thousand yards, the maximum effective range of the B-17's defensive guns.[18]

American crews debated whether it was useful to open fire before the enemy was close in, speculating that tracer rounds flashing by would discombobulate a hesitant attacker. One German pilot put his own spin on the practice: "The bomber guns usually start to fire when we were still out of range, 2000 m from them. It was obvious that they were just as scared as we were. Shaken by the slipstream of the B-17s and blinded by the condensation trails, we were subject to machine gun fire for minutes or seconds that seemed endless before being able to see the results of our attack. Despite the armor plating over cockpits, we had good reason to dread the defensive fire of the bombers."

Until the B-17's powered nose turrets became common in 1944, the Germans favored frontal attacks with a half-dozen or more fighters in a row. They closed to within a few hundred yards—or fewer—and opened fire for a couple of seconds before throwing their planes into sharp dives. A successful attack was one that not only damaged or destroyed a bomber but also shocked B-17 pilots into breaking formation.

On April 17, 1943, FW 190 pilot Hans Ekkehard Bob missed a bomber on his first pass: "I started a new attack and approached the lead group of Fortresses from the front. I fired at the aircraft on the right of the leading element from 550 yards, getting good hits on the cockpit and number two engine." Then he misjudged his speed and distance, and "when I tried to dive beneath the B-17 I hit the bomber." The two aircraft collided. "I lost much of my fuselage, while the bomber lost a wing."[19] His aircraft spun out of control and Bob bailed out and saw the B-17 stagger on before its crew took to parachutes.

The FW 190 fighter was originally armed with only two rifle-caliber machine guns and one 20mm cannon, inadequate armament for their task. The Germans turned to the heavier MG 131, equivalent to the Browning .50 caliber, standoff rockets were introduced along with a 30mm automatic cannon that could blow off a bomber's wing with one shell. The increase in armament created a different set of problems. A fighter loaded up with guns and ammunition certain to take down the B-17 was slow, sluggish, and susceptible to the P-51 or the P-47.

By May 1944, the American escort fighters produced dramatic results. Bomber losses per mission dropped to 2.7 percent as compared with 9.7 percent in October 1943. A few months later they fell to below 1 percent.

Now it was the German pilots' turn to face the high probability of death. Fighter losses soared, and while production of aircraft increased, Germany didn't have the pilots or fuel to train new aviators. By the early spring of 1944, American fighters were conducting low-level sweeps to destroy German airfields and airplanes in advance of the invasion. By June, tens of thousands of American troops were in Normandy, armed squad by squad with Browning .30-caliber machine guns, driving tanks and half-tracks mounting up to four .50-caliber guns, carrying BARs and wearing holstered Colt 1911 pistols. And carrying the M-1 carbine traced to brother Ed.

They also had the advantage of the lessons learned from ground combat in the Pacific, which began in 1942 on Guadalcanal, when three soldiers with a Browning water-cooled machine gun broke the first major Japanese counterattack of that island campaign.

CHAPTER THIRTEEN

SOLDIERS AT WAR

In the spring of 1942, on a hitherto obscure spot in the south-west Pacific, the Japanese began construction of a naval base on an atoll called Tulagi, and an airfield on a jelly-bean-shaped, jungle-covered island called Guadalcanal.

American commanders paid quick attention. Japanese air and sea attacks from those bases could cut supply lines to Australia and threaten American plans for a western Pacific offensive. An invasion fleet was rapidly assembled and dispatched across the Pacific. In the nine months of combat since Pearl Harbor, Imperial Japanese troops had delivered embarrassing defeats to every Western army in their path. In February, eighty thousand British soldiers surrendered the supposedly impregnable strong-hold of Singapore to a force of only thirty thousand Japanese soldiers, only to discover the Japanese had all but exhausted their ammunition. It was the worst military defeat in British history. In May, American and Filipino troops defending the island fortress of Corregidor were overwhelmed after six months of combat, cementing Japanese occupation of the Philippines.

But in June, as Americans wondered if the Japanese could be stopped, let alone thrown back, the Navy sank four Japanese aircraft carriers at the Battle of Midway with the loss of only one American flattop. It was a turning point in the naval war, and the hitherto undefeated Japanese Navy never fully recovered. Next up was a test of the Marine Corps, as fourteen thousand troops, most newly recruited, freshly trained, and totally untested, arrived off Guadalcanal and Tulagi on August 6, 1942, for the first American ground offensive of the Pacific War. Within days the Marines armed with Browning machine guns would repel a major Japanese assault and preserve their narrow beachead.

Tulagi was quickly occupied by three thousand troops, while another eleven thousand from the First Marine Division seized the partly constructed airfield on Guadalcanal's flat north shore. The few Japanese defenders were easily brushed aside, but two days later a Japanese task force sank four American cruisers, killed 1,077 servicemen, and chased the American invasion fleet out if its anchorage. The Marines were left stranded and short of supplies, and a starvation diet was only averted because fleeing Japanese abandoned a supply depot stuffed with rice, canned beef in soy sauce, crabmeat, fruit, and stores of beer and saki, the latter quickly consumed by the Marines. They subsisted on two meals a day and struggled to complete the runway, fend off scattered attacks by the remaining Japanese, and set up a defensive perimeter for the inevitable Imperial counterattack.[1]

Leading that assault was a skilled tactician and "all-purpose firebrand," Col. Kiyonao Ichiki, who began with a mistake—on August 19 he landed only 916 troops from his regiment's 2,500 men. It was an error born of "victory fever," a psychological malady characterized by excessive hubris that was widespread among Japanese officers. Before a shot was fired, Ichiki set August 24 as the date of his victory. By then he was dead, as were most of his soldiers, thrown back and slaughtered by Marine defenders, most famously by three men wielding a single Browning machine gun.[2]

Ichiki's second mistake was ignoring a wake-up call on August 20, when a 38-man Japanese patrol was wiped out in a skirmish east of the island airstrip, now renamed Henderson Field in honor of a Marine aviator killed at the Battle of Midway. Ichiki was nevertheless convinced a nighttime bayonet charge by his veteran troops would scatter the untested Marines. He readied 800 men for an assault westward along the shoreline, where the

Marines' defensive line stretched inland from the beach, follow-ing the bank of a shallow tidal lagoon, erroneously identified on American maps as the Tenaru River. In fact, the sluggish, muddy water bore the more appropriate name of Alligator Creek, and Marines would soon watch a crocodile—alligators prefer fresh water—crawl up the far bank to eat the corpse of a Japanese soldier.[3]

A sandbar along the beachfront linking both sides of the tidal stream offered a bridge across the water, so there on their left flank the Marines set up a 37mm antitank gun supplied with canister rounds, essentially cannon-sized shotgun shells packed with marble-sized lead balls. Heading inland along the creek, Browning water-cooled machine-gun positions were set up at one-hundred-yard intervals, each .30-caliber gun with a gun commander, a gunner, and an assistant gunner.

The Browning closest to the .37mm cannon was manned by three Marines who were seemingly selected by central casting, and indeed Hollywood made a film chronicling their fate.

The corporal in command was LeRoy Diamond, considered a veteran as he had enlisted in 1940, which earned him the nick-name of "Pappy." The son of Jewish emigrants from Europe, Dia-mond commanded a total team of five men. When the gun went into action he chose the targets and oversaw the gunner and assis-tant gunner. The gunner was Pvt. John "Jack" Rivers, who joined in early 1942. Marine records list him as a Native American, but in fact his roots were Hawaiian, explained nephew Bill Freedman, a historian who assembled a detailed account of his uncle's short life and twice interviewed Diamond before the Marine's death in 2009. Rivers was the son of a native Hawaiian who immigrated to the New Jersey area in search of work and there married Lillian Godwin. Later Jack was placed in a foster family and graduated from high school in Quakertown, Pennsylvania. Prior to joining the Marines, Rivers spent four years as an amateur boxer, where promoters played up his supposed "Indian" roots.[4]

The third man was another recent volunteer, assistant gunner Al Schmid, the son of an ethnic German father and Irish mother, raised in a Philadelphia row house, who was an unpleasant brawler in civilian life. "Jesus Christmas how I loved to fight," he told his official biographer.[5] Other Marines considered him a bully whose favorite targets were "anyone who was dark or perceived as not white, or Jewish," said Freedman. Schmid had the "common prejudices" of that era, as one biographer put it. Aboard the troopship USS *George F. Elliott* on their way to Guadalcanal, the dark-skinned Rivers, fed up, ended up in a brawl with Schmid, which was broken up by a lieutenant. A ring was set up on deck and the two men fought it out with gloves on. "My uncle toyed with him and literally cut him to pieces," Freedman said. Schmid subsequently decided his former foe was now his best friend. In combat, Schmid's job was to reload the gun with fresh ammunition belts..

The three were not close—after the war Diamond and Schmid never met—but their personal animosity evaporated when confronted by the Japanese.

By the evening of August 20, Diamond's gun was set up a few yards back from the waterline, where the Marines dug out a half-circle trench about four feet deep, with the Browning mounted in the center, so that the barrel extended over the rim a foot or two above ground level. Stacked around them were five crates of .30-caliber ammunition, a total of some six thousand cartridges loaded into belts each holding 250 rounds. They erected frontal and overhead defenses of sandbags and freshly cut logs. Then they waited.

Around midnight the first shots rang out, and English-speaking Japanese yelled insults from across the water where they were forming up amid the rows of a palm tree plantation owned by Lever Bros., the soap manufacturer. Japanese machine-gun fire began raking the Marine lines, and at 12:30 a.m. Ichiki sent troops with fixed bayonets charging down the sandbar and across the lagoon. As the Japanese advanced, Diamond climbed out of the machine-gun pit and cleared away sandbags so that Rivers could traverse the gun left toward the sea. Diamond ordered Rivers to rake the flank of the Japanese attackers crossing the sandbar. Meanwhile, Japanese were spotted preparing to attack across the lagoon. The Browning a hundred yards to the right of Diamond's position opened up, and the machine gunners and Marine riflemen lining the creek fired in short, quick bursts at the advancing enemy troops or at the enemy machine guns dug in across the creek. Then the Marine gun to Diamond's right abruptly ceased firing, and the beachfront antitank gun fell silent.

Schmid kept loading fresh ammunition belts as Rivers fired. Regulations called for about 125 rounds a minute in aimed bursts of 5 or 7 rounds. About ten minutes into the fighting, Rivers suddenly slumped over the gun. His finger was stuck on the trigger and the Browning pounded away for fifteen or twenty seconds, a continuous roar that drowned out human voices and the sounds of combat.

Schmid and Diamond pulled a motionless Rivers off the gun. "A rifle round went right through his helmet and into his head," Diamond told Freedman, in a voice so emotion laden he sounded "like he was back in 1942 on Guadalcanal," recalled Rivers's nephew. "He said that my uncle's trigger finger froze and he fired off the whole 200 round belt in his death grip." The long burst of fire was even noticed at the Marine command post to the rear.

With Rivers's body laid to one side, Schmid took over the gun while Diamond loaded and directed fire by punching him in one arm or the other, "really hitting him" to swing the gun upstream where a Japanese machine gunner had opened up on their position. At some point a string of bullets punctured the Browning's water jacket, the coolant spurted out, and the exposed barrel began overheating. The Browning kept firing. "The gun got red hot but for some reason it didn't jam the way it was supposed to when it didn't have water," according to Schmid's account. His return fire silenced the Japanese gun. Then Diamond was shot in the arm and knocked to the ground as the first assault was thrown back.

A second massed charge began around 2:00 a.m. Schmid again fired to the left, toward the beach and across the creek at charging Japanese troops. Diamond was apparently able to direct fire and may have been able to help reload the Browning.

An account of the battle written by a *Life* magazine correspondent reported that during a lull in combat Diamond and Schmid heard the sound of men scrambling up the bank. Diamond leaned over the edge of the sandbagged position and with his good arm lifted a Reising submachine gun, an experimental automatic weapon issued to a few Marines, and fired a burst toward the noise. Three dead Japanese were found the next day. Other accounts don't mention that incident.

What did happen was that a Japanese soldier crawled up and tossed a hand grenade that bounced off the Browning and exploded in the trench. Diamond now found both his arms immobilized by shrapnel. Schmid lost one eye and was partially blinded in the other.

As Freedman tells the story, "Lee Diamond says, 'I can't load,' and Schmid replied, 'No problem, tell me which way to traverse the gun.' Lee is standing behind him and hitting him with his shoulders." A push with his right shoulder on Schmid's back meant swing right, and a nudge with his left meant swing left.

The final Japanese attack came through the surf as the enemy tried to outflank the Marine line. That, too, failed. By dawn, firing had ceased, and in daylight the Marines launched a counterattack. All but thirty of the Japanese were killed. Ichiki's exact fate is unknown. Some Japanese survivors said he was killed in combat, while other reports suggest he committed ritual suicide.

The next day, on the sandbar swept by Diamond, Rivers, and Schmid's machine gun and along the lagoon in front of their pit, stunned Marines walked among bodies piled one atop each other. They counted two hundred dead Japanese. Diamond and Schmid received the Navy Cross, second only to the Congressional Medal of Honor. Rivers's medal was posthumous, and after the war some Marines complained that Rivers's role was minimized in favor of an emphasis on Schmid, the blinded survivor.

Subsequent publicity made much of the battle and the machine gunners, and a book and film were produced about Schmid's life. He never regained significant sight in his damaged eyes.

Diamond received little attention, and after his wounds healed he was returned to duty. Eventually he was transferred back to the States to train Marine recruits and was finally discharged in late 1945. As the nation grappled with the flood of returning veterans, he struggled to find work and an apartment for himself, his wife, Helen, and their daughter, Linda.[6] Diamond became a plumber and died in 2009.

The "heavy" Browning machine guns used on Alligator Creek were so called because along with the water jacket, tubing, and condenser to recycle steam from the hot gun, the weapon was mounted on a complex tripod that weighed fifty-two pounds. Moving the weapon into combat was ideally done by four or five men. One carried the gun, another the tripod, the third the cooling equipment, and the fourth, and sometimes fifth, the ammunition.

The air-cooled version weighed far less at thirty-one pounds, but in 1939 the Ordnance Department began looking for a lighter replacement, as post–World War I infantry tactics had abandoned trench warfare for small-unit maneuvers. Tactical theory was also edging away from the infantry rifle in favor of automatic weapons.

In America movement in that direction was slowed by the adoption of the eight-round Garand M-1 semiautomatic rifle, which by increasing individual soldiers' firepower was thought to reduce the need for crew-served weapons. Nevertheless, five air-cooled machine guns were tested. All failed to meet the Army's criteria, so the Army stuck with the Browning in hand. Its official designation was the 1919A4.

In Germany the resurgent Wehrmacht still issued bolt-action rifles but organized its small-unit tactics around lightweight, fast-firing air-cooled machine guns. In contravention of the Versailles

Treaty's limits on military weapons Germany had secretly poured time and money into a surreptitious machine-gun program that became public after Hitler took power in 1933. One resulting gun was the MG 34, which fired 900 rounds a minute but was delicate and expensive to manufacture. By 1942 it was being replaced by the MG 42, largely made of stamped steel and which fired a very remarkable 1,200 rounds a minute, producing a sound so vicious it was nicknamed Hitler's buzz saw. The barrel reciprocated back and forth like a Browning, but the internal action was an original design that used small steel rollers to speedily lock and unlock the barrel and breech. The MG 42 used a thin, lightweight barrel only good for 250 rounds of continuous fire, but it could be changed out in thirty seconds or less. To do so in a slower-firing Browning required removing the grips and the bolt and pulling the barrel assembly out of the rear. It couldn't be done in combat.

An American attempt to copy the MG 42 ended up a failure due to a simple mathematical error. Adding a new machine gun to the American manufacturing and supply chain was only practical if it used ammunition already in production, so the German gun was redesigned to accept the 30.06 cartridge used in the M-1 rifle, the BAR, and the Browning machine guns. Somehow engineers failed to correctly compensate for the difference in the length—the American cartridge was slightly longer than the German ammunition—so the prototypes malfunctioned and the project was dropped. That mistake prevented America from copying the enemy's machine-gun design and doing to the Germans in World War II what Pershing feared the Germans would do in World War I.

The U.S. Army admitted the sound of the MG 42 working at 1,200 rounds, even for a few seconds, meant a few seconds of terror for inexperienced recruits. It taught tactics to counter the gun, including the example seen in *Saving Private Ryan*, the film set during World War II, where troops led by Tom Hanks attack a German machine gun from the flanks, waiting for the Germans to change out the barrel before making a final charge. The rate of fire wasn't the only standard by which to judge a weapon, however. The faster gun required a higher degree of skill and training, and the brutal recoil easily threw it off target. The slower-firing Browning, at some 600 rounds per minute, was easier to keep on target and the American Army preferred the better accuracy—and lower ammunition consumption—that came with short bursts of 5 to 7 rounds. That, of course, is enough to kill a man. A skilled operator with Browning's air-cooled gun could fire twenty-two aimed bursts in a minute for a total of 154 rounds and sustain that rate without damaging the barrel.

That gun received a firm endorsement by the Marines. In December 1943 Marine lieutenant colonel Vincent H. Krulak, a veteran of Guadalcanal and other Pacific campaigns, briefed ordnance officers in Washington, D.C., on the pros and cons of American combat arms. He praised the M-1 rifle, saying, "It is magnificent. We will stop here." He thought the Thompson submachine gun mostly useless in jungle fighting, as the low-velocity .45-caliber bullets were thrown askew by thick vegetation and the gun itself was "much too heavy, it is uncomfortable to carry, and it does not function well."

Krulak criticized the BAR's weight, but as the briefing meandered onto other topics Krulak suddenly interjected, "It has come to my mind at the moment that I've done Mr. Browning a terrible injustice in omitting one of the finest pieces of ordnance that has ever been designed and that is the 1919A4 light machine gun which we used to prodigious effect. It is the most dependable weapon that ever came down the road. My only comments are those of humility." Krulak was referring to the air-cooled version of the water-cooled gun. He considered the latter too heavy and awkward for mobile combat in the Pacific. The Army described the air-cooled version of Browning's gun as the "backbone" of the American infantry. Krulak agreed: "We have no need for water-cooled machine gunners so long as we have that splendid weapon in our possession."

●　●　●

But he was right about the BAR. As the only hand-carried American automatic weapon firing a high-velocity bullet, it was relied upon by squad, company, and platoon. Krulak conceded it was a "very fine weapon"—for World War I. "It is in our mind outmoded. It is a dead duck," even though no Marine would give it up, and the number of BARs per squad steadily increased throughout the war. Krulak complained, correctly, that Ordnance Department "improvements" increasing the weight to twenty pounds from Browning's original sixteen pounds were marginal if not useless. The magazine still held 20 rounds, and it lacked a quick-change barrel, unlike the heavier but similar British Bren gun, based on a Czech design.

Krulak praised a little-known automatic weapon called the Johnson light machine gun after its inventor, Melvin Johnson Jr., a Boston attorney and Marine reservist. It was more of an automatic rifle than a light machine gun, but it had two advantages over the BAR—it weighed only fourteen pounds and had a quick-change barrel. Only a few thousand were ever built, as ordnance tests raised doubts about its durability and its very long magazine, mounted on the side, made it hard to maneuver through underbrush. Most important, the BAR was already in mass production. With the demands already facing the American industrial base the Johnson gun, though good, wasn't good enough.

To address the BAR's weight gain, troops in the field removed the Ordnance Department's two-pound bipod and a steel shoulder brace on the stock. The flash suppressor was also tossed aside, getting the weight down to seventeen pounds, close to what Browning intended. "In the original form the Browning automatic rifle was a pretty good infantry weapon, and until the modification hounds loused it up it was portable and practical," wrote Roy Dunlap, an Army Ordnance sergeant from Illinois and self-described "confirmed American gun crank." He wrote an entertaining account of his military service in North Africa and the Pacific called *Ordnance Went Up Front*, in which he observed: "I hated the Army, but the war I didn't mind so much."[7]

It was common for every soldier in a squad to carry extra magazines for the BAR man and when combat demanded sustained fire magazine after magazine was loaded and fired until the barrel burned up or the gun jammed. Then the BAR man picked up another one.

In September 1943, that's what Charles "Commando" Kelly did in the small southern Italian town of Altavilla, about ten miles inland from the coastal city of Salerno.

Kelly was one of nine children who grew up in a run-down home on a run-down alley in Pittsburgh with no running water, electricity, or indoor toilet. He dropped out of school and in 1942 joined the Army, which jailed him in a base stockade for going AWOL.[8] The thin, diminutive Kelly trained as a BAR man and landed in Italy with the Thirty-Sixth Infantry Division on September 9, 1943. The first few days were touch-and-go. Altavilla was captured by American troops, then recaptured by the Germans, and on September 13 two battalions from the Thirty-Sixth were ordered to retake the town.

Kelly volunteered for a reconnaissance patrol and crawled two miles under fire to scout the German line. Once the attack began, Kelly used his BAR to knock out two German machine guns that were halting his unit's advance. Needing more ammunition, Kelly was dispatched to the unit's ammunition dump in a nearby home. He arrived to find a German attack underway and took up a defensive position at the rear door, where he spent the night. Combat resumed at dawn. He moved up to a second-floor bedroom window with his automatic rifle as the Germans advanced. He aimed and fired, emptying 20-round magazines one after the other.

"I worked my BAR so steadily that when I put the next load of cartridges in it wouldn't work anymore. I laid it against a bed and went back to get another BAR, but when I came back the bed was on fire. That first gun was so hot that it touched off the sheets and blankets. I worked the new BAR until the steel of the barrel turned reddish-purple with heat and it became warped. I couldn't find another BAR, so I went upstairs and scouted around until I found a Tommy gun with a full magazine. Then I went to the window and gunned for some more Germans," Kelly said.[9]

Again out of ammunition, he picked up 60mm mortar shells, pulled out the safety pins, and used them as hand grenades, killing a group of five enemy. Then he picked up an M-1 carbine. By that time German troops were about to overrun the house, so Kelly volunteered to cover the retreat, apparently with a third BAR, a bazooka, or both. He got out alive, and his exploits were chronicled in the army newspaper, *Stars and Stripes*, which bestowed the "Commando" nickname. Congress voted him the Medal of Honor, the first received by an American soldier in the European Theater. Witnesses said Kelly killed at least forty Germans.

In a 1957 interview CBS correspondent Mike Wallace asked Kelly if he found "any real satisfaction out of killing another man."

"That group of men, yes," Kelly said. "When I was sitting in the front line with your buddies, just waiting for the attack, when you see your buddies being cut down, screaming for help, and you can't help them, blood running out of them, the rest of the men pinned down that they can't move you sort of get an urge. Well, I got that urge and took off. I went back and I got the 40 Germans. And I'm never sorry . . . But I had the urge to kill and I killed. It was just one of the things. We didn't want to do it but we did anyhow."[10]

Kelly never found his way in life after the war. He was paid tens of thousands for the movie rights to his life and $15,000—well over $100,000 today—for a single magazine article. He was fêted by Pittsburgh, married, and purchased a gas station that went bust in two years. His wife died of cancer in 1950 and he bounced from place to place despite multiple offers of jobs and financial help. In 1984 he was admitted to a Pittsburgh VA hospital, said he had no living relatives even though five brothers had homes within a few miles, and then pulled intravenous tubes out of his body to die alone.[11]

Appropriately for the end to a biography of John Moses Browning is the story of Audie Murphy, a baby-faced nineteen-year-old, one of twelve children born into a family of Texas sharecroppers. Browning's rise from a childhood on the newly settled frontier to an inventor whose machines became woven into the fabric of American life and world history is barely credible as a novel, which is also true of Audie Murphy, who rose from private to first lieutenant by dint of a rare combination of skill as a fighter and leader—and a measure of luck. He was the most decorated American in World War II, serving as a foot soldier in Italy, France, and Germany. His survival during those eighteen months of combat is extraordinary in and of itself, and his exploits might be written off as exaggerations if his deeds weren't done in full view of his fellow soldiers, and with dead German soldiers for evidence. Murphy lived every Hollywood combat cliché and later portrayed himself in a movie about himself. While Murphy is largely forgotten by popular history, his real-world exploits have provided the factual backbone for decades of Hollywood war movies and action films. One example suffices. In 2014 Brad Pitt starred in *Fury*, the grim tale of an American tank crew who chose near-certain suicide to halt a German advance. In the penultimate scene Pitt stands astride a knocked-out tank, cutting down Nazi troops with a Browning .50-caliber machine gun, until he is felled by a sniper's bullet.

That act of screen heroism occurs in chapter 19 of Murphy's autobiography, *To Hell and Back*, except that Murphy lived to receive the Congressional Medal of Honor. He went on to star in Hollywood Westerns, write and sing country and western tunes, and author a raw, compelling account of his life in combat, made into the 1955 movie when he still looked young enough to plausibly play his nineteen-year-old self.

Murphy's father abandoned the family when he was a child, and Murphy left school in the fifth grade to pick cotton. His mother died when he was sixteen years old. He was bright, if a loner with mood swings and a quick temper. World War II was an escape from the poverty of rural Texas, and an older sister falsified paperwork so that the seventeen-year-old would be eligible for the armed services. The short, childish-looking Murphy was rejected by the Navy and Marine Corps before he finally landed a bunk in the Army, which grew from a few hundred thousand troops to 8 million by 1945. Casualties were enormous. Between D-Day on June 6, 1944, and the end of the European war on May 8, 1945, there were twelve thousand to eighteen thousand GIs and Army Air Force crewmen killed every month and forty thousand to sixty thousand wounded.[12]

Murphy's war started when his unit, the Third Infantry Division, landed in Sicily on July 10, 1943. His aggression was instant and fearless and coldly rational, and within five days he was promoted to corporal. The first time he killed a man was on a reconnaissance patrol. "We flushed a couple of Italian officers. They should have surrendered. Instead, they mounted magnificent white horses and galloped boldly away. My act is instinctive. Dropping to one knee, I fired twice. The men tumbled from the horses, roll over and lie still." Murphy was bawled out by the commanding officer—obviously new to combat—who demanded to know why Murphy shot two fleeing men. "They would've killed us if they had the chance," he replied. The Sicilian campaign wrung out any sense of romanticism. "I've seen war as it actually is, and I do not like it," Murphy wrote. "Experience has seasoned us, made us battle wise and intensely practical. But we have much to learn." The first lesson was that soldiers who didn't control their fear ended up dead.

He had a keen sense for reading the ground, crucial to picking out camouflaged German positions, which was crucial to staying alive. His accurate rifle fire was learned hunting for food as a child with a .22-caliber rifle, when ammunition was so scarce each bullet fired had to bag a squirrel or rabbit. By January Murphy was a staff sergeant with B Company:

> If I discovered one valuable thing during my early combat days, it was audacity, which is often mistaken for courage or foolishness. It is neither. Audacity is a tactical weapon. Nine times out of 10 it will throw the enemy off balance and confuse him. However much one sees of audacious deeds, nobody really expects them.[13]

Company B landed at St. Tropez, France, on August 15, met little resistance, and in forty minutes was inland moving north. Murphy was on his way to becoming "a hero of ultimate reality," wrote Don Graham, author of *No Name on the Bullet*, a 1989 biography. "What he did in France is simply incredible. His personal crusade—it almost seems that—to rid the world of German soldiers (or was it simply to get the war over and return home?) took on extraordinary proportions the day of the landing."

A mile inland of the beach two of Murphy's men were cut down by German fire from a fortified hilltop position. Murphy worked his way forward, step by step. He surprised two Germans and shot them both. He came upon an American machine-gun squad, pinned down and not moving but still armed with a Browning .30-caliber air-cooled machine gun. He took the gun and set it up so he could fire uphill but remain hidden from German fire coming downhill. He cleared the hill foot by foot, each time carrying the gun forward, setting up, and killing the enemy. As he neared the top Murphy's best friend, Lattie Tipton, joined him and they continued up the hill.

Two Germans fired, missed, and Tipton killed both with two shots. Murphy and Tipton moved farther up the hill, under heavy fire, and two more Germans appeared at "point blank range" and shot off a piece of Tipton's ear. Tipton's aim was better, and he again fired just twice to kill both Germans. Still moving upward, they came under fire from a German machine gun. Murphy replied with the Browning machine gun, and a moment later a German appeared with a white handkerchief. Over Murphy's advice Tipton stood to accept the supposed surrender. "Keep down," Murphy yelled. "Don't trust them." But Tipton did and was shot through the chest.

In his biography Murphy writes that he was possessed by a "demon." He threw a grenade into the machine-gun pit, killing the Germans, picked up their gun, and ran up the hill firing it from the hip until he came to the German machine-gun nest that fired the fatal shot. He fired until he ran out of ammunition. The hill was taken, and Murphy returned to Tipton's body and cried.

For his actions that day, Murphy received the Distinguished Service Cross. Soon Murphy's skill and reputation was such that he earned a battlefield promotion to second lieutenant, which he tried to stave off by noting that he had only a fifth-grade education. He had, however, taken educational courses offered to the troops.

Murphy's war wasn't over. On the morning of January 26, 1945, he was Company B's only surviving officer, and one of only eighteen men from the original complement of 235. They were fighting in central Alsace, the French-speaking province bordering Germany that the Nazis had incorporated into the "Greater German Reich."

Just before dawn Murphy's men were ordered to a position on the edge of a clearing to fend off an expected German attack. The ground was frozen solid, and attempts to dig foxholes only succeeded in warming the freezing troops. A unit that was supposed to protect their flank never arrived, though clanking into place were two tank destroyers, lightly armored, tracked vehicles with high-velocity cannon mounted in open, rotating turrets. Then one slid into a ditch and had to be abandoned. At 2:00 p.m. German troops appeared, two hundred men and six tanks, badly outnumbering the Americans. Murphy ordered up an artillery barrage via a field telephone, but moments later the Germans knocked out the surviving tank destroyer and a German shell killed his entire machine-gun unit. In his autobiography Murphy wrote: "At that moment I know that we are lost."

He ordered the rest of his troops back into the woods and stayed on the phone directing artillery fire. He emptied his carbine at the approaching Germans and was about to sprint away when he saw that atop the smoldering tank destroyer was "a perfectly good machine gun and several cases of ammunition." It was a Browning .50 caliber, five feet long, eighty-four pounds, mounted atop the turret and in full view of the approaching enemy. Murphy climbed up with the field telephone, pushed aside the body of a dead American, and while German bullets and tank rounds narrowly missed him called in artillery fire. Then he turned the Browning on anything that moved. He also told jokes. A soldier on the other end of the phone asked how close the Germans were. "Just hold the phone and I'll let you talk to one of the bastards," Murphy said.

Smoke from the burning tank destroyer provided him cover, and Murphy said flames warmed his feet for the first time in days. Then through a gap in the haze he saw twelve Germans crawling toward him. "I turned the machine gun on them and stacked them up by cordwood." The worried artilleryman on the other end asked if was injured. "I'm all right, Sergeant. What are your postwar plans?" Murphy said.

A forward artillery observer, Lt. Walter W. Weispfenning, who witnessed the action, said, "I saw hundreds of Germans swarming from the woods. They all had automatic weapons. He was all alone out there, except for a tree and a tank destroyer that was about 10 yards to his right. The artillery fire he directed had a deadly effect. I saw Germans disappearing in clouds of dirt and snow." With the Germans 100 yards away, "he climbed onto the tank destroyer turret and began firing its .50 caliber machine gun at the Krauts. He was completely exposed to the enemy fire and there was a blaze under him that threatened to blow the destroyer to bits."[14]

Twice the tank destroyer was hit by enemy shells, and Weispfenning saw Murphy engulfed in clouds of smoke and spurts of flame, his clothes riddled by flying fragments of lead. How long Murphy stood on the tank, firing the Browning .50-caliber gun and calling in artillery rounds, is difficult to calculate. Some said the engagement lasted an hour; others said thirty minutes.

Later Murphy said he found that time slowed to a crawl. Every object and movement became "very clarified." Smashed by artillery fire and riddled by Murphy's machine gun, the German advance faltered and collapsed. Murphy, wounded by shell fragments in one leg, crawled off the tank and limped away into the sudden quiet.

EPILOGUE

When Audie Murphy mounted the tank, a seemingly futile gesture that morphed into a courageous stand worthy of the Medal of Honor, he used a .50-caliber machine gun that had been invented by John Browning a half-dozen years before Murphy was born. When his men pulled back into the forest they carried Browning Automatic Rifles, which appeared in 1917. And as an officer Murphy would have been issued a Colt pistol, adopted by the Army in 1911.

The machine-gun crew from Murphy's B Company, First Division, killed by shrapnel from a German artillery shell, was armed with Browning's .30-caliber machine gun, first conceived in 1900.

All four Browning firearms remained in service through the Korean War, where the obsolete BAR was praised as the infantry's "indispensable" weapon by army historian S. L. A. Marshall.

Few other twentieth-century firearms, from any nation, remained effective through decades that saw aircraft evolve from cloth-covered biplanes to aluminum-skinned jets. If Browning's firearms weren't perfect, they were always good enough for the bitter business of war.

Browning didn't set out to invent battlefield weapons. The majority of his 128 patents, 35 shared with Matt, were for civilian arms—hunting rifles for deer, shotguns for ducks or trap, and compact, mechanically inventive pistols for police or for self-defense. He found the mechanical challenge of automatic arms impossible to ignore, however, and to that end Browning applied the concepts imagined and mastered over a lifetime to arm American troops. In a letter to his son Val, firearms historian George Chinn wrote in 1986, John Moses Browning was "the world's greatest inventor of every <u>successful</u> automatic weapon principle of operation."

Browning, driven by an unquenchable need to invent and explore the limits of his mechanical imagination, also saw his contribution to military arms as a patriotic duty—the duty of any citizen—and an acknowledgment of humankind's imperfectability. If there were going to be wars, there had to be guns, and Browning was going to give his country the best.

Replacing them has been a challenge.

In 1957 Browning's .30-caliber machine gun and the BAR were retired in favor of the M60, a belt-fed machine gun "inspired" by the fast-firing German MG 42. The new gun was compact, cheap to manufacture, mechanically simple, and sported a quick-change barrel. As one small-arms historian noted, however, "The M60 was lightweight, but correspondingly flimsy, prone to damage and relatively quick to wear out critical parts." Looking for a replacement, the Army organized a shoot-off between the M60 and a machine gun from FN called the M240. Each fired 50,000 rounds. The FN gun experienced a failure about every 6,442 rounds, while the M60 failed at about every 1,669 rounds, making the FN gun three times more reliable. The Belgian weapon was adopted and remains in use today. What didn't get much attention, then or now, was that the M240 is essentially Browning's World War I–era BAR, only with the action turned upside down and fed by a belt rather than a box magazine.[1]

By the 1980s the Army's 1911 pistols, most manufactured during World War II or earlier, were worn out. Their replacement was the Italian-designed Beretta M9, which, rather than the storied .45-caliber cartridge, fired the standardized NATO 9mm pistol round. Unsurprisingly, many complained that the smaller, lighter bullet was a poor substitute for the larger .45-caliber bullet with its "stopping power," even as critics acknowledged that the Beretta had distinct advantages. The smaller round meant its magazine held fifteen cartridges compared to the 1911's seven.

The 9mm cartridge produced less recoil, making it less intimidating to inexperienced troops. Safety features designed into the gun also minimized unintended discharges from careless handling, a potential hazard with the 1911.

The M9 used the slide invented by John Browning, though not his tilting barrel. The Beretta was a good gun, despite complaints about its size and weight. When it was replaced in 2017, the Army chose a gun designed by SIG Sauer, a Swiss-German company that pioneered "modular" construction, meaning that the mechanical action can be quickly switched into small, medium, or large frames, to better fit the shooter's hand. Even the caliber can be changed.

The new SIG Sauer, called the M17 and sold in the civilian market as the P320, uses the tilting barrel and slide Browning invented in 1896.

The .50-caliber machine gun has also come up for periodic reevaluation, and at least four major attempts have been made to develop a lighter gun with less recoil. One was produced by General Electric, specifically for tank turrets, but lasted only a brief time before it was replaced with the old M2. Alternatives proposed by various other manufacturers have never made it past field tests. Today about fifty thousand Browning M2 machine guns remain in use by the American military. Its longevity has been extended by a quick-change barrel system, finally rectifying the gun's only significant shortcoming. Almost 2 million M2s were made during World War II. Total worldwide production is now estimated to be 3 million, and it is used by some 100 nations. In America it is still manufactured by General Dynamics, U.S. Ordnance, a private firm in Nevada, and Ohio Ordnance Works.

Lever-action rifles remained the quintessential American long arm for generations of hunters, so while Browning's lever-action Winchester rifle designs are advanced in years they still function as he intended and are still manufactured, though not by the original Winchester company and not in America. In 1931 the Great Depression sent Winchester into bankruptcy. Eventually the Olin Corporation took over, and it prospered arming America for World War II. Afterward the cost of producing rifles to Browning's original, nineteenth-century designs led to labor strife and in 1980 the New Haven complex was sold off to the employees. They continued doing business as U.S. Repeating Arms and sold firearms under the Winchester name until the company was sold to FN. In 2006 the factory that made Winchester rifles and shotguns for 140 years was closed. The brick buildings are now apartments called the Winchester Lofts, each unit featuring at least two of the tall, wide windows that provided light to the factory floor in the era before electricity.

Today most of Browning's rifles, from the first single shot through the 1895 box-magazine rifle that Theodore Roosevelt favored, remain in small-scale production but are manufactured in Japan and in Italy. Olin still sells ammunition for rifles, shotguns, and handguns under the Winchester name.

Colt suffered through its own management missteps, financial crises, and a succession of owners. In the 1980s workers went on a five-year-long strike that ended with the company's sale to private investors. Colt now manufactures M-4 carbines for the U.S. Army, along with revolvers, including the original nineteenth-century Single Action Army of western fame, and the 1911 pistol. Unfortunately for Colt, the Browning patent is long expired and more than two dozen American firms, plus others overseas, produce Browning's pistol in dozens of varieties. There are 1911s made in at least seven different calibers and four different sizes, at prices that range from $500 to over $5,000 for an exquisitely handcrafted model. A small industry produces parts and frames for upgrading and partial manufacture at home. The trigger John Browning created remains the best handgun trigger mechanism in the world, as it can be tuned so that pressing the trigger works the action as sharp and quickly as a hammer cracking a pane of glass. The 1911's biggest drawback was that it only held seven rounds, so in the 1980s Browning's action and slide was used as the basis for "2011" competition firearms with rounds stacked in two columns for greater capacity.

FN produces Browning's .50-caliber machine gun as well as other military and civilian rifles and pistols and still manufactures highly crafted shotguns based on the Superposed. A large bronze plaque in the company boardroom pays homage to Browning, and his photograph hangs in the room where he was struck down by a heart attack. Outside, a block to the north of the main entrance, is a street named in his honor, Rue John Moses Browning.

After John Browning's death, Val and Marriner Browning created Browning Arms, which imported rifles and shotguns from Belgium and, after World War II, from the Miroku company in Japan. In 1977 the company became embroiled in a federal tax dispute involving rifles purchased from FN and Miroku for resale in America. In what FN later conceded was something of a "hostile" takeover it purchased the Browning company, ending family involvement.[2] Val's relationships with Colt and Winchester improved with time, and he became a major philanthropic donor as did other descendants of John and Matthew. He died at age ninety-eight in 1994. Marriner Browning died in 1966 at age seventy-six. He left the Browning company before World War II— he and Val disagreed on the company's direction—to work in banking and ranching. Ed was hospitalized and died of appendicitis in 1939 while in New Haven for a meeting with Winchester.

Exactly how many of John M. Browning's firearms have been produced is difficult to calculate. There are many knock-offs manufactured across the globe, and many other firearm designers have been influenced by his work. The famed Soviet AK-47, for example, uses an unusual safety lever that strongly resembles the mechanism on Browning's Remington-made Model 8 rifle. In the mid-twentieth century the former Soviet Union produced more than 1.5 million Tokarev TT-33 pistols, a close copy of Browning's Colt 1903. FN stopped making Hi-Power pistols in 2017, but that slack was picked up by the Turkish company TİSAŞ, which began producing copies in 2014, along with its own version of the 1911.

So a very, very conservative estimate—indeed, most certainly too low—is between 35 and 40 million firearms of all types. That figure encompasses American military contracts and major civilian manufacturers, through the twentieth century, such as Winchester, Colt, FN, Remington, and the Ithaca Gun Company, an unfamiliar name to many but one that serves to underline Browning's historic longevity. More than a decade after Browning's death, Ithaca started manufacturing its Model 1937 shotgun after the patents expired on a 1913 Browning design. Elements of the Model 1937 have been revised in the intervening decades, but it is essentially the same firearm. It remains widely used, favored by police departments and hunters alike, and is said to be the only pre–World War I shotgun design still in mass production. Why? Another Browning idea. It's sleek, easily handled, and the shells are loaded and ejected out the bottom, rather than the side, making it comfortable for left- and right-handers alike. Production is more than 2 million and counting.

ACKNOWLEDGMENTS

There are thousands of books, articles, and YouTube videos describing or demonstrating John Moses Browning's firearms, but there is only one previous biography, written in the 1950s by Browning's eldest son, John "Jack" Browning, and then re-written and edited in the 1960s by the late author Curt Gentry, with a final review likely done by Jack's younger brother Val Browning. The published version is poetic and folksy but provides a sometimes less-than-accurate and incomplete account of Browning's life. Much of it is presented through conversations Jack reconstructed decades after the fact. Its emphasis is on the inventor's early years in Utah, making it the primary source on Browning's story for the first decades after his birth in 1855. My own research and writing were greatly aided by an uncut and unabridged version of Jack's manuscript graciously provided by John Moses Browning's granddaughter Judith Browning Jones and her husband, Leon, and Browning's late grandson Bruce W. Browning, who along with his wife, Barbara, twice hosted me for interviews and lunch. Bruce and Judith are the children of Val and Ann Chaffin Browning.

Bruce Browning was an enthusiastic supporter of my effort, hoping for a book that introduced modern readers to his grandfather's work. Though at age ninety-one he found it difficult to walk, Bruce was a sharp and helpful source on firearms and family history. Unfortunately, he passed away in December 2019, though not before reading the previously unknown transcript of the 1901 deposition of John, Matt, and Ed. "The document was very moving," he wrote in an email. "For the first time in my life

ACKNOWLEDGMENTS

I had words directly from John M. The document answers many questions for me."

Judith Jones asked that I sidestep the mythmaking that often surrounds John M. Browning, and she offered important insights into John and his wife, Rachel, passed on by her aunts, John and Rachel's daughters. Her husband, Leon, was particularly encouraging. No review of the manuscript was asked or offered.

Other Browning family members were also very helpful. Steven E. Lindquist, a descendant of John's brother Matthew, graciously provided historical detail about that often-overlooked Browning brother, along with documents gleaned from his own research. Betseylee Browning, who runs the Browning family Facebook page and has shelves of binders on the extended family's history—there are many branches of the Browning family— welcomed me to her home and shared her relevant files. Her husband, Deven Kay, is a descendant of a son from Jonathan Browning's first marriage. Quentin Smith, a descendant of Jonathan "Ed" Browning and now living in Texas, was kind enough to write two long emails recounting stories from older relatives and provided me with letters and newspaper clippings.

I received early access to forty boxes of family and company documents, previously in Bruce Browning's basement and recently donated to Weber State University. Sarah Langsdon, curator of special collections at the Stewart Library on the Ogden campus, along with her staff, provided me with enthusiastic assistance.

The breadth of Browning's inventions has been the subject of many extraordinarily detailed technical histories by writers who specialize in Browning's military and civilian firearms. Those volumes on military arms often included lengthy excerpts from Army Ordnance reports, which saved me much research time. Particular thanks go to Dolf L. Goldsmith and his five-volume history of Browning machine guns, and Frank Iannamico, who in addition to his own work, *Hard Rain: History of the Browning Machine Guns*, coauthored with Goldsmith an important book on the development, testing, and deployment of the .50-caliber Browning machine gun, *Semper Fi FIFTY!*, volume 4 of *The Browning Machine Gun*.

Similar thanks are due Edward Scott Meadows, whose 558-page *U.S. Military Automatic Pistols,* volume 1: *1894–1920* not only encompasses the lengthy development of Browning's .45-caliber 1911 pistol but also describes its many competitors.

The late author of an important history of Winchester and Browning, Herbert G. Houze, gave me more than an hour of his time for an interview. Dan Shea, editor-in-chief of *Small Arms Review* and *Small Arms Defense Journal,* provided a tour of his firearms collection and explained the design innovations that made Browning's machine guns the primary Allied automatic weapons of World War II.

Archivists and librarians in America and Belgium were crucial to this book. Bob Beebe at National Archives at Kansas City found century-old patent documents. Thanks are also owed to Tim Reidy, of Reidy Historical Consulting in Kansas City, who saved me an airplane flight, and archivist Jennifer Audsley-Moore.

At the National Archives in New York City, Kelly McAnnaney provided additional patent documents that included a second Browning deposition.

Anyone interested in the Browning story should visit two museums. At the John M. Browning Firearms Museum in Ogden, I received much-welcomed help from Lee Witten and particularly Robert Geier, who after an hour's conversation about Browning and his firearms passed my contact information on to Leon Jones. Also in Ogden is Jim Alvey of the Alvey Media Group who gave me a tour of John Moses Browning's second-floor workshop, now part of his company's private offices. Real estate agent Sue Wilkerson took time from her schedule to escort me through Browning's Ogden home.

In Cody, Wyoming, the unparalleled Buffalo Bill Center of the West has detailed nineteenth-century records from Winchester Repeating Arms held at the McCracken Research Library. Thanks to its staff, which includes Mary Robinson, Karen Roles, and Karen Preis.

In the same complex is the recently redesigned Cody Firearms Museum. Its collection spans centuries and includes the many John M. Browning prototypes purchased but never produced by Winchester. Ashley Hlebinsky, curator emerita and senior firearms scholar, and Danny Michael, assistant curator, welcomed me and offered insights on an earlier version of this book. My thanks.

Also, Eugene Golubtsov, aka LugerMan, in Langhorne, Pennsylvania, who produces excellent reproductions of the rare .45-caliber Luger used in the early-twentieth-century military trial.

Two extraordinary well-researched YouTube channels played an important role in my firearms education: Ian McCallum's popular *Forgotten Weapons*, and *C&Rsenal*, where host Othais and "designated markswoman" Mae serve up history and demonstrations of World War I–era firearms.

Others who assisted in my research were Samuel Williamson and Jenny Fienberg at the Augusta-Richmond County Public Library system; Cori Sparks, Lumpkin County, Georgia, geographer; Chris Worick, Lumpkin County Historical Society; Valerie D. Glen, University of Georgia Libraries; Susannah Carroll, assistant director of collections and curatorial at the Franklin Institute; and Jennifer Duncan, special collections librarian at Utah State University. Also, Jim Davis, from This Is the Place Heritage Park; Vivian Rogers-Price, research director at the National Museum of the Mighty Eighth Air Force. Thanks to Raphael Sagalyn for suggesting a "social history."

Linda Harris read and critiqued these chapters. Others who helpfully weighed in on all or parts of this book were Ned Warwick, Wayne Urquhart, Nell Boeschenstein, Greg Muennich, Jane Friedman, Tom Graham, Jonina Schonfeld, Michael DeLeo, and Azriel Shiloh. Susan Barr Toman very helpfully read the original proposal and early chapters. Also, Shane Healey.

Becca Flemer is much thanked for her support and encouragment. Also Jonina (Gorenstein) Schonfeld and her husband, Jonathan.

Domenica Newell-Amato translated the many French-language memos, letters, articles, and documents on Browning and FN, and Marla Hess, a freelance American editor living in Belgium, did research in advance of my arrival in Belgium. That trip would not have been nearly as successful without the help of interpreter Pauline Mercier, of Liège, who translated and assisted with research in Belgium.

Much appreciation is due to the staff of FN's Ars Mechanica Foundation in Herstal, who hosted me for much of a week, providing documents, meals, and a tour of the FN facilities. They include the late Robert Sauvage, former CEO of the Ars Mechanica Foundation, the historical institute created by FN; Pascal Pruvost, who made a special search of the archives; and Anne-Marie André. My thanks also to Dr. Bernard Wilkin, chief archivist at the state archives Belgium Liège division. Shane Healey of FN, now retired, discussed the technical nature of Browning's work, and Adrien Marnat took time from his schedule to conduct a tour of the Grand Curtius Museum in Liège.

Assistance was also provided by Jay G. Burrup, a history specialist with the LDS Church History Library in Salt Lake City, Utah; William Brown, director of the Eli Whitney Museum in Connecticut; and Scott Davison, education director at the fascinating American Precision Museum in Windsor, Vermont, who offered me a tour on a cold winter morning. Anyone vacationing in Vermont should visit.

Taigh Ramey runs the Stockton Field Aviation Museum in Stockton, California, and organizes the annual "Bomber Camp," a one- or two-day immersion into World War II bomber aircraft. I was fortunate enough to spend a day, including an hour flying in a B-17 operated by the Collings Foundation prior to that aircraft's tragic crash in 2019.

There would be no book without my agent, Alice Fried Martell of the Martell Agency; Rick Horgan, vice president and executive editor at Scribner; and his editorial assistant, Beckett Rueda. Thanks to all.

GLOSSARY

Action—The internal mechanism of a firearm that loads and fires ammunition.

Automatic weapon—A firearm that, once the trigger is pulled, will keep firing until the trigger is released or the gun runs out of ammunition. See *semiautomatic*.

Block or breechblock—The part that seals the end of the barrel after the ammunition is loaded into the chamber. It contains the firing pin.

Bolt—A type of block that reciprocates horizontally to open and close the breech.

Bore—The interior of a gun barrel through which the bullet travels out the muzzle.

Breech—The rear of the barrel where the ammunition is inserted.

Bullet—The projectile that exits the barrel when a gun is fired.

Caliber—The internal diameter of a barrel; also used to refer to the diameter of a bullet. A .50-caliber bullet is produced for a barrel bore .5 inches in diameter.

Cartridge—The combination of metallic casing, primer, propellant, and lead bullet.

Chamber—The breech end of the barrel where the cartridge is loaded. When a barrel bore is drilled the breech end is shaped to the dimensions of a specific cartridge. The chamber is sealed by the block or bolt.

Firing pin—The spring-loaded steel pin that strikes the primer and ignites the propellant.

Gas operation—The use of hot gas drawn off from burning propellant to power the mechanism of an automatic weapon.

Gunpowder—Usually refers to black powder, a mixture of saltpeter, charcoal, and sulfur, used as the propellant in firearms until the 1890s.

Heavy machine gun—A term applied to Browning's .30-caliber water-cooled machine gun, but which now refers to other large-caliber, tripod-mounted automatic weapons.

Lever action—A rifle that uses a lever at the trigger to load and eject a cartridge; the type made popular by Winchester.

Light machine gun—In World War II usually a tripod-mounted automatic weapon without a water-cooling system.

Mainspring—A spring, flat or coiled, that powers a firearm's hammer.

Primer—A catalyst at the base of a cartridge ignited by the firing pin, and which ignites the propellant in the cartridge.

Receiver—The steel frame of a pistol, rifle, or machine gun, which contains the action. It "receives" the ammunition.

Recoil—The force pushing a firearm rearward in reaction to the propellant pushing the bullet forward.

Recoil spring—A spring in a handgun slide that is compressed when the gun fires and slide moves backward. When the slide reaches the end of its travel the stored energy in the recoil spring throws the slide forward.

Rimfire—A type of cartridge ignited by a firing pin striking a priming compound in the rim of the cartridge case.

Round—Another name for a cartridge.

Semiautomatic—Also called *self-loading.* A firearm that fires only one shot each time the trigger is pulled, even if the trigger is held down after the first shot. It's different from an automatic weapon.

Slide action—A term to describe a handgun mechanism, specifically the steel shell that encloses the barrel and includes an integral block and firing pin. The slide reciprocates on rails cut into the frame, ejecting the spent cartridge as it retracts, then cocking the gun and loading a fresh cartridge for the next shot as it moves forward. (Tradtionally, "a slide action" refers to a pump-action shotgun, and the handgun slide system is a "short-recoil" action.)

Smokeless powder—A powerful, clean-burning propellant that replaced black powder in the 1890s.

NOTES

Prologue

1. There are many accounts of the archduke's assassination. This is drawn from publications that include: Tim Butcher, *The Trigger: Hunting the Assassin Who Brought the World to War*, reprint ed. (New York: Grove Press, 2014), and Charles River Editors, *The Assassination of Archduke Franz Ferdinand: The History and Legacy of the Event That Triggered World War I* (Charles River Editors, 2014).

2. Or try to kill a revolutionary. In August 1918 a Browning pistol was used in a near-successful attempt to assassinate Vladimir Lenin in Moscow. A disillusioned follower, Fanny Efimovna Kaplan, fired three shots from an FN 1900, one through Lenin's coat, one through his neck, and one into his left lung. Kaplan, 28, was executed five days later. As history shows, Lenin survived until 1924, though apparently never fully recovered.

3. All production figures are from published manufacturers' data or records in the Browning Family Collection, unless otherwise noted. Also relied upon is data collected by Browning grandson Bruce Browning and included in the biography written by his uncle, John "Jack" Browning, and Curt Gentry, *John M. Browning American Gunmaker*, 1st ed. (New York: Doubleday, 1964), and Anthony Vanderlinden, *FN Browning Pistols, Side Arms That Shaped the World History*, expanded 2nd ed. (Greensboro, NC: Wet Dog, 2013).

4. Browning became the subject of glowing profiles in magazines and newspapers across the country. One of many examples was the June 1918 article, "The Greatest Inventor of Guns in the World," in *American Magazine*, a popular publication with a national circulation.

Chapter One: Frontier Lessons

1. Excerpts are from the original, unpublished version of John "Jack" Browning's biography of his father, John M. Browning, written in the 1950s. It contains material not included in the 1964 published book. By the early 1960s, Jack Browning was in ill health and his text was rewritten by co-author Curt Gentry, who in an apologetic letter after his first attempt

told Jack he was unfamiliar with firearms. Val Browning, Jack's younger brother, headed the Browning company and purchased rights to the manuscript from his brother before publication. Val probably had final control of the text.

2. Noland F. Nelson, *Waterfowl Hunting in Utah* (Utah Department of Fish and Game, 1966).

3. Dates for Jonathan Browning's life were in large part taken from Family Search.org, https://www.familysearch.org/tree/person/details/K2W3 -743. Much research was done by Betseylee Browning, whose husband, Deven Kay, is a descendant of patriarch Jonathan Browning's son David Elias. Susan Easton Black, "Jonathan Browning, Mormon Gunsmith," *Pioneer* 59, no. 2 (2012), was also useful in compiling this history, as was Betseylee Browning, "Matthew Sandefur Browning," in the same publication.

4. It is on display at the John M. Browning Firearms Museum in Ogden, Utah.

5. "Orville H. Browning (1806–1881)," *Mr. Lincoln and Friends* (blog), http:// www.mrlincolnandfriends.org/members-of-congress/orville-browning/; The Diary of Orville Hickman Browning, Illinois State Historical Society Library, 1927.

6. Ibid.

7. Old-fashioned black powder is for all practical purposes an explosive, while modern "smokeless" powder burns, or "deflagrates," to produce the hot gas that propels a bullet down the barrel.

8. John M. Browning to Seymour & Earle, attorneys, New Haven, Connecticut, April 28, 1900, Browning Family Collection (hereafter BFC), MS 493 Special Collections, Weber State University, Ogden, Utah.

9. Some accounts indicate Jonathan Browning married a second wife, named Polly Rippy, around 1830, long before he joined the Mormon faith. If so, there are no known records to substantiate the union.

10. Pioneer Personal History Questionnaire T. Samuel Browning, Works Project Administration, Federal Writers Project, August 2, 1941, Utah State Historical Society.

11. Original Jack Browning manuscript.

12. Richard C. Roberts, *Ogden: Junction City*, 1st ed. (Northridge, CA: Windsor, 1985).

13. Lyle J. Barnes, *Notorious Two-Bit Street* (West Conshohocken, PA: Infinity, 2009).

14. Browning's curse words were omitted from the published version, as was the reference to the customer's intoxication.

15. Lucian Cary, "Genius Gun Designer," *True* magazine, 1952.

16. A bullet's size, based on the diameter of the barrel's bore, is called its caliber, which corresponds to inches, so a .50-caliber bullet has a half-inch diameter, though the actual dimension can vary. A bullet may be a thousandth of an inch or so larger to better grip the rifling.

17. Copy of sales contract, dated January 7, 1879, courtesy of Steven Lindquist.

NOTES

Chapter Two: Land of Invention

1. "The Hoosac Tunnel Disaster of 1867," *New England Historical Society* (blog), 2020, https://www.newenglandhistoricalsociety.com/hoosac-tunnel -disaster-1867/; "Workers Complete Hoosac Tunnel," https://www.mass moments.org/moment-details/workers-complete-hoosac-tunnel.html. Estimates of the number of dead range between 180 and 200.
2. George W. Wingate, *Why Should Boys Be Taught to Shoot* (Boston: Sub-Target Gun Co., 1907), p. 1.
3. *Harper's Weekly*, October 10, 1874, p. 838.
4. S.I. Staff, "The Great Rifle Match," Sports Illustrated Vault | SI.com, September 13, 1954, https://vault.si.com/vault/1954/09/13/the-great-rifle -match.
5. History of Creedmoor Match, National Rifle Association of Ireland, http://nrai.ie/creedmor-history.html.
6. Herbert G. Houze, *Arming the West: A Fresh New Look at the Guns That Were Actually Carried on the Frontier*, 1st ed. (Woonsocket, RI: Andrew Mowbray, 2007).
7. William Temple Hornaday, *The Extermination of the American Bison* (Washington, DC: Smithsonian Museum, 1889).
8. The external hammer was mounted on the right side of the receiver. It didn't fall directly on the cartridge but instead struck a lever that transferred the force sideways, then forward onto the firing pin. The firing pin didn't retract between shots, a sought-after safety feature. Loading the gun took five steps: pulling the hammer back to half cock, dropping the lever, loading the cartridge into the chamber, raising the lever, and pulling the hammer back to full cock. It wasn't a rifle conducive to quick second shots.
9. Reloading it was less tedious than reloading the Sharps. The hammer was pulled back first; then the block was rolled open, the cartridge loaded, the block closed, and the trigger pulled.
10. Directory of Ogden City and Weber County, 1870, p. 181.
11. "In the Matter of the Estate of Jonathan Browning, Deceased, in the Probate Court of Weber, Territory of Utah," Utah State Archives. The file contains 204 pages; the estate was not finally settled until 1893.
12. Ibid., Joseph Wright, Affidavit of Auctioneer to Sales of Personal Property.
13. Author interviews with Browning descendants. Various dates 2018 and 2019.
14. Rushton was a good shot. He tied with Browning for first place at an Ogden rifle club pigeon shoot in 1883, though a short while later lost the second finger of his left hand in a shotgun hunting accident. He left the Brownings' employ and went into business in Provo, Utah, for himself and in 1888 "skipped" town with his creditors in pursuit. In 1904 he was back in Ogden and declared bankruptcy.
15. Laura Trevelyan, *The Winchester: The Gun That Built an American Dynasty* (New Haven, CT: Yale University Press, 2016).
16. *Record of Service of Connecticut Men in the Army and Navy of the United States*

During the War of the Rebellion, Connecticut Adjutant-General's Office, 1889, p. 815.

17. A. H. Newton, *Out of the Briars: An Autobiography and Sketch of the Twenty-Ninth Regiment, Connecticut Volunteers* (Philadelphia: A.M.E. Book Concern, 1910).

18. Ibid., p. 56.

19. Ron Soodalter, "The Great Beefsteak Raid," *Opinionator* (blog), September 21, 2014, https://opinionator.blogs.nytimes.com/2014/09/21/the-great-beefsteak-raid/.

20. Herbert G. Houze, *To the Dreams of Youth: Winchester: .22 Caliber Single Shot Rifle,* 1st ed. (Iola, WI: Krause, 1993), and *Winchester Repeating Arms Company: Its History & Development from 1865 to 1981,* 1st ed. (Iola, WI: Krause, 1994).

21. Robert Bennett to wife, Jennie, morning, December 10, 1883, Connecticut State Historical Society.

22. Robert Bennett to wife, evening, December 10, 1883, Connecticut State Historical Society.

Chapter Three: Conquering the East

1. New York Public Library's Digital Library, digital ID 3fa04b30-c530-012f-91ea-58d385a7bc34.

2. Felicia Johnson Deyrup, *Arms Makers of the Connecticut Valley: A Regional Study of the Economic Development of the Small Arms Industry, 1798–1870* (Northampton, MA: Smith College Studies, 1948); Edwin A. Battison, *Muskets to Mass Production: The Men & the Times That Shaped American Manufacturing,* 1st ed. (Windsor, VT: American Precision Museum, 1976).

3. David A. Hounshell, *From the American System to Mass Production, 1800–1932: The Development of Manufacturing Technology in the United States* (Baltimore: Johns Hopkins University Press, 1985).

4. Ibid.

5. Harold Francis Williamson, *Winchester: The Gun That Won the West* (New York: A.S. Barnes and Co., 1952).

6. Edwin Pugsley, speech, Winchester Museum in Hartford, Connecticut, circa 1950s.

7. John Campbell, *The Winchester Single-Shot* (Lincoln, RI: Andrew Mowbray, 1995).

8. Bruce Browning, interview with the author, January 7–8, 2019.

9. Report of the Secretary of the Navy, 1885, p. 233.

10. Ned H. Roberts, *Roberts on Rifles,* p. 32.

11. "Bear Hunt in the Himalayas," *Forest and Stream* 29 (August 1887–January 1888): 404.

12. "Two Bears with One Ball," *Forest and Stream* 35 (October 28, 1890): 271.

13. Frank M. Canton, *Frontier Trails: The Autobiography of Frank M. Canton,* 1st paperback ed. (Norman: University of Oklahoma Press, 1972).

14. Phil Spangenberger, "The Dalton Death Rifle?," *True West Magazine* (blog), November 5, 2012, https://truewestmagazine.com/article/the -dalton-death-rifle/; "Coffeyville, Kansas: The Town That Stopped the Dalton Gang (Teaching with Historic Places)," National Register of Historic Places, National Park Service, Washington, DC, 2002.
15. Brent Craven, museum curator, interview with the author; Bob Boze Bell, "Dalton Debacle," *True West Magazine* (blog), https://truewestmagazine .com/article/dalton-debacle/.

Chapter Four: Trekking through Georgia

1. Lumpkin County, Georgia, Assessor's Office records.
2. John M. Browning to LDS president John Taylor, February 17, 1897, LDS Archives.
3. Heather M. Seferovich, "History of the LDS Southern States Mission, 1875–1898," Brigham Young University, Scholars Archive, 1996.
4. Reid L. Nielson, "The Nineteenth-Century Euro-American Mormon Missionary Model," in *Go Ye into All the World: The Growth & Development of Mormon Missionary Work*, ed. Reid L. Nelson and Fred E. Woods (Provo, UT: Religious Studies Center, 2012), 65–90, https://rsc.byu.edu/; Heather M. Seferovich, "Hospitality and Hostility: Missionary Work in the American South, 1875–98," in Nelson and Woods eds., *Go Ye into All the World*, 317–40, https://rsc.byu.edu/.
5. *John Moses Browning*, LDS missionary archives, https://history.churchof jesuschrist.org/missionary/individual/john-moses-browning-1855?lang =eng.
6. Judith Browning Jones, interview with the author, January 24, 2019.
7. "John Carver, of Eden, was arrested on the charge of unlawful cohabiting with his wives . . . $1,500 . . . bonds were furnished by J.H. Shaw and Matt S. Browning," *Ogden Herald*, December 8, 1886.
8. Child's diary.
9. Judith Browning Jones, interview with the author.
10. John Kimball Alexander, "Tarred and Feathered: Mormons, Memory, and Ritual Violence" (MA thesis, University of Utah, 2012).
11. Letter from Jedediah Ballantyne, *Deseret News*, September 28, 1887.
12. *Dahlonega Signal*, May 29, 1887.
13. Ballantyne, *Deseret News*, November 21, 1888.
14. Williamson, *Winchester: The Gun That Won the West*.
15. In 1884 Matthew, twenty-four, married Mary Ann Adams, twenty, on December 17, in a joint ceremony with his brother Ed, twenty-five, and Mary Ann Roxanna Jones, who turned twenty years old six days after her wedding. Betseylee Browning in *Pioneer* magazine wrote: "There is a family story that after the wedding, the boys were sitting around chatting so long that the brides went to bed in the same bedroom, leaving the bridegrooms behind."

16. *Ogden Daily Standard,* June 1, 1890, and various articles.
17. "ICI Paints Division, Stowmarket" (5 series, 1979 1871), HC411, Suffolk Record Office, Ipswich Branch, UK.
18. Michael Bussard, *Ammo Encyclopedia,* ed. John B. Allen and David Kosowski, 6th ed. (Minneapolis: Blue Book Publications Inc., 2017).

Chapter Five: Thinking in Three Dimensions

1. *Ogden Standard,* December 3, 1889, p. 1.
2. Bussard, *Ammo Encyclopedia.* Browning used a Winchester 1873 firing the .44-40 cartridge, a low-velocity round by then considered more suited to revolvers. The peak gas pressure was a relatively modest 16,000 pounds per square inch.
3. *Salt Lake Herald Republican,* November 17, 1888.
4. *Ogden Semi-Weekly Standard,* October 26, 1889.
5. John Browning and Curt Gentry, *John M. Browning American Gunmaker,* 1st ed. (New York: Doubleday, 1964), p. 149.
6. As Matt realized the import of John's inventions he began keeping irregular notes about John's life and work that are quoted in Jack's manuscript. Matt's notes have apparently since been lost.
7. "James Watt, Father of the Modern Steam Engine," December 30, 2017, https://interestingengineering.com/james-watt-father-of-the-modern-steam-engine; "James Watt Biography—Science Hall of Fame—National Library of Scotland," https://digital.nls.uk/scientists/biographies/james-watt/index.html.
8. Albert Einstein, *Ideas and Opinions,* reprint ed. (New York: Broadway Books, 1995), p. 27; "Einstein on Creative Linking/Music and the Intuitive Art of Scientific Imagination," *Psychology Today,* March 31, 2010, https://www.psychologytoday.com/us/blog/imagine/201003/einstein-creative-thinking-music-and-the-intuitive-art-scientific-imagination.
9. Philip H. Brownell, "Turning Something Over in the Mind," *Scientific American* 251, no. 6 (December 1984): 106.
10. Bruce Browning, interview with the author.
11. Ibid.
12. An anecdote not included in Jack Browning's published book.
13. The $10,000 is an estimate based on incomplete accounts in various public reports. It probably errs on the low side.
14. Jack's version of this anecdote appears to be based on a written account by Matt.

Chapter Six: America's Deer Rifle

1. "Pioneer Personal History, Alex Brewer | Works Progress Administration Biography Sketches," https://collections.lib.utah.edu/details?id=699748.

NOTES

2. Patents were filed in June and December 1885, July and September 1886, two in May 1888 and June 1889.

3. Judith Browning Jones, interview with the author.

4. *Complainants' [sic] Rebuttal Proof Continued, John M. Browning and Colt's Patent Fire Arms Manufacturing Company vs Albert H. Funke*, United States District Court for the Southern District of New York, deposition taken October 7, 1907, in Ogden, Utah, p. 40.

5. Letter to Frank M. Browning, Ed's son, June 24, 1939, by Col. S. G. Green, courtesy of Quentin Smith.

6. "Pioneer Personal History."

7. William Frederick Schulz, Fairfield Osborn, and James H. Duff, *Conservation Law and Administration: A Case Study of Law and Resource Use in Pennsylvania*, Literary Licensing, LLC, 2012.

8. The North American Model of Wildlife Conservation, Technical Review, December 2012.

9. William Thomas Sherman, *Benjamin Rush: The Revolution's Doctor of Medicine and Universal Humanitarian* (Seattle: 2013), p. 5.

10. "The Return of the White-Tailed Deer," *American Heritage*, https://www.americanheritage.com/return-white-tailed deer.

11. The diameter of the .30-30 bullet is .308 inches, and hunters now typically choose a bullet of 125 or 150 grains. The original bullet was 160 grains. The second "30" stands for 30 grains of the original smokeless powder. "Probably more deer have been harvested with a .30-30 Win than all other rifle cartridges combined" (Bussard, *Ammo Encyclopedia*).

12. Edwin Pugsley offered another description of the problem in a September 1955 speech to the New Haven meeting of the American Society of Arms Collectors: "Due to the frequency of hang fires in the early shotgun ammunition, too often the shot shell that was in the chamber would be ejected before the slow primer ignited the charge, which gave it certain undesirable sales features," meaning the shell could ignite as it was being ejected, "and the gun was withdrawn from the market," until fixes were in place.

13. T. C. Johnson, *MS 020—Winchester Repeating Arms Company Archives Collection, 1857–1980 | McCracken Research Library*, http://centerofthewest.libraryhost.com/index.php?p=collections/findingaid&id=21&q=&rootcontentid=9616#id9162.

14. Dennis Adler, *Winchester Shotguns*, 1st ed. (Edison, NJ: Book Sales, 2008), p. 34.

15. The .405 Winchester bullet weighed three hundred grains. Its recoil bruised shoulders, but it had a modest effective range of about 150 yards when shot at large game animals.

16. Theodore Roosevelt, *African Game Trails*, appendix: "List of Game Shot with the Rifle During the Trip," originally published in 1910. There are now a number of editions by various publishers.

17. Iain McCalman, Annual Lecture, Australian Academy of the Humanities, 2004, p. 96.

NOTES

Chapter Seven: The Mustachioed Man

1. Contract, BFC.
2. Browning to Seymour, 1901, BFC.
3. Lucian Cary, *Genius Gun Designer, True* magazine, 1952.
4. Judith Browning Jones, interview with the author.
5. Bruce Browning, interview with the author.
6. Investigative Reports of the Bureau of Investigation [forerunner of the FBI], 1908–22. Berg was investigated by Naval Intelligence and the Department of State in 1918, in part because he was reported, erroneously, to be involved in the production of mustard gas, a weapon used in World War I trench warfare. He was cleared after an agent interviewed Paul Fuller Jr., chairman of the nation's War Trade Board, and reported: "Says Berg is a shrewd operator of the better classes. . . . Mr. Fuller knows the subject to be a good patriotic citizen of the United States."
7. In 1907 Berg was the European representative of the New York firm Flint & Company, the sales representative for the Wright Brothers, and accompanied Wilbur Wright during his famous European tour. Berg was by now a French Chevalier of the Legion of Honor. Berg's then-wife, Edith (he was married three times), became the first American woman to fly in an airplane, with her ankle-length skirt fastened tightly. "A photograph of Madame Berg seated on the Flyer at Wilbur Wright's side, beaming with pleasure in advance of takeoff, made an unprecedented magazine cover, and the famous Paris dress designer Paul Poiret, quick to see the possibilities in the rope about the ankles, produced a hobble skirt that became a fashion sensation" (David McCullough, *The Wright Brothers* [New York: Simon & Schuster, 2015], p. 204).
8. *Boston Sunday Globe,* March 18, 1900, p. 16, via *New York World.*
9. Browning to attorney George Seymour, 1900, BFC.
10. Recent research has suggested another German inventor, Theodore Bergmann, may have some claim to that title. Https://Www.American-rifleman.Org/Articles/2018/1/4/in-the-Beginning-Semi-Automatic-Pistols-of-the-19th-Century-Google Search."
11. Hans Tauscher, American sales manager for Fabrique Nationale (hereafter FN) and Deutsche Waffen- und Munitionsfabriken (hereafter DMW), deposition, 1901. (See chapter 8 note 13.)
12. There is an extensive history on Borchardt and Luger. Accounts here are drawn from: John Walter, *Luger: The Story of the World's Most Famous Handgun* (New York: Skyhorse, 2018); Fred Datig, *The Luger Pistol: Its Development and History from 1894 to 1945* (Alhambra, CA: Borden, 1962). Also, the massive three-volume history by Joachim Gortz and Dr. Geoffrey Sturgess, *The Borchardt & Luger Automatic Pistols,* vols. 1–3: *A Technical History for Collectors from C93 to P.08* (Galesburg, IL: Brad Simpson Publishing & G L Sturgess, 2012).
13. *Lugar* [*sic*] *v. Browning,* deposition, 1901, p. 33. (See chapter 8 note 13.)
14. Ibid., p. 42.

15. *Browning, Colt, v. Funke,* deposition, 1907, p. 35. (See chapter 8 note 13.)

16. Bruce Browning, with the help of family members, used the patent application and single existing model to construct a working copy, which functioned smoothly but was impractical to produce for the modern market. Bruce Browning, interview with the author.

17. A "slide action" technically refers to the "pump action" as in a shotgun or Browning's .22-caliber 1890 rifle.

18. The slide picked up a fresh cartridge from the magazine contained in the grip and loaded it into the barrel, which rose up and locked to the slide. Once the barrel and slide clicked together the gun was ready to fire another round.

19. With the smaller bullet's lower velocity and a stiff recoil spring, the mass of the steel slide was enough to keep the breech sealed until the bullet emerged from the muzzle, at which moment the slide began its backward movement to eject, cock, and reload the gun.

20. *Lugar* [*sic*] *v. Browning,* deposition, 1901, p. 4. (See chapter 8 note 13.)

21. This account is offered in the published and original version of Jack Browning's memoirs and is the basis for the account used in the many books published about Browning's firearms.

22. *Lugar* [*sic*] *v. Browning,* p. 6.

23. Tom Clancy, *Op-Center 01* (New York: Penguin, 1995), p. 297.

24. Dagmar Ellerbrock, "Gun Violence and Control in Germany 1880–1911: Scandalizing Gun Violence and Changing Perceptions as Preconditions for Firearm Control," in *Control of Violence. Historical and International Perspectives on Violence in Modern Societies,* ed. Wilhelm Heitmeyer, Heinz-Gerhard Haupt, Andrea Kirschner, and Stefan Malthaner (New York: Springer, 2011), pp. 185–212; "Generation Browning," *History in the West* (Geschichte Im Westen), vol. 26, 2011. The author is the chair of modern and contemporary history at the Technische Universität, Dresden, Germany.

25. "Anarchists' Favorite Weapon," *Ogden Daily Standard,* September 19, 1906. There is an extensive literature on pre–World War I anarchists, and Parisian criminal mobs, that often cites the Browning pistols as their weapon of choice. In the summer of 1914 one of Browning's nephews was arrested in Belgium on suspicion of being an anarchist and had to call on "representatives of the Browning's interests," presumably FN, to get released.

26. "The Automatic Gun," *Ogden Daily Standard,* December 1, 1908.

27. George J. Lankevich, *New York City: A Short History* (New York: NYU Press, 2002), p. 140.

Chapter Eight: Georg's Luger and John's Shotgun

1. "Ogden Marksmen Rank with Greatest Trap Shooters in Entire United States," *Ogden Standard-Examiner,* January 9, 1921, https://newspapers.lib.utah.edu/details?id=7230721.

NOTES

2. Elmer Keith, *Shotguns* (Sportsman's Vintage Press, 2013, 1988), p. 8.

3. *Lugar* [*sic*] *v. Browning*, deposition, May 17, 1901, p. 2. (See note 13.)

4. *Browning and Colt v. Funke*, deposition, October 8, 1907, p. 53.

5. Ibid., p. 64.

6. Jennifer Price, *Flight Maps*, new ed. (New York: Basic Books, 2000), p. 3.

7. *Lugar* [*sic*] *v. Browning*, deposition, 1901, p. 61. (See note 13.)

8. Contract dated "20th day of May 1899," BFC.

9. The team at LugerMan in Langhorne, Pennsylvania, who produce high-quality copies of the otherwise rare Luger pistol in .45 ACP, graciously showed me around their shop, explaining the process and techniques used to create precise and reliable firearm replicas.

10. As noted, the Luger Parabellum had distinct visual elements. In his redesign Luger moved the bulbous Borchardt recoil spring into a new, slanted handgrip. He shrank the Borchardt's pistol size further with the revised toggle link. Luger retained the knobs on either side of the toggle-link joint, used to pull the action open by hand, and gave them a second purpose. Now when the gun was fired and the toggle link recoiled, the knobs struck the curved metal ribs projecting on their side of the frame. That impact kicked the joint skyward, "breaking" the toggle link. That change allowed him to reduce the toggle link's overall length.

    Four or five years earlier Browning confronted the same toggle-link size problem when he began work on his first automatic shotgun design in 1894. Shotgun shells are nearly three inches long. This would mean a six-inch-long steel toggle link, too large and too heavy. His solution was to incorporate a triangular steel shape on the bottom of the toggles to strike a steel protrusion on the frame and "kick" open the toggle link. That significantly shortened the rear legs of the toggle mechanism.

11. *Luger v. Browning*, deposition, 1901, p. 3; Decision, United States Patent Office, *Luger v. Browning*, October 5, 1901. (See note 13.)

12. George O. Seymour to John M. Browning, March 23, 1900, BFC.

13. Transcripts of Browning's deposition and other records of the Browning–Luger patent dispute are found in three sets of documents: *Lugar* [*sic*] *v. Browning*. Case no. 20547: National Archives at Kansas City, Kansas City, MO. Container ID 148; *Browning et al v. Funke*, Equity Case S-9074, U.S. Circuit Court for the Southern District of New York, National Archive at New York City. The third set is an exchange of letters and patent filings between Browning and his various patent attorneys. Those documents are part of the Browning Family Collection, MS 493, Weber State University Special Collections. At the time of this writing that collection, donated to the university by Browning grandchildren Bruce Browning and Judith Browning Jones, was being processed, and it may not yet be available for public viewing.

14. *Browning, Colt v. Funke*, finding and decree, Judge George C. Holt, United States Court, Southern District of New York, October 7, 1908.

15. Bennett to Browning, July 23, 1900, BFC.

16. Ibid.

17. Browning to Bennett, August 14, 1900, BFC. The Weber State archive includes a fascinating exchange of ten letters between Bennett and Browning recording Winchester's ultimately unsuccessful, or abandoned, effort to turn the toggle-link shotgun into a production-ready weapon.
18. John Henwood, *The Great Remington 8: And Model 81 Autoloading Rifles*, 3rd ed. (Cobourg, Ontario: Collector Grade, 2003).
19. Maxim published a lengthy diatribe in which he complains about Colt without mentioning Browning. "The Automatic System of Fire-Arms: Its History and Development" was presented in a speech in London on December 11, 1896. It is not known if Browning replied. Colt responded, "Mr. Maxim might as well claim a patent on the wind that blows." In 1896 Maxim did build a gas-operated machine gun, which was tested to good reviews in 1899. Only four were produced.
20. Bennett's letter, with Browning's comments scribbled on the reverse, is in the BFC.
21. *Browning v. Luger* deposition and BFC files.

Chapter Nine: A Mechanism for the Ages

1. *Report of the Philippine Commission to the Secretary of War* (Washington, DC: Govt. Print. Off., 1901–16), Exhibit T, p. 489.
2. James R. Arnold, *The Moro War: How America Battled a Muslim Insurgency in the Philippine Jungle, 1902–1913*, first American ed. (New York: Bloomsbury Press, 2011).
3. Robert Lee Bullard, *The Caliber of the Revolver*, Robert Lee Bullard Papers, Library of Congress, Washington, DC.
4. Detailed accounts of the development of what became the Colt 1911 are available from a number of sources. Particularly useful was the history of the U.S. Army's pistol trials in Edward Scott Meadows, *U.S. Military Automatic Pistols*, vol. 1, *1894–1920* (Moline, IL: Richard Ellis, 1993), a very complete volume, which includes verbatim excerpts from Ordnance Department reports. Also very useful to anyone seeking a detailed history of Colt and the 1911 is Donald B. Bady, *Colt Automatic Pistols* (Union City, TN: Pioneer Press, 2000).
5. Colt's Patent Fire Arms Manufacturing Company Records, circa 1810–1980 (RG 103), Connecticut State Library.
6. A lengthier explanation may be useful for those interested in the mechanical details.

    Colt's famous 1873 revolver was the Single Action Army, the gun seen in innumerable Westerns. Rounds were loaded into the rear of the revolving cylinder. The shooter cocked the hammer with a thumb, which revolved the cylinder, lining up a round with the barrel. Pulling the trigger dropped the hammer, firing the round down the barrel. To rotate the cylinder for a second shot the hammer had to be cocked again with the thumb.

The double-action revolver, popular by the early twentieth century, combined cocking, revolving, and firing with one pull of the trigger. No thumb was needed for the first or subsequent shots.

Browning's semiautomatic pistol is loaded by pressing the rounds into a spring-loaded rectangular magazine, which is inserted into the hand-grip. But—and this was a major change from a revolver—inserting rounds into the magazine did not make the gun ready to fire. To put a bullet into the barrel the shooter had to grip the gun with one hand and pull the slide back with the other, so the spring in the magazine pushed a bullet up into the slide. Then the shooter released the slide. It snapped forward and pushed the bullet into the barrel. The slide, as noted earlier, includes the block and firing pin.

When the pistol trigger was pulled the gun fired a round and the slide retracted, ejecting the spent casing as it traveled. As the slide returned it snatched up a fresh round from the magazine, making the gun ready to fire. Each subsequent trigger pull fired one shot. Carrying early versions of Browning's pistols with a round already loaded in the chamber was considered dangerous for a soldier on horseback (or anyone). Browning, as will be seen, addressed that problem with an improved safety system.

7. Information on Browning's travels to Europe is drawn from reports in the Ogden newspapers, FN historical documents, patent case depositions, and letters in the BFC from Browning and FN executives.

8. "Mayor Browning Home Again," *Ogden Daily Standard*, December 24, 1900, https://newspapers.lib.utah.edu/details?id=7684574.

9. "Released from Quarantine," *Ogden Evening Standard*, March 27, 1912.

10. Marcel Conradt, *Histoires des Hôtels de Liège, 1850–1975* (Belgium: Noir Dessin, 2011), pp. 73–76; various letters from Browning to FN, FN archives, 1904 and 1908; *Maisons recommandees, Guide du Touriste, au pays de Liège* (Belgium: 1891).

11. Henri Chevalier, "Les relations de la FN avec la famille Browning de 1897 à 1914," *Revue, Organe Mensuel du Personnel de la Fabrique Nationale D'Armes de Guerre de Herstal*, 1962. Chevalier, an FN executive who worked with Browning, wrote a series of articles about Browning published in the FN employee magazine.

12. John Potocki, *The Colt Model 1905 Automatic Pistol* (Lincoln, RI: Andrew Mowbray, 1998). Potocki's book includes a copy of the Thompson and La Garde report, p. 122.

13. Meadows, *U.S. Military Automatic Pistols*, vol. 1, *1894–1920*, p. 60.

14. Ibid., p. 100.

15. A cam is a metal part that by impact causes movement in another metal part. In modern refinements to Browning's design the link is replaced by a machined rectangle that is forced down as the slide recoils, tilting the barrel.

NOTES

Chapter Ten: Arming the Army

1. That figure is calculated from population figures drawn from B. R. Mitchell, *European Historical Statistics 1750–1970* (London: Macmillan, 1975), pp. 19–24. If Czarist Russia is included there was one Browning gun per every 362 people.
2. "Browning Is Back from Liège," *Ogden Daily Standard*, September 2, 1909. When an Ogden reporter eager for some detail of Liège buttonholed Browning he offered this observation on the FN workforce: "It might be interesting that most of the work is done by women and girls. They handle the machinery, do the milling and drilling and many other things calling for rather heavy work. They roll up their sleeves and go out like men. It is quite amusing to hear them, clunky clank, over the wooden floors as they go about the work in heavy wooden shoes."
3. "Une Grande Fête a la Fabrique Nationale, La Grande Manufacture de Herstal celebre en un Banquet monster le 1,000,000 Browning et son Inventeur [A big party at the National Factory. The large manufacturer in Herstal celebrates the 1,000,000th Browning and its inventor in a monstrous banquet]," *La Meuse*, February 2, 1914, p. 1. This is the most detailed account of the banquet.
4. As his children grew, Browning made more time for them. His daughter Carrie was a professionally trained pianist. In 1912 when Browning was in Liège she was taking lessons in Berlin, Germany. Browning booked a voyage home for both with the White Star Line but canceled when Carrie was unexpectedly scheduled for a recital. The voyage they never made was the first and last voyage of the *Titanic*. (Judith Browning Jones, interview with the author).
5. Val to Rachel Browning, February 3, 1914, courtesy of Judith Browning Jones.
6. "Plat du Jour: A la gloire du cityen Browning," February 3, 1914, p. 1. A front-page daily commentary. "Plat du Jour" is a play on the restaurant term "Today's Special."
7. Auguste Francotte, Claude Gaier, and Robert Karlshausen, *ARS Mechanica: The Ultimate FN Book* (Herstal, Belgium: FN Herstal Group, 2008), pp. 98–99.
8. "Browning Fears for Liège Gun Factory, Doubts Germans Will Operate the Plant," *Salt Lake Tribune*, August 8, 1914.
9. Ibid. Browning said the plant had little military use. "As the German army is not equipped with the same arms that are being manufactured at the Belgium plant I cannot see any reason why they should desire to take over the factory." The plant could be easily disabled by "blowing up" the factory's stand-alone power plant.
10. Terence Zuber, *Ten Days in August: The Siege of Liège 1914*, 1st ed. (Stroud, UK: Spellmount, an imprint of The History Press, 2014), p. 26.
11. "While these losses would be quite extensive, I do not care to state the exact amount," Browning told the *Salt Lake Tribune*.

12. Thanks to Steve Lindquist for maps and research by Bob Creamer forwarded by Steve.

13. Dolf L. Goldsmith, *The Browning Machine Gun*, vol. 1, *Rifle Caliber Brownings in U.S. Service*, edited and produced by R. Blake Stevens (Cobourg, Ontario: Collector Grade, 2005), pp. 66–77.

14. Gerard and Buffetaut Yves Demaison, *Honour Bound: Chauchat Machine Rifle*, 1st ed. (Cobourg, Ontario: Collector Grade, 1995). "It seems clear from the existing record that the Chauchat . . . long recoil autoloading and machine rifle designs were inspired by the principles and some of the details of the 1900 Browning patent" (p. 7).

15. J. E. Browning to Edwin Pugsley, vice president, Winchester Repeating Arms Company, February 20, 1939, BFC.

16. The photo, on the cover, at the Browning museum in Ogden, was located by Tom Laemlein, who has published a series of photo books about World War II and related firearms.

17. James L. Ballou, *Rock in a Hard Place: The Browning Automatic Rifle*, produced and edited by R. Blake Stevens (Cobourg, Ontario: Collector Grade, 2000).

18. J. E. Browning to Edwin Pugsley, vice president, Winchester Repeating Arms Company, February 20, 1939, BFC.

19. The "Edison of Guns" appellation has its roots in a March 1, 1917, *Ogden Daily Standard* news story, "Wonderful Gun Invented by John M. Browning to Revolutionize Warfare," which says: "He is as great in his line of work as is Thomas A. Edison in electrical invention. In certain personal characteristics, Mr. Browning is like Edison. He has the same power of absolute mental concentration." On November 17, 1917, the article "Utahn [*sic*] 'Edison of Firearms' Army Accepts Browning Guns Weapons Will Destroy Huns" was distributed by the Ohio-based newspaper chain owned by E. W. Scripps. Articles from Scripps's influential newspapers were syndicated across the country—to hundreds of papers—by the Newspaper Enterprise Association. Scripps's chief Washington, DC, correspondent, Harry B. Hunt, wrote: "He has been to the development of firearms what Edison has been to electricity," a line picked up by a 1918 Congressional Resolution honoring Browning.

20. Postwar application for reparations was eventually rejected by an Allied commission, BFC.

21. Browning was recognized for his slide action–pistol design in 1905 when he received an award from the Franklin Institue in Philadelphia, but it was little noticed by the public.

22. "Conversations from July 20," an undated letter, likely from 1920, from the FN archives in Herstal, Belgium. It was written by an FN executive following a meeting in New York City with the vice president of Colt. The full paragraph, translated from the French, reads as follows: "During the war, the Brownings did not receive any license fees, and for their famous machine gun, they had an enormous disappointment, in fact the govern-

ment dealt with them for a set sum, payable once. Yet, after having payed, they reclaimed 60% in taxes on the said sum. John Browning almost died from it."

23. Matthew S. Browning to daughter Telitha, July 7, 1918, courtesy Steven Lindquist.

24. Judith Browning Jones, interview with the author.

25. Val Browning to Marriner Browning, August 1918, BFC.

26. Val to Marriner, August 1918, from American training base in France, BFC.

27. The Germans protested on September 19, 1918, with a threat to execute any American captured carrying a shotgun. The Army replied: "Inasmuch as the weapon is lawful and may be rightfully used, its use will not be abandoned by the American Army. . . . [I]f the German Government should carry out its threat in a single instance, it will be the right and duty of the . . . United States to make such reprisals as will best protect the American forces, and notice is hereby given of the intention of the . . . United States to make such reprisals." No American prisoners are known to have been executed for carrying a shotgun. W. Hays Parks, Special Assistant for Law of War Matters, Office of Judge Advocate General, U.S. Army, "Joint Service Combat Shotgun Program," *The Army Lawyer*, October 1997.

28. Frieman's wartime diary is available at the Veterans History Project, part of the American Folklife Center at the Library of Congress, http://memory .loc.gov/diglib/vhp/story/loc.natlib.afc2001001.23600/.

29. "What Were the Causes of the Delay of the 79th Division Capturing Montfaucon during the Meuse-Argonne Offensive in World War I?" Thesis, 2011, Paul B. Mitchell III, Major, U.S. Army, Southern Illinois University.

30. Alvin York, *Sergeant York: His Own Life Story and War Diary*, ed. Tom Skeyhill, introduction by George E. York, foreword by Gerald E. York (New York: Racehorse, 2018), chapter 18: "Conscientious Objector."

31. Ibid., chapter 24: "The Argonne Fight, October 8th."

32. Douglas V. Mastriano, *Alvin York: A New Biography of the Hero of the Argonne*, illustrated ed. (Lexington: University Press of Kentucky, 2014).

Chapter Eleven: The Sixty-Fourth or Sixty-Fifth Voyage

1. Adney's story is included in the text of a three-page undated letter. A note at the top, added later in pencil, is "Remarks on John by C.G. Adney." It appears to be a letter to one of Browning's children. BFC.

2. Efforts to ban the autoloading shotgun continued into the 1920s, and this was the only time Matt responded to a public criticism of Browning guns. The brothers lobbied Utah's U.S. senator Reed Smoot on that and other firearm-related issues, and Matt engaged in a public debate in the

letters column of *Forest and Stream*. An unsigned letter in the Browning archive, dated 1912, argued that the greatest threat to "song birds etc. that the Audobon [*sic*] Society have been shedding so many tears about" was not the relatively small number of Browning autoloaders, rather "the immense number of single shotguns in the hand of boys and foreigners accounts for nearly all the bird killings." Italian emigrants were faulted for importing the old-country custom of hunting small birds. The writer argued strict game laws, not firearm restrictions, was the answer.

3. Browning to FN, dated January 26, 1921. It is addressed to "Gentlemen" rather than to an individual at FN. BFC.

4. Ibid.

5. All the letters quoted in this chapter are found in the BFC. Specific dates are cited when relevant.

6. Benjamin Ballantyne's father was James Edward Ballantyne. James was a half brother of Jedediah Ballantyne. Their father was Richard Ballantyne, thrice married, according to Ancestry.com and Familysearch.org. James was the son of his second wife, Mary Pearce, while Jedediah was the son of his third wife, Caroline A. Sanderson. Benjamin would therefore be a first half cousin of Jedediah Ballantyne.

7. Details of the murder and trial are drawn from dozens of articles published by the *Ogden Standard Examiner* and the *Salt Lake Telegram* in 1923.

8. BFC.

9. Printed text of remarks at Matt's funeral, BFC.

10. The letter, dated September 19, 1923, is on Heublein Hotel stationery, with a penciled note that Marriner responded on September 24. That letter is apparently lost.

11. French-language memo from FN representative in NYC to FN in Belgium, "Generalities on the Brownings," June 6, 1924. The writer is not identified, but Joassart, who had known Browning for more than two decades, was in the United States and met Browning in Chicago on August 9 and 10.

12. "Passagers Ville de Liège," May 23, 1922, and January 18, 1926, Ministère de la Justice, Administration de la Sûreté Publique, Police des Etrangers; Archives Générales du Royaume Afdeling 5, Brussels, Belgium.

13. Typed memos in BFC.

14. Ibid.

15. FN archive, memo dated February 4, 1925.

16. Probate, 3888 and 4309, Second Judicial District of the State of Utah, Utah State Archives.

Chapter Twelve: Twenty Thousand Feet High

1. Battle of Britain Transcript, Imperial War Museum, Roland Beamont, IWM SR 10128, and oral history recording.

2. Loss estimates for the battle vary widely depending on what units and

aircraft are included. These figures only include fighter planes and pilots for the British, and all aircraft for the Germans.

3. G. F. Wallace, *The Guns of the Royal Airforce, 1939–1945* (London: William Kimber, 1972), pp. 9–11. Also, Dolf L. Goldsmith, *The Browning Machine Gun*, vol. 2, *Rifle Caliber Brownings Abroad* (Cobourg, Ontario: Collector Grade, 2006). Goldsmith's five volumes on *The Browning Machine Gun* are the gold standard, forgive the pun, for Browning machine-gun history.

4. Ibid, p. 68.

5. Goldsmith, *Browning Machine Gun*, vol. 2, p. 41.

6. Those arms are the .50-caliber machine gun, the .30-caliber machine gun, the BAR, and the 1911 pistol. Ed's contribution was the initial design of the M-1 carbine, which fired a light .30 cartridge. The other major arms were the Garand M-1 rifle and the Thompson submachine gun. Also, the "grease-gun," the slow-firing .45-caliber submachine gun introduced late in the war as a cheap-to-make replacement for the Thompson.

7. Frank Iannamico and Dolf L. Goldsmith, *The Browning Machine Gun*, vol. 4, *Semper Fi FIFTY!*, 4th ed. (Cobourg, Ontario: Collector Grade, 2008), p. 31.

8. There is an extensive history on the development of the B-17, strategic bomber theory, and the World War II battles of the Eighth Air Force. This account primarily relies on: *The Army Air Forces in World War II*, ed. Wesley Frank Craven and James Lea Cate (Washington, DC: Office of Air Force History, 1983); Edward Jablonski, *Flying Fortress: The Illustrated Biography of the B-17s and the Men Who Flew Them* (New York: Doubleday, 1965); Donald L. Miller, *Masters of the Air: America's Bomber Boys Who Fought the Air War Against Nazi Germany* (New York: Simon & Schuster, 2007); Thomas H. Green, *The Development of Air Doctrine in the Army Air Arm, 1917–1941* (Washington, DC: Office of Air Force History, 1985); Stephen L. McFarland, *To Command the Sky* (Washington DC: Smithsonian Institution, 1991); and the U.S. Air Force's various postwar studies of the bomber offensive and development of long-range fighters. Very useful was William R. Emerson's 1962 lecture to the U.S. Air Force Academy, "Operation Pointblank: A Tale of Fighters and Bombers."

9. Author flight, June 2019, in a B-17 built in 1944 and operated by the Collings Foundation, Hudson, Massachusetts.

10. Theo Boiten and Martin W. Bowman, *Jane's Battles with the Luftwaffe: The Bomber Campaign Against Germany 1942–45* (London: Collins Reference, 2001), p. 136.

11. Emerson, "Operation Pointblank," p. 3.

12. Anthony G. Williams and Dr. Emmanuel Gustin, *Flying Guns World War II: Development of Aircraft Guns, Ammunition and Installations 1933–45* (Wilshire, UK: Airlife, 2003), p. 224.

13. Excerpt from "My 1st Tour of Duty" on the website of the Ninety-First Bomb Group, http://www.91stbombgroup.com/airmen_diaries/diaries .html.

14. Warmer's story is told in John Hinds, *"Big Ben": Sergeant Benjamin F. Warmer III Flying Ace.* Air Force Historical Foundation, vol. 50, Fall 2003, p. 14. "Fortress Gunner Downs 7 Planes," *New York Times*, July 7 and August 29, 1943.

15. Emerson, "Operation Pointblank," p. 17.

16. Craven and Cate, eds., *The Army Air Forces in World War II*, p. 63.

17. Williams and Gustin, *Flying Guns World War II.*

18. Donald Caldwell and Richard Muller, *Luftwaffe over Germany: Defense of the Reich* (Barnsley, UK: Frontline, 2014), chapter 3.

19. Ibid., chapter 4.

Chapter Thirteen: Soldiers at War

1. Richard Tregaskis, *Guadalcanal Diary* (New York: Random House, 1943), chapter 2.

2. William H. Bartsch, *Victory Fever on Guadalcanal: Japan's First Land Defeat of World War II* (College Station: Texas A&M University Press, 2014), p. 245.

3. Robert Leckie, *Helmet for My Pillow: From Parris Island to the Pacific, a Marine Tells His Story* (New York: Random House, 1957), p. 74.

4. *BoxRec, Boxing's Official Record Keeper,* reports that "Indian Johnny Rivers" fought 26 bouts in Pennsylvania and New Jersey between 1940 and 1941 and 23.08 percent were won with a knock-out (https://boxrec.com/en/pro boxer/073705).

5. Roger Butterfield, *Al Schmid: Marine* (New York: W. W. Norton, 1944), p. 23.

6. "A Guadal Hero Today: No Job and No Home," *Brooklyn Daily Eagle*, April 6, 1947, p.7.

7. Roy F. Dunlap, *Ordnance Went Up Front: Some Observations and Experiences of a Sergeant of Ordnance* (Plantersville, SC: Samsworth/Small-Arms Technical Publishing, 1993), p. 304.

8. Duane Schultz, "Commando Kelly's War," *World War II History*, December 2014, p. 2.

9. Ibid., p. 3.

10. "Charles "Commando" Kelly, *The Mike Wallace Interview*, June 20, 1957, Harry Ransom Center Digital Collections.

11. Steve Levin, "North Side's Battlefield Hero Found Life's Wounds Too Deep," *Pittsburgh Post-Gazette*, May 31, 1999.

12. Those figures do not include the U.S. Navy or Marines. In total 407,316 Americans were killed and 671,278 wounded, casualty figures dwarfed by the estimated 15 million Soviet and German combat deaths in Eastern Europe and Chinese combat casualties, estimated at more than 3 million. Total civilian deaths in World War II are estimated at 50 million.

13. Murphy's quotes are from his autobiography, *To Hell and Back*, written with David McClure (New York: Henry Holt, 1949). Particularly useful was

NOTES

Don Graham, *No Name on the Bullet: A Biography of Audie Murphy* (New York: Penguin, 1990).

14. Graham, *No Name on the Bullet*, p. 91.

Epilogue

1. Shane Healey, FN Herstal operational marketing manager, retired, interview with the author.
2. Francotte, Gaier, and Karlshausen, *Ars Mechanica*, p. 338.

BIBLIOGRAPHY

Adler, Dennis. *Winchester Shotguns*. 1st ed. Edison, NJ: Book Sales, 2008.

Anderson, James, and Lee Kennett. *The Gun in America: The Origins of a National Dilemma*. Reprint ed. Westport, CT: Praeger, 1975.

Armstrong, David A., and Jay Luvaas. *Bullets and Bureaucrats: The Machine Gun and the United States Army, 1861–1916*. 1st ed. Westport, CT: Praeger, 1982.

Bady, Donald B. *Colt Automatic Pistols*. Union City, TN: Pioneer Press, 2000.

Barnes, Lyle J. *Notorious Two-Bit Street*. West Conshohocken, PA: Infinity, 2009.

Bijlefeld, Marjolijn. *The Gun Control Debate: A Documentary History*. Westport, CT: Greenwood, 1997.

Boiten, Theo, and Martin W. Bowman. *Jane's Battles with the Luftwaffe: The Bomber Campaign Against Germany 1942–45*. London: Collins Reference, 2001.

Bowman, Martin. *B-17: Combat Missions: Fighters, Flak, and Forts: First-Hand Accounts of Mighty 8th Operations over Germany*. New York: Greenhill Books, 2007.

Bowyer, Chaz. *Guns in the Sky: The Air Gunners of World War Two*. 1st ed. New York: Scribner, 1979.

Brown, M. L. *Firearms in Colonial America: The Impact on History and Technology 1492–1792*. 1st ed. Washington, DC: Smithsonian Institution, 1980.

Browning, John. *History of Browning Guns from 1831*. Ogden, UT: Browning, 1942.

Browning, John, and Curt Gentry. *John M. Browning American Gunmaker*. 1st ed. New York: Doubleday, 1964.

Butcher, Tim. *The Trigger: Hunting the Assassin Who Brought the World to War*. Chatto & Windus, 2014. Reprint, New York: Grove Press, 2018.

Caldwell, Donald, and Richard Muller. *The Luftwaffe over Germany: Defense of the Reich*. Barnsley, UK: Frontline 2014.

Campbell, John. *The Winchester Single-Shot*, vol. 1. Lincoln, RI: Andrew Mowbray, 1995.

———. *The Winchester Single-Shot*, vol. 2, *Old Secrets and New Discoveries*. 1st ed. Lincoln, RI: Andrew Mowbray, 2000.

Charles, Patrick J. *Armed in America: A History of Gun Rights from Colonial Militias to Concealed Carry*. Illustrated ed. Amherst, NY: Prometheus, 2018.

Charles River Editors. *The Assassination of Archduke Franz Ferdinand: The History and Legacy of the Event That Triggered World War I*. Charles River Editors, 2014.

BIBLIOGRAPHY

Coffey, Thomas M. *Decision over Schweinfurt: The U.S. 8th Air Force Battle for Daylight Bombing.* New York: D. McKay 1977.

Colt's Patent Fire Arms Manufacturing. *A Century of Achievement 1836–1936—Colt's 100th Anniversary.* 1st ed. Colt's Patent Fire Arms Manufacturing Co., 1937.

Cornish, Paul. *Machine-Guns and the Great War.* South Yorkshire, UK: Pen & Sword Military, 2009.

Dizard, Jan E., Robert Muth, and Stephen P. Andrews, eds. *Guns in America: A Historical Reader.* Paperback ed. New York: NYU Press, 1999.

Dobie, Duncan. *Dawn of American Deer Hunting: A Photographic Odyssey of Whitetail Hunting History.* 1st ed. Iola, WI: Krause, 2015.

Dunlap, Roy F. *Ordnance Went Up Front.* Plantersville, SC: Samsworth/Small-Arms Technical, 1948.

Emmerson, Charles. *1913: In Search of the World Before the Great War.* 1st ed. New York: PublicAffairs, 2013.

Francotte, Auguste, Claude Gaier, and Robert Karlshausen. *ARS Mechanica: The Ultimate FN Book.* Herstal, Belgium: Herstal Group, 2008.

Frank, Richard B. *Guadalcanal: The Definitive Account of the Landmark Battle.* Reprint ed. New York: Penguin, 1992.

Freeman, Roger A. *B-17 Fortress at War.* Book Club ed. New York: Charles Scribner's Sons, n.d.

Fulton, Robert A. *Moroland: The History of Uncle Sam and the Moros 1899–1920.* 2009 ed. Bend, OR: Tumalo Creek Press, 2007.

Gangarosa, Gene, Jr. *FN . . . Browning Armorer to the World.* Wayne, NJ: Stoeger, 1999.

Garavaglia, Louis A., and Charles G. Worman. *Firearms of the American West, 1866–1894.* 1st ed. Albuquerque: University of New Mexico Press, 1985.

Giltner, Scott E. *Hunting and Fishing in the New South: Black Labor and White Leisure After the Civil War.* Baltimore: Johns Hopkins University Press, 2008.

Goldsmith, Dolf L. *The Browning Machine Gun,* vol. 1, *Rifle Caliber Brownings in U.S. Service.* Cobourg, Ontario: Collector Grade, 2005.

———. *The Browning Machine Gun,* vol. 2, *Rifle Caliber Brownings Abroad.* Cobourg, Ontario: Collector Grade, 2006.

———. *The Browning Machine Gun,* vol. 5, *Dolf's Notebook.* 5th ed. Henderson, NV: Chipotle, 2016.

Grant, Neil. *The Bren Gun.* 1st ed. Botley, UK; New York: Osprey, 2013.

Hatcher, Julian S. *Machine Guns: Part I. Mechanism; Part II. The Practical Handling of Machine Gun Fire; Part III. Machine Gun Tactics.* London: Forgotten Books, 2018.

Hatcher, Julian S., and Ned Schwing. *Hatcher's Notebook.* 2nd rev. ed. Mechanicsburg, PA: Stackpole Books, 2008.

Hatcher, Julian S., Glenn P. Wilhelm, and Harry J. Malony. *Machine Guns. Part I. Mechanism—Scholar's Choice Edition.* Wolcott, NY: Scholar's Choice, 2015.

Henshaw, Thomas, ed. *The History of Winchester Firearms 1866–1992.* Subsequent ed. Clinton, NJ: Winchester Press, 1993.

Henwood, John. *The Great Remington 8: And Model 81 Autoloading Rifles.* 3rd ed. Cobourg, Ontario: Collector Grade, 2003.

BIBLIOGRAPHY

Herman, Daniel Justin. *Hunting & American Imagination*. 1st ed. Washington, DC: Smithsonian Institution, 2001.

Hickman, Orville Browning. *The Diary of Orville Hickman Browning*. Illinois State Historical Society Library, Springfield, 1927.

Hill, J. J. *A Sketch of the 29th Regiment of Connecticut Colored Troops*. Baltimore: Daugherty McGuire, 1907.

History of Creedmoor Match. National Rifle Association of Ireland. http:// nrai.ie/creedmore-history.html.

Hodges, Robert R., Jr. *The Browning Automatic Rifle*. 1st ed. New York: Osprey, 2012.

"Hoosac Tunnel Disaster of 1867, The." *New England Historical Society* (blog), October 18, 2014. https://www.newenglandhistoricalsociety.com/hoosac -tunnel-disaster/.

Hornaday, William Temple. *The Extermination of the American Bison*. Washington, DC: Smithsonian Institution, 1889.

Hounshell, David A. *From the American System to Mass Production, 1800–1932: The Development of Manufacturing Technology in the United States*. Baltimore: Johns Hopkins University Press, 1985.

Houze, Herbert G. *Arming the West: A Fresh New Look at the Guns That Were Actually Carried on the Frontier*. 1st ed. Woonsocket, RI: Andrew Mowbray, 2007.

———. *To the Dreams of Youth: Winchester: .22 Caliber Single Shot Rifle*. 1st ed. Iola, WI: Krause, 1993.

———. *Winchester Repeating Arms Company: Its History & Development from 1865 to 1981*. 1st ed. Iola, WI: Krause, 1994.

Husband, Julie, and Jim O'Loughlin. *Daily Life in the Industrial United States, 1870–1900*. Westport, CT: Greenwood, 2004.

Iannamico, Frank. *Hard Rain: History of the Browning Machine Guns*. Harmony, ME: Moose Lake, 2002.

Iannamico, Frank, and Dolf L. Goldsmith. *The Browning Machine Gun*, vol. 4, *Semper Fi FIFTY!* 4th ed. Cobourg, Ontario: Collector Grade, 2008.

Johnsen, Frederick A. *Warbird Tech*, vol. 7, *Boeing B-17-Flying Fortress*. Revised ed. North Branch, MN: Specialty Press, 2002.

Johnson, Nicholas. *Negroes and the Gun: The Black Tradition of Arms*. 1st ed. Amherst, NY: Prometheus, 2014.

Kassab, Rob, and Brad Dunbar. *Winchester Model 1895: Last of the Classic Lever Actions*. Boca Raton, FL: Buffalo Cove, 2019.

Keith, Elmer. *Shotguns by Keith*. Sportsman's Vintage Press, 2013.

Kuhnhausen, Jerry. *The .45 Automatic*, vol. 1. New expanded 10th ed. McCall, ID: Heritage Gun Books, 2015.

Leckie, Robert. *Helmet for My Pillow: From Parris Island to the Pacific, a Marine Tells His Story*. New York: Random House, 1957.

Lindsay, Merrill. *The New England Gun: The First Two Hundred Years*. 1st ed. New Haven, CT: New Haven Colony Historical Society, 1975.

Marcot, Roy. *The History of Remington Firearms: The History of One of the World's Most Famous Gun Makers*. New York: Chartwell Books, 2011.

BIBLIOGRAPHY

Marshall, Evan, and Edwin J. Sanow. *Handgun Stopping Power: The Definitive Study*. 1st ed. Boulder, CO: Paladin Press, 1992.

Mastriano, Douglas V. *Alvin York: A New Biography of the Hero of the Argonne*. Lexington: University Press of Kentucky, 2014.

McCallum, Iain. *Blood Brothers: Hiram and Hudson Maxim: Pioneers of Modern Warfare*. 1st ed. London: Greenhill Books, 2006.

McCullough, David. *The Wright Brothers*. Reprint ed. New York: Simon & Schuster, 2016.

McFarland, Stephen L. *To Command the Sky*. Washington, DC: Smithsonian Institution, 1991.

Meadows, Edward Scott. *U.S. Military Automatic Pistols, vol. 1, 1894–1920*. Moline, IL: Richard Ellis, 1993.

Miller, David. *The History of Browning Firearms*. New York: Chartwell Books, 2014.

Miller, Donald L. *Masters of the Air: America's Bomber Boys Who Fought the Air War Against Nazi Germany*. Reprint ed. New York: Simon & Schuster, 2007.

Morris, Craig F. *The Origins of American Strategic Bombing Theory*. Annapolis, MD: Naval Institute Press, 2017.

Newton, A. H. *Out of the Briars: An Autobiography and Sketch of the Twenty-Ninth Regiment, Connecticut Volunteers*. Philadelphia: A.M.E. Book Concern, 1910.

"Orville H. Browning (1806–1881)." *Mr. Lincoln and Friends* (blog). http://www.mrlincolnandfriends.org/members-of-congree/orville-browning/.

Pegler, Martin. *Winchester Lever-Action Rifles*. New York: Osprey, 2015

Porterfield, James D. *Dining by Rail: The History and Recipes of America's Golden Age of Railroad Cuisine*. New York: St. Martin's Griffin, 1998.

Posewitz, James. *Rifle in Hand: How Wild America Was Saved*. Helena, MT: Riverbend, 2004.

Potocki, John. *The Colt Model 1905 Automatic Pistol*. 1st ed. Lincoln, RI: Andrew Mowbray, 1998.

Pursell, Carroll. *The Machine in America: A Social History of Technology*. 2nd ed. Baltimore: Johns Hopkins University Press, 2007.

Reiger, John F. *American Sportsmen and the Origins of Conservation*. Revised, expanded 3rd ed. Corvallis: Oregon State University Press, 2000.

Roberts, Richard C. *Ogden: Junction City*. 1st ed. Northridge, CA: Windsor, 1985.

Roosevelt, Theodore. *African Game Trails*. New York: Charles Scribner's Sons, 1910.

Rose, Alexander. *American Rifle: A Biography*. Illustrated ed. New York: Delta, 2009

Rottman, Gordon L. *Browning .50-Caliber Machine Guns*. New York: Osprey, 2010.

Rottman, Gordon L., Johnny Shumate, and Alan Gilliland. *Browning .30-Caliber Machine Guns*. New York: Osprey, 2014.

Ruffin, Paul, and Bob Conroy. *Browning Automatic Rifle*. 1st ed. Huntsville: Texas Review Press, 2015.

Shirley, H. M., Jr., and Anthony Vanderlinden. *Browning Auto-5 Shotguns: The Belgian FN Production*. Revised 2nd ed. Greensboro, NC: Wet Dog, 2010.

BIBLIOGRAPHY

SI Staff. "The Great Rifle Match." September 13, 1954. Sports Illustrated Vault | SI.com. Accessed April 2, 2020. https://vault.si.com/vault/1954/09/13 /the-great-rifle-match.

Soodalter, Ron. "The Great Beefsteak Raid." *Opinionator* (blog), September 21, 2014. https://opinionator.blogs.nytimes.com/2014/09/21/the-great-beef steak-raid/.

Thompson, Leroy, Adam Hook, and Alan Gilliland. *The M3 "Grease Gun."* New York: Osprey, 2016.

Tregaskis, Richard. *Guadalcanal Diary.* New York: Open Road Media, 2016.

Trevelyan, Laura. *The Winchester: The Gun That Built an American Dynasty.* New Haven, CT: Yale University Press, 2016.

True Magazine Gun Editor. *The New Lucian Carry On Guns.* New York: Fawcett, 1957.

Turner, John G. *Brigham Young: Pioneer Prophet.* Cambridge, MA: Belknap Press, 2012.

Vanderlinden, Anthony. "The FN Browning 1910 Pistol and the Great War." September 5, 2014. https://www.americanrifleman.org/articles/2014/9/5 /the-fn-browning-1910-pistol-and-the-great-war/.

———. *FN Browning Pistols, Side Arms That Shaped the World History.* Expanded 2nd ed. Greensboro, NC: Wet Dog, 2013.

Walter, John. *Luger: The Story of the World's Most Famous Handgun.* New York: Skyhorse, 2018.

Warren, Louis S. *The Hunter's Game: Poachers and Conservationists in Twentieth-Century America.* 3rd ed. New Haven, CT: Yale University Press, 1999.

Wilson, R. L., and Sid Latham. *Colt: An American Legend.* Sesquicentennial ed. New York: Artabras, 1985.

Winkler, Adam. *Gunfight: The Battle over the Right to Bear Arms in America.* 1st ed. New York: W. W. Norton, 2013.

"Workers Complete Hoosac Tunnel." https://www.massmoments.org/moment -details/workers-complete-hoosac-tunnel.html.

York, Alvin. *Sergeant York: His Own Life Story and War Diary.* Edited by Tom Skeyhill. Introduction by George E. York. Foreword by Gerald E. York. New York: Racehorse, 2018.

Zuber, Terence. *Ten Days in August: The Siege of Liège 1914.* 1st ed. Stroud, UK: Spellmount, an imprint of The History Press, 2014.

INDEX

INDEX

INDEX

INDEX

INDEX